D1638975

THE SECOND MOST IMPORTANT JOB IN THE COUNTRY

Niall Edworthy

This edition first published in Great Britain in 2000 by
Virgin Publishing Ltd
Thames Wharf Studios
Rainville Road
London W6 9HA

First published in Great Britain in 1999

A catalogue record for this book is available from the British Library.

ISBN 1 7535 0374 3

Typeset by TW Typesetting, Plymouth, Devon

Printed and bound in Great Britain by
Mackays of Chatham PLC

Contents

Acknowledgements

I am indebted to a host of people for their help in putting this book together – not least the dozens of players, managers, FA officials and journalists who gave up their time to give me their views on the subject. The only reluctant interviewees were those players still involved in the game today. Unless you are prepared to empty your wallet of your hard-earned, you may as well forget about trying to talk to football players in the 1990s. If you are privileged enough to receive some form of response from their control-freak, cash-mad agents, the answer to your request for a short five-minute interview will inevitably be 'a polite no'. That said, those who had been involved in the game before the era of the agent could not have been more helpful and I would like to extend special thanks to the following: Sir Walter Winterbottom, Sir Tom Finney, Johnny Haynes, Bobby Robson, Jimmy Armfield, Ronnie Clayton, Allan Clarke, Ron Greenwood, Martin Peters, Geoff Hurst, Alan Mullery, Alan Ball, Gerry Francis, Mick Channon and Howard Wilkinson. Former and current employees of the FA I would like to thank are David Barber, David Davies, Alan Odell, David Bloomfield and David Teasdale. I am also heavily indebted to a number of the country's leading sports journalists (in order of the alphabet rather than merit): Mihir Bose, Bryon Butler, Mike Collett, Brian Glanville, Colin Malam, Rob Shepherd, Henry Winter and Brian Woolnough.

I was also fortunate to have an outstanding editor in Jonathan Taylor, who joined Virgin Publishing as their senior sports editor while I was in the middle of writing the book. His constructive suggestions, eye for detail and patience as I battled with my deadline, all helped make this a better book than it would have been otherwise.

Author's note

Readers will notice that I have made a number of references to contemporary newspaper accounts in the chapter on Walter Winterbottom and to a lesser extent in the chapter on Alf Ramsey. I have done this for two reasons. Firstly, newspapers are the most reliable source of information from the period as the reactions of correspondents were made within minutes, hours, or at most days, of the events described. Furthermore, with the exception of the people I have quoted in those chapters, I found that many people's memories, 40 or 50 years on, have grown understandably hazy on the specifics of what happened. Secondly, one of the main themes of this book is the relationship between the England managers and the press and I wanted to draw attention to the huge changes in newspaper coverage between then and now.

Introduction

How Glenn Hoddle must wish that he had been born forty years earlier and gone on to manage England at a time when the nation's sports reporters – and the Prime Minister – would not have given a flying farthing for his views on life, the after-life or any other matter not relating to the business of beating Johnny Foreigner in the next match. Hoddle, though, is by no means the first England manager to be hounded out of office after the smiles and upbeat talk of a bright new future had turned to scowls and recriminations. Not one England manager has walked out of Lancaster Gate a happier man than when he first arrived.

Walter Winterbottom, the officer and a gentleman who had helped drag England into the modern era, making possible England's triumph in 1966, left in unhappy circumstances feeling he had been snubbed after so many years of loyal service. Alf Ramsey, the only man to have steered England to World Cup glory, and knighted for his efforts, was sacked by the Football Association and palmed off with a niggardly pension. Don Revie, one of the greatest club managers in the history of English football, fled to the Middle East for a fistful of dollars amid cries of 'traitor' after deserting England in the middle of a World Cup qualifying campaign. He ended up fighting his former employers in the High Court, safe from the bilious scorn of his countrymen only in his adoptive Leeds. Ron Greenwood, as reasonable and decent a man as you will find in the unreasonable, ruthless world of football – and a highly respected, innovative coach to boot – left the job depressed by the unrelenting snipings and the thanklessness of his office. 'The Impossible Job' he called it, and nowadays he can barely bring himself to talk about his experiences. Bobby Robson, a highly personable, enthusiastic, honest man who left the small-town comfort of his beloved Ipswich to steer England into the 1986 World Cup quarter-finals and then the semi-finals at Italia 90 four years later, broke down in tears towards the end of his eight-year stint, a near broken man after enduring as bitter a tabloid campaign against him as can be imagined. Graham Taylor: need we say more than 'turnip-head' or 'Norse manure', or recall that his wife was spat at in the street? Terry Venables, one of the most respected coaches in world football, got it right with the public and most of the press, but was out on his ear after just two years as a result of his murky, writ-bound business activities.

Hoddle, the youngest England manager in history at the age of thirty-eight, full of new ideas and the inheritor of a much improved squad, lasted just six months longer. One of the most admired footballers of his generation, Hoddle was a laughing stock by the time the press, the public and the FA decided that his 'crackpot' views on life and the universe were just as embarrassing as some of Venables' friends in the world of London commerce. 'HOD OFF GLENN!', screamed the papers, and so he did – pursued by a pack of pressmen delighted that the man who seemed to relish making their job more difficult had finally got his comeuppance. Hoddle failed to see the importance of having the press on his side – and they crucified him.

It was an irony that Hoddle's fateful, final interview with *The Times* was the start of an orchestrated charm offensive to win back some respect after the controversies over his World Cup diary and use of faith-healer Eileen Drewery. It was also an irony that Hoddle's passing from the scene was a minor cause of lament in some quarters of Fleet Street. He made great copy and even better headlines. A football manager with an eccentric potful of half-baked, inarticulate spiritual beliefs in charge of an unsuccessful team might just as well have been sent from the God of Nasty Headlines himself. And with a surname which when abbreviated rhymed with sod, odd and God, sub-editors and headline writers barely had to engage their imaginations to bring a smile to the nation's newspaper readers the following morning ('HODBALL!', 'OFF WITH

HIS HOD!', 'IN THE NAME OF HOD, GO!', 'HE'S OFF HIS HOD!', etc.).

Only Venables, with his bar-room banter and cheeky Cockney smile, knew how to seduce the Fourth Estate. Always good for a quote, apparently candid in his answers, funny, upbeat, serious-faced when he needed to be, loyal to his players, tactically astute, Venables gave his critics very little rope with which to hang him. In the end, it was battles in the boardroom and the courtroom and not the boot room that cost him his job.

Ramsey, in contrast to his fellow East Ender Venables, made no secret of his contempt for the press. Why should he kow-tow to the men in grubby macs and pork pie hats after getting his hands on the Jules Rimet trophy, and then steering an even better England side to the quarter-finals four years later only to go out in what were regarded as unfortunate circumstances? He was Sir Alf. His players loved him (give or take the odd Jimmy Greaves). He had nothing to prove to anyone. But when results failed to go England's way, as they inevitably do for all teams at some point, the press were not there to support him when their backing might well have kept him in the job.

Nor does there appear to be much of an after-life, in this world at least, for those who have held the top job in English football. Winterbottom returned to the relative anonymity of his first loves, physical education and general coaching, while Ramsey headed for oblivion and back to his semi-detached home in Ipswich, via forgettable spells in Birmingham and Greece. Ramsey became something of a recluse in the last twenty years of his life and rarely appeared in public, even at Wembley. He died at the end of April 1999 following a long illness. Revie spent his last few years fighting to clear his name in the courts before dying a painful death from motor neurone disease. Greenwood, who had to be talked out of resigning by his own players in the middle of England's 1982 World Cup qualifying campaign, bolted into virtual retirement on the south coast and has barely been seen in football circles since. Taylor went to Wolverhampton and was sacked, and then returned to the comforting bosom of Watford in the Second Division. Venables went to spend some quality time with his lawyers and then headed for the other side of the planet to coach Australia, a squirrel of a team in international terms compared to the lion of England. He tried his tricks at Portsmouth and Crystal Palace before leaving both stricken clubs with considerably more money in his own pockets than they had had in theirs. Hoddle, meanwhile, sought solace in his spirituality as he pondered an uncertain future. Only Robson can be said to have thrived after leaving the England job, bouncing off away from the glare of the tabloids first to PSV Eindhoven, then the sunshine of Porto and Sporting Lisbon, Barcelona, and back to PSV for a second spell, all the time reportedly courted by a number of leading Premiership clubs.

Before Hoddle was appointed to the England post, as many as eight high-profile candidates were reported to have either turned it down or ruled themselves out of the running for it. And it is not difficult to see why. Who wants to be caricatured as a tasteless root vegetable? Who would want his children to be mocked in the school playground, or his wife to be spat at? Who would want lurid and steamy details of his private life splashed over the front page of national newspapers? Why leave the relative (and better paid) comfort of club football where, it can be assumed, he had enjoyed enough success to be considered for the national job in the first place?

There are nearly 400 countries in the world and only one of them can win the World Cup every four years. For that, a manager needs at least four or five or six great players, a dozen very good others, the luck of the draw, luck on the day, the improbability of all his players being fit, high morale in a squad of players drawn from a dozen different clubs, an unbeaten run of about eight matches against the best teams in the world, and the hope that there is not an opposition team out there with all of the above and more. Only a madman or a character of astonishing fearlessness and self-belief, or perhaps vanity, can believe everlasting glory and eternal peace of mind is about to be thrust upon him when he settles down before a forest of microphones for his first press conference as the new England coach.

Rightly or wrongly, the decisions of the England manager and the fate of the national team have an enormous impact on English society. Just ask the police. On the night of England's defeat at the hands of Germany in the semi-finals of the European Championships, police reported a 400 per cent increase in wife-beatings, riots broke out up and down the country, central London was brought to a standstill as riot squad officers battled to contain a mob in Trafalgar Square, cars were overturned and set alight, a Russian student was stabbed in the mistaken belief he was German, and a group of England fans had to be rescued by lifeboatmen after throwing themselves off Brighton pier at the final whistle. The aftermath of England's elimination from France 98 told a similar story.

The importance of a successful England football team to the country's morale has been well understood at the highest political level in recent years. Margaret Thatcher was an exception to this rule, and once famously said she 'loathed' football and could not understand why some of her ministers would want to spend their weekends at a match. She did, however, provide one of football's better anecdotes. Shortly after West Germany beat England on penalties in the semi-finals of the 1990 World Cup, one of her aides entered her office to tell her that a tongue-in-cheek Chancellor Kohl had passed on Germany's apologies for beating England at its national sport. The Iron Lady is said to have looked up from her desk and replied, poker-faced: 'Well, you can tell Herr Kohl from me that twice this century we have played the Germans at their national sport and beaten them on both occasions.' But whereas Thatcher was happier to be photographed with her head sticking out of a Challenger tank, John Major and Tony Blair were quick to understand that they might be seen in a more favourable light by playing 'keep-it-uppie' with Kevin Keegan or Alex Ferguson and a group of grinning school children.

It does not take a political clairvoyant to work out that when half the public settles down to watch an England match, the nation's 'feel-good' factor will swing one way or the other according to the result. It is a well-documented fact that consumer spending on the high street increases when England are successful and falls when the team fail. There is a growing realisation in political circles that by being seen to be associated with football, politicians come across as being in touch with the people. In the frenzied days leading up to Hoddle's dismissal in early 1999, Tony Blair took time off from saving the world to appear on the Richard and Judy *This Morning* show to say he believed Hoddle should step down. The following day, the front page of the *Daily Telegraph* ran the headline: 'BLAIR GIVES HODDLE THE RED CARD'. (To appreciate how far football has come in the world, try and imagine a similar headline from, say, 45 years ago: 'CHURCHILL GIVES WINTERBOTTOM THE RED CARD'.) The experience of France after the World Cup in 1998 bears out the truth that a successful national football team not only lifts national morale, it also serves to give the impression to outsiders of a country that is strong, confident, happy, well-organised and perhaps even stylish and inventive – and certainly worth investing in or taking a holiday there.

So why does anyone want to manage the England team? The truth is that no one really does any more. Barely had Hoddle been shown the door when half the prospective candidates for the vacant post were rushing to their fax machines to issue statements saying they were perfectly happy where they were or they were too inexperienced, or simply 'you must be joking'. Howard Wilkinson held the post just long enough to see himself caricatured as Mr Spock on the front page of one national newspaper, and then watched as England were outclassed by the world champions at Wembley and his job application was pushed into the FA shredding machine. Nor was it with the greatest enthusiasm that Keegan was brought to the negotiating table. He had to be virtually dragged out of the relative obscurity of the English Second Division, kicking and screaming that he had no intention of breaking his contract and deserting his beloved Fulham. Even when the inspirational former England captain finally cracked under the pressure of his popularity among the public and the press, he agreed only to take charge of England's four matches until June and then would only consider taking the job on a part-time basis.

Shortly after taking over the England job, Keegan said that one of his priorities was to try and improve the relationship between the England set-up and the media which, during

Hoddle's time in charge, had become the worst any journalist could remember. If nothing else, and whether people like it or not, the experiences of the England managers down the years have dramatised the ever-increasing importance of the media. It was a fact lost on Hoddle – to his cost.

1 The End of England's Football Empire

Sir Walter Winterbottom 1946–1962

T IS OFTEN WRITTEN that Walter Winterbottom, England's first manager, suffered a newspaper campaign to remove him from his post as vicious as any experienced by the men who were to follow him into the job. But trawling through the newspaper archives of the day, there is very little evidence to support this until we reach the end of his sixteen-year tenure in office in the early 1960s. Up to then it is very difficult to find any direct and personal attacks on him, or even a headline carrying his name. The match reports in the first half of his reign barely refer to him. When criticism was dished out, it was at the team as a whole, at the captain (Billy Wright for most of his time in charge), at the Football Association and the Football League, and, most frequently, at the committee of selectors.

There is nothing at all surprising about the players themselves being blamed for failure or that commentators should scrutinise the entire structure and administration of English football, but what strikes modern readers as strange is that the captain was considered a more significant figure in the England hierarchy than the manager. Today, it is inconceivable that newspapers would call for the head of the skipper following defeat. The notion of the football manager as the most influential figure in a team set-up was still only in its infancy during Winterbottom's reign. The idea of having a panel of selectors to choose the team also strikes us as bizarre (it should be said that it also struck many contemporaries as just that). But the existence of these committee men – most of them directors or chairmen of League sides, or amateur sides like the Army – almost certainly saved Winterbottom from a greater grilling in the press. Though he had a considerable say in the selection process, no journalist could ever refer to England as 'Winterbottom's team'. When Alf Ramsey took over from Winterbottom, he did so on the condition that he alone would choose the team. This was regarded as a sensible and overdue development. But from that moment on, the press had a direct target they have been firing at ever since.

After the upheaval of the six years of the Second World War, it would inevitably take some time before anything like 'normality' returned to British life. Food rationing was in operation and time was needed for industry to adapt to civilian rather than military ends. In order not to disrupt the output from factories and distract the nation from its regeneration, there was no midweek football. Football, like so many other areas of British life, was in a serious state of disrepair in the post-war years, even though it had survived in skeleton form at club and international level throughout the hostilities. Military conscription and the employment laws under the Enforced Works Order deprived clubs of some of the best young talent available. But after years of despair, bereavement and privation, the British people clamoured for entertainment just as they had after the First World War. Interest in football boomed in the immediate aftermath of the conflict and crowds reached record levels. On 9 March 1946, this nationwide lust for football sparked one of the worst tragedies in the history of the game when 33 people were killed and over 400 injured after the crush barriers gave way in an FA Cup tie at Burnden Park between Bolton Wanderers and Stoke City.

Football was about to enter the most turbulent period of its history when the face of a game which would have been recognisable to the Victorians was transformed, by the early 1960s, into one which we largely recognise today. During this period, floodlighting was introduced, European club competition began, baggy shorts and heavy boots were replaced by lightweight, synthetic alternatives, television broadcast its first live matches, the use of white balls was legalised, the maximum wage for players was abolished, and substitutes were allowed.

The coverage of football at this time varied from paper to paper. The broadsheets, or 'qualities', devoted far less space to sport than their more populist rivals. On Friday, 20 September 1946, news of the England team to play Northern Ireland and related comment was given just four paragraphs in *The Times*; next to it, in the 'Points from Letters' columns, Mr R.B. Charlton from Hexham, Northumberland, was given nearly twice as much space to expound his views on pit ponies, whose lot he thought 'simply marvellous'.

A few days later, the same paper allocated just two paragraphs to the news that Stanley Matthews, the most celebrated footballer of the day, was injured and would be replaced by the uncapped Tom Finney. Under the spectacularly unsensational headline 'CHANGE IN THE ENGLAND TEAM', the paper reported: 'The Football Association announced yesterday that Finney, the Preston North End outside-right, will replace Matthews of Stoke City, in the England team to play Ireland at Belfast on Saturday.' In the only other football news reported that day a paragraph beneath the England news read: 'Accrington Stanley will meet Carlisle United in a Third Division (North) match at Accrington this afternoon, kick-off 3.15.' In the column next to the football news is the headline 'INTERNATIONAL IDEAS IN PLANNING: ARCHITECTS FROM MANY COUNTRIES'. Elsewhere on the page is the racing programme from Lanark, while other sports news that day reported the departure of the Indian cricket team from London docks by cargo boat, the venue for the Army squash rackets championship, the teams for a golf match between Admirals and Air Vice-Marshals, and the composition of the Oxford University hockey team.

The page makes interesting reading for modern readers only in so far as it reveals how little importance was attached to the coverage of professional sport in the nation's more serious-minded newspapers. There is also an element of class division reflected in the fact that the paper gives prominence to amateur sports like rugby and semi-amateur ones like cricket, as well as to matches involving the services and Oxbridge universities. Its readers, presumably, had little interest in the proletarian pursuit of Association Football. The contrast with today, when all the broadsheets devote several pages to sport, not to mention whole weekly supplements, could not be greater.

On the Monday of that week the entire Football League programmme from Saturday was written up in a single 300-word piece, mentioning in its introduction that QPR, of the Third Division (South), were one of only four teams to remain unbeaten in the opening weeks of the new season. The defeat of leaders Manchester United by Stoke (3–2) was given just one sentence, and there was not a word about the goalless Merseyside derby. Curiously, though, the report found space to devote a long paragraph (one of just four in the entire round-up) to describe the action from a match between an amateur team from Iceland and non-League Dulwich Hamlet. On the Saturday, *The Times* ran a short preview of the entire League programme under the headline 'SOME INTERESTING GAMES'.

England's match against Northern Ireland on that same day 28 September 1946 was reported under the headline 'ENGLAND BEAT IRELAND' and began: 'The first full international to be played since 1939 was decided at Windsor Park, Belfast, on Saturday and a record crowd of 57,000 people was there to see England overwhelm Ireland by seven goals to two.' The second paragraph carried news of a major disturbance : 'The prelude was one of intense excitement. The swirling crowd invaded the touchlines and for some moments there was the threat of a cancelled match.' (For the record, the team that day was: Swift, Scott, Hardwick, Wright, Franklin, Cockburn, Finney, Carter, Lawton, Mannion, Langton – a line-up which today Finney describes as the best team he ever played in and one of the best of all time.)

Football and other sports, though, were written up in a far more lively way in those papers which, though still broadsheet in design, were 'tabloid' in editorial style. The circulation of these papers was huge. The 1951 edition of the *Newspaper Press Directory* records that the *News of the World* had a circulation of 8,443,917, the *People* 5,089,455, the *Daily Express* 4,192,650, the *Sunday Pictorial* 5,093,935, the *Daily Herald* 2,071,289, the *Daily Mirror* 4,566,930, the *Daily Mail* 2,245,286, and the *Sunday Dispatch* 2,377,609; by way of contrast, the *Daily Telegraph*'s figure was put at 975,891 and *The Times*' at 253,502. The style was broadly similar to today's tabloids: opinionated, didactic and colourful, although there is little of the irreverence and occasional viciousness familiar to modern-day readers. All the 'tabloid' newspapers devoted at least one and often two pages to sport, increasing coverage steadily over the years; the leading writers, who were given picture by-lines, were almost as well known in the nation's households as the heroes they wrote about. There was no cult of the sports writer as a personality in his own right in the 'qualities', where stories were more often than not attributed to 'Our Special Correspondent', who relied on the national and local news agencies for much of his material. Match reports rarely carried quotes from the manager or players as the comments of the reporter were authority enough. The opinion of the best-known journalists in the popular press was considered all-important. In a commentary piece on Monday, 9 December 1946, the main sports headline in the *Daily Express* declared, 'YOUNG HOOLIGANS YELL "SEND HIM OFF" ', and the report began: 'The reaction of dim-wits on every sports ground is to boo at some time on general principles. That's all right, an occasional boo is human. But something should be done about the young hooligans in the pen reserved for schoolboys at Anfield, writes HENRY ROSE. Their concerted booing and continual cries of "Send him off!" in the Liverpool v. Wolves match horrified me. I suggest the Liverpool board close the pen for a few weeks and bring them to their senses – if any.'

On Saturday, 28 November 1946 Frank Butler, the chief football writer for the *Daily Express*, reported on an easy win for England over Holland. Some two months earlier, on 30 September, England had scraped a 1–0 win over unfancied Eire in Dublin, provoking a barrage of criticism back home. Butler wrote: 'England regained some lost Soccer prestige by routing a weak Holland team at Huddersfield yesterday, by eight goals to two. The Dutchmen were even more disappointing than I expected.' Further on, he continued: 'Langton is still lacking in international class and I shall want to see Harry Johnston against sterner opposition.'

Today, no reporter would use 'I' in a match report. The use of the first person tells us much about the change in the relationship between the press and the world of football. Football writers felt entitled to voice their opinions without fear of footballers or managers or the public scoffing, 'Well, what does he know, and what do we care what he thinks anyway?' Nowadays, the press is regarded with the greatest suspicion by players, coaches and much of the public who believe – often rightly – that newspapers will write anything, even make it up, merely to make a more sensational impact on the reader. 'Exclusives' appear daily in all the tabloids, but rarely are the claims supported by a quoted source. Of course, now, just as then, reporters are given information 'off the record' by players and club officials, but many exclusives or 'splashes' amount to nothing so that the players and coaches feel they can no longer trust the reporters. The stock of the football journalist has perhaps never been lower than it is today.

Another significant moment in the breakdown of trust between the two sides came when editors of the news pages began to be interested in the behaviour of football stars off the pitch. From the time when footballers were first treated and paid like film and pop stars, interest in them spread beyond the back pages of the papers to the front where the news journalists, with little interest in the fragile bond of trust which needs to exist between sports writers and the people they write about, began to run exposés on the private lives of the stars. Understandably, footballers do not differentiate between types of journalists, but with the modern news lust for lurid details of the lifestyles of the rich and famous, sports journalists have been tarred with the same brush as their less scrupulous colleagues on the news pages of some of the papers.

Sir Tom Finney, one of the greatest forwards in the history of English football and a man who experienced the press from the inside when his playing career ended, as a reporter for the *News of the World*, recalls that during his playing days for England and Preston in the 1940s and 1950s players and press mingled happily. 'In those days people writing about football were footballing people. They really understood the game. Certainly in Lancashire there was a generation of outstanding journalists, several of whom, sadly, were killed in the Munich air disaster. They were legends within the game because they brought something to it rather than took something away. It is a very different set-up nowadays. From what I can gather from players now they don't dare say anything to anybody for fear of being misquoted. Terrible things are written about the players these days. All the trust has gone. It all changed at the start of the sixties when you began to read these headlines and then read through the story itself and more often than not there's nothing in it. Everything is taken out of context. It's just cheap, bad journalism. When I was playing you could talk to a reporter man to man. We just used to say, "I'll tell you this but it's just for your knowledge" or "It's off the record" and you could trust the fellow implicitly.'

On the subject of the press coverage of the England team, Finney says: 'I played my last game for England against Russia in 1958 and I can honestly say that during my twelve years playing for England I did not see a single headline saying "Winterbottom must go". When I saw the headlines they did about Robson and Taylor it made me shudder. They were absolutely hunted out of the job, just as they continue to have been. I have always felt that the treatment the England manager receives is terribly unfair. The manager can only do so much. He puts out what he sees as the best team available and if they don't perform then he's the one who gets the blame. If he has chosen a terrible team then some criticism would be justified, but most of the time they roughly get it right. More often than not the ones to blame are the players who didn't perform. I often say to reporters, "wouldn't it be great if you lot were asked to put out a team and see how they get on?" Then they might change their tack a bit. And nowadays the press come at them from all angles. They attack them for what they eat, drink and do in their private lives. If you go out with your wife or girlfriend, everyone is watching you. Their lives are not their own. They've become public property. That was true to some extent in our day, but it was never, never anything like it is today. I cannot recall any player in my generation going for a drink and it being written about in the next day's papers. But in the sixties that all changed. Footballers began to be treated like pop stars.'

It was in this climate of trust that Winterbottom went about his job – or, more accurately, both his jobs. Winterbottom was not only the manager of England but also the FA's Director of Coaching, a post regarded by his employers as more important than looking after the national team. With selectors to choose the team and a standard team formation of 2–3–5, it was felt that, in a playing sense, the England team looked after itself to a large extent. 'Certainly when he first started as England manager after the war, it was very much a case of Walter letting us just go out and play,' says Finney. 'It was a brilliant team that picked itself, and he felt there was very little he needed to tell us. That changed later as Walter grew into the job and the great players like Lawton, Mannion, Carter, Swift, Hardwick and Mortensen left the team.' Players, it was thought, knew what was expected of them. Stan Matthews even went into print, shortly after Winterbottom's appointment, to say he could see no need for a national manager.

Winterbottom's brief from the FA was to oversee the occasional training session when the clubs would allow the release of their players, inform the team about key players in the opposition, and, when on tour, look after all the travel and accommodation arrangements. The role, however, changed in the mid-1950s after the morale-shattering defeats against Hungary in 1953 and 1954 when it was brought home to everyone in English football that a major overhaul in the preparation of the national team, as well as in the whole structure of the domestic game, was vital to future success. But in the beginning, Winterbottom was almost a peripheral figure in the England set-up, a fact reflected by the lack of reference to him in the nation's newspapers. The coaching job, which involved the establishment of coaching schools, giving lectures and the production of handbooks, was seen as the more important of Winterbottom's twin responsibilities.

Winterbottom himself saw the coaching post as the more important of the two. 'People tend to forget that my main job was as Director of Coaching,' he recalls. 'I had no hesitation in accepting it as I had a good knowledge of sports science. I was a coach and lecturer, I could handle groups of people and I had run plenty of coaching courses at Carnegie College [the Centre of Physical Education]. But as for the job of England manager, I had no idea what I was meant to do. Nobody knew or said what it would involve. The concept of the manager/coach was just coming into being, but I knew that coaching was part of my brief. That was it. That was what I was good at. Nobody believed in coaches at this time. I wanted to change the whole attitude to coaching in this country.' He had been aware since the early days of the post-war years that English football was in need of a more scientific and modern approach. 'When I first took over as England coach, I put the players through some pretty severe training which I think was a bit of a shock to some of them. I used to say, "Come on chaps, you have to be realistic if you want to play these international matches. We have to be fit as a team. We can't be slapdash, living it up in hotels and having late nights in the casino." '

On 13 November 1946, the day England beat Wales in the Home Championship, the *Daily Express* reported that on the eve of the match England had 'loosened up with spells of football and dancing ... Team coach Walter Winterbottom gave a short talk on tactics and a long talk on the rules of Soccer.' In-depth tactical analysis and thorough physical conditioning in the build-up to matches were alien concepts in the immediate post-war years, but the *Express* report showed that attitudes were changing, albeit in a modest way, at the highest level of English football. The pre-match report continued: 'The FA is appointing an official trainer to the England team – a development of the policy which saw Walter Winterbottom becoming team manager.'

All the headlines following the Wales match, which England won 3–0, were dominated by the continuing absence of Stan Matthews, who had lost his place to Finney, 'the young plumber from Preston' as the papers liked to call him. But it was the selectors and not Winterbottom who came in for a battering from the critics. Frank Butler, one of dozens clamouring for the reinstatement of Matthews, wrote in the *Daily Express*: 'Whatever the tactics, the faces of the England selectors must have glowed with embarrassment.' Winterbottom may be considered to have been unfortunate in not being able to select his own teams, but at least it was not his head the snipers sought when plans were seen to go awry. The existence of the England selectors acted as a protective shield for Winterbottom, deflecting the blame on to a panel of faceless suits. Disgruntled hacks could rail only against the system. If it all went wrong on match day, Winterbottom needed to do no more than raise a quizzical eyebrow and say, 'Well, don't look at me, I didn't choose the team.'

Winterbottom remembers the selectors well. 'When I first started there were eight of them plus a chairman. We would all meet in the Victoria Hotel, Sheffield, because it was a central location. We would all sit down around a big table and the chairman would say, "Now, gentlemen, it's time we picked the team. Let's have the nominations for goalkeeper" – and there would be five or six names put forward. Then we would have to whittle it down to one. That's how it was done. It often went on for hours as the selectors, some of whom had not even watched the player talked about, would argue it out. A lot of it in those days was recognition for loyalty to a club. A player might be given a cap if the selectors felt he had been a faithful servant of the club. Over time I tried to change things. A lot of the selectors would nominate players without having seen them play that season, and I thought that had to change. Many of the selectors were relying on the managers for information, so the information was coming through second-hand. 'Another problem was that the northern selectors wanted northern players, the southern ones wanted southern players, and the Midlands ones wanted Midlands players. This was clearly unsatisfactory, so we arranged for the selectors to watch players in "neutral" games – that is, not their own clubs. I suppose nowadays it seems amazing that selectors could select a player without having seen him play.

'After a while the system began to improve, but it was never entirely satisfactory. I even encouraged the selectors to ask the press what they thought, as reporters went to as many, if not more, games as they did. The selectors became better at selecting, and over time they began to consult me more and more for my thoughts on certain players. Eventually it got to the point where I would propose a team, but I did not want to push it too far and say, "This is my team." If there were two players I wasn't sure about I would leave the selectors to make the choice. This allowed them to think they were still selecting the team, but I felt that it gradually became my team. But there were always times when they would resist me. I remember after the 1958 World Cup the selectors insisted we recall Nat Lofthouse against Russia. We thrashed them 5–0, but I felt we had taken a step backwards because he would not be around for the next World Cup. The selectors had chosen a team just for that match – a friendly – but I was trying to build one capable of winning in Chile.'

Winterbottom was famously unflappable, even when facing the press after England's humiliations at the hands of the United States in the 1950 World Cup, and Hungary – the worst results in 130 years of England's history. Ever courteous, if a little suspicious, towards the press, he knew that any weaknesses shown by the national side were simply a reflection of much deeper problems in the domestic game – and the public and the press were far more interested in club football than they were in international matches (another factor that helps to explain why Winterbottom was handled by the press with relatively soft hands). 'There was little enthusiasm for international competition,' says Winterbottom. 'I had to force the FA to enter the World Cup, though [FA secretary] Stan Rous would have seen to it anyway. Our idea of international football was a couple of friendlies on a summer tour of the continent after a long season. In those days, come the season's end, footballers thought they should be on holiday like their friends in other professions.

'Club managers, too, were extremely keen that their assets were given a long rest before the new season. The idea of me taking away top players on a tour was anathema to the whole culture of the day. A lot of the players simply did not want to go, partly because of the pressure being exerted on them by their clubs. I remember a doctor at Preston North End telling me, "I'm afraid Tom Finney won't be going on any of your tours." "Why not?" I asked. "Because he's got varicose veins and I'm going to see that they are treated," he said. Of course, there was no chance of them being treated in the club's time, only in England's.

'The clubs weren't solidly behind England like they were in Brazil. There, the national team was everything, just as it was throughout South America. They suspended their matches in the season of the World Cup so that the national team took priority and they could come on tours of Europe, train together intensively and build up a sense of unity and understanding. That would never happen here as the clubs are so powerful, though there are now a lot more England get-togethers than in my day.'

The inaugural European Championship was still over a decade away, and it was not until 1958 that the World Cup was considered to be a truly meaningful event. A combination of political bickering, an unsophisticated qualifying system and a lack of real interest in the tournament meant that Hungary, Austria, Scotland, West Germany (not yet readmitted to FIFA), Belgium, France, Russia, Czechoslovakia and Argentina did not make it to Brazil in 1950, and only 31 countries competed in the qualifying rounds. The 1954 tournament in Switzerland was an improvement, but worldwide interest in the event would not be truly fired until Sweden four years later when the rapid expansion of television coverage meant that the event could be beamed into millions of homes around the world. Television played a central role in the boom of interest in international football. It also meant that there was no hiding place for the teams and their coaches. In the immediate post-war years only a handful of households in the developed world could afford the luxury of a television set. Most fans' experience of football came from standing on the terraces of their local club on a Saturday afternoon or from reading about events elsewhere in the national and local newspapers whose sports editors were far more interested in relaying news from Huddersfield than Hungary.

Since then, the massive expansion of football coverage in newspapers, magazines, television and radio, as well as the emergence of new media like websites and text services and new technology like action TV replays, has given every football follower the opportunity to consider himself an expert. 'Half the country suspects they can pick a better team than the England manager. The other half *knows* they can,' says the *Daily Telegraph*'s veteran football writer Bryon Butler. No longer is the football fan's vision of the game limited to his perspective from behind the goal of his local team. He can now see right around the world – from his armchair.

When football resumed after the war, most Englishmen believed that their representatives in the national side were the undisputed masters of world football. England had never been beaten by a Continental side on their own territory. Summer tours abroad were regarded more as a holiday and defeats there rarely sparked a national outcry. But there had been warning signs in the 1930s that England's hegemony on the world stage was not the incontrovertible truth most people understood it to be. Hugo Meisl's Austrian Wunder team and Vittorio Pozzo's Italy had both shown before the war that the rest of the world was starting to close the gap on the country that introduced the sport to the world seventy or so years earlier. At the same time, the South American teams were improving rapidly, but virtually nothing was known of them in England. England's first match against a South American team was not played until they met Chile in the 1950 World Cup. The outstanding England team of the immediate post-war years sustained the illusion that English football would continue to dominate the world for years to come. It was a cruel deception. English football needed a radical overhaul. But it would not be until a crisp November afternoon at Wembley in 1953 when Puskas' mighty Magyars demolished what was considered a powerful England team with some breathtakingly scientific and skilful football that the nation finally woke up to the fact that Johnny Foreigner could also play a bit.

Winterbottom was not the only man in the country to realise that England's days as the world's pre-eminent football team were numbered. The journalists who travelled with England on their summer tours had seen the threat from abroad at first hand. On Monday, 5 May 1947, two days after England had beaten France 3–0 at Highbury, the *Daily Express* announced the England tour party to play Switzerland and Portugal later in the month. Frank Butler took the chance to fire a warning shot about England's international standing. Of the French game he said: 'As an exhibition of football the game became a farce. It served one useful purpose: to show an English crowd what our boys are up against in these Continental tours and to explain why we lose matches abroad.'

On 10 May, the day Great Britain took on a Rest of Europe team to celebrate the return to FIFA of the four British associations, the following headline appeared in the *Express*: 'BRITAIN MUST BEAT EUROPE: OUR PRESTIGE AT STAKE'. Butler's preview of the match struck an alarmist note. In a very far cry from the claim of future England managers that 'there are no easy games in international football', Butler wrote : 'Great Britain's £150,000 Soccer team must not only beat the Rest of Europe at Hampden Park, Glasgow, today, but go all out to overwhelm the representatives of Babel United. There must not be any easing up if the British team score early goals because a draw would be regarded as a moral victory by the Continentals and leave us the laughing stock of Europe.' Great Britain won 6–1 and Butler was happy to report on the Monday that Europe was now convinced that Britain are the 'bosses of Soccer'.

A week later England lost 1–0 to Switzerland in Zurich. The defeat was seen in most quarters as an aberration, a one-off that could be explained away by a number of reasons. Fatigue at the end of the season and dubious refereeing were the excuses most frequently cited on England's behalf, but John MacAdam of the *Express* came up with one of the more original explanations in his assertion that England had been overfed by over-hospitable hosts. Under the headline 'EXTRA FOOD MAKES ENGLISH SLUGGISH', MacAdam wrote: 'Seldom has an England side of high-class players been made to look so ordinary as this one was, and the only possible explanation is that our boys were sluggish from a too-sudden immersion in an ocean of food.'

Nine days later England played a much-improved Portugal side for the first time. The match generated a good deal of publicity in the build-up and many – not least in Portugal – predicted that England's shortcomings were about to be exposed by an emerging power in European football. As it turned out, England produced one of the greatest performances in their entire history, swamping their bemused and increasingly ill-tempered hosts and thrashing them 10–0, then their biggest victory since beating Austria 11–1 in 1908. With Finney on the left and Matthews on the right causing havoc down the flanks, Lawton and Mortensen bagged four goals apiece as President Carmona, the Prime Minister and 100,000 of their compatriots looked on in uncomfortable awe. The result appeared to confirm that, when the mood took them, England had the pedigree to overwhelm lesser breeds of football nations. 'It was like we could see into each other's minds,' says Finney. Winterbottom recalls that the match became painful to watch after a while. 'I watched Portugal disintegrate and you felt sorry for them,' he says. 'I think some of their players were so shocked that they stopped playing by the end. They were demoralised, rubbished. Their goalkeeper was rated the best in Europe. When he came on to the field he took a bow and then he was replaced. It was sad really.'

The demolition of the unfortunate Portuguese prompted glowing reviews in the nation's papers which unanimously claimed that the prestige of English soccer had been fully restored. But even though England's results over the three seasons leading up to the 1950 World Cup rank among the best of the post-war years, the press were not entirely happy. England won 17 of their 21 matches over that time and lost just three. They had played a total of 29 matches since the war, winning 23 of them and scoring 100 goals at an average of 3.5 per game. They were beaten 3–1 by Scotland at Wembley in April 1949, but defeat at the hands of the Auld Enemy had never been regarded as a disgrace, especially as so many of the opposition were 'Anglos' earning their wage in the English Football League. England also lost 3–1 to Sweden in Stockholm a month later, but the result could easily be passed off as little more than a fluke at the end of an exhausting season. Likewise, the 2–0 defeat against Eire at Goodison Park in September 1949 – strictly speaking England's first home defeat by a non-British country – was explained away by some on the grounds that the Irishmen were adopted Englishmen who had learned their trade in the Football League.

Only a year earlier, England had thrashed reigning world champions Italy 4–0 in Turin in what must rank as one of the finest moments in the country's footballing history. 'Italy were technically the world champions,' says Winterbottom. 'They thought they were going to demolish us. There was little TV in those days, so after arriving in Turin we went to the cinema and watched the newsreel. The president of Italian football came on and said he thought Italy would win 4–0. I remember the match well; it was terribly hot and humid and there was a huge, very excitable crowd. Of course it was us who won 4–0 – and we had a couple of goals disallowed by the Spanish referee.' Memories, though, appeared to be short as England prepared for their first World Cup finals (or, more accurately, they waited for the tournament to begin). England's victories were rarely convincing enough to satisfy the press. A month before they set out for Brazil, England beat Portugal 5–3 thanks largely to the brilliance of Finney, who scored four of the goals. The *Daily Mirror* was unimpressed by England's effort: 'THIS VICTORY WASN'T NEARLY GOOD ENOUGH' moaned the headline.

The World Cup squad was announced on Tuesday, 24 May, and included the names of Ramsey, Wright, Dickinson, Milburn, Finney, Matthews, Mannion, Mullen and Mortensen. Compared to the great circus which attends the World Cup and its qualifying campaigns today, the build-up to the 1950 tournament was a distinctly low-key affair. Today, papers are packed with previews, profiles, supplements and daily reports of England's preparations, but in 1950, between the announcement of the final squad and its arrival in Brazil over three weeks later, there is virtually no mention of England in the nation's newspapers. One piece in the *Daily Mail* of 7 June, a paragraph long, informed readers that the squad would train at Dulwich Hamlet for a few days the following week before returning to their families. The next mention of England in the *Daily Mail* comes on 19 June, the day England flew out, when the paper's chief football writer Roy Peskett reported that the flight would take 27 hours, that the trip would cost the FA £22,000, and that the 'trainer/baggage man' was Bill Ridding of Bolton. The reader is also told that state-of-the-art kit will replace the baggy shorts and heavy boots of old: '. . . newly designed lightweight shirts and Continental shorts will be worn for the first time . . . Most of the players will wear the new type lightweight boot – a pair weighs five ounces less than the familiar type.' Winterbottom is referred to halfway down the dispatch and, intriguingly, appears to be introduced to readers: 'In charge of the Rio invaders is team manager Walter Winterbottom, dietician and planner. His is the job of training what we hope will be the winning team; of pairing up the players, some of whom can be as temperamental as prima donnas; of planning their diet, and of copy-indexing the play of the opponents. He has a card index of the tactics of almost every star in the world.'

So it was against a backdrop of cautious optimism that England boarded the aeroplane for Rio de Janeiro to participate in their first World Cup. England, the mother country of football and joint favourites with the hosts to collect the Jules Rimet trophy, were treated as superstars when they arrived in the Brazilian capital. Crowds greeted the party at the airport and at their hotel, desperate for a glimpse of the legendary figures of Matthews, Finney, Wright, Mortensen and Mannion.

Nearly fifty years after the event, Winterbottom admits that England were ill-prepared for the tournament. 'We were ignorant,' he says. 'I had no realisation of what taking part in a World Cup – especially in a foreign country – would entail, and nor had the players. Arsenal had been out there to play and they recommended we stay in a hotel which they used, right on the Copacabana beach. It was absolutely ludicrous because all the players wanted to do was go and have a swim on the beach and I had to keep them away from it. The hotel was rowdy and the food was awful. It was all a very sad experience, the accommodation and the organisation, and it probably did have some effect on morale. They weren't bad lads, the players. They didn't complain too much and they never used the conditions as an excuse. But we spent a lot of time trying to get things rearranged, especially the menus, which were dreadful. I also had to try and stop crowds coming into the hotel to try and talk to the players, who found themselves besieged. What we failed to do in Brazil was go and reconnoitre the place first, to check out the whole business of hotels, training facilities and food, and so on.' England did not even have their own team doctor, though a certain Victor Jaime de Sa was appointed by the Brazilian Sports Federation to attend to their guests throughout the tournament. His tasks, according to the press, were to 'advise the players on vitamin pills and perhaps also give them sleeping tablets so that they can get rest despite the din of firecrackers which boys are expected to explode outside the hotel this coming week'.

The contrast with the Brazilian camp could not have been greater. John Thompson filed his 'first cable from Rio' for the *Daily Mirror* on Saturday, 17 June under the headline 'THEY'RE GOING NUTS ON SOCCER IN BRAZIL'. His story began: 'In a millionaire's home, hidden on the hills behind this fabulous Soccer-crazy city, are twenty-two young men whose hearts are set on resisting England's bid to take home the World Cup. They are brilliant, highly paid Brazilian stars, joint favourites with England for football's most coveted prize.' Thompson reported that the Brazilians had a lavishly equipped medical room with two doctors, two masseurs and three chefs. Brazil's coach, Flavio Costa, apparently feared England more than any other team. He was quoted in the English press as saying: 'When I saw England play in Glasgow I was so excited, and there was so much I wanted to tell my boys about the fine England play that I dashed back to Brazil long before I meant to return.'

England were clearly held in some awe by the host nation, who had yet to encounter a team from the mother country of the sport. Headlines in the local press announced: 'THE KINGS OF FOOTBALL HAVE ARRIVED!' England were considered to be robust, even brutal, in their style. A former president of the Brazilian Sports Federation, Vargas Netto, had been to see the FA Cup final and told reporters: 'I do not refer only to the using of the body or strong tackling and the use of the legs to put the man off the ball. I saw many feet in the air which caught opponents above the knee. There was systematic rushing of the goalkeepers with excessive energy. Forwards threw themselves with all their weight, like tanks or racing cars.'

England's first group match was against Chile in Rio's newly built 130,000-capacity Maracana Stadium, where all the seats had been painted blue because the colour was thought to have a calming effect on volatile fans. On the eve of the match Winterbottom told the press: 'It is difficult to stop the training, they are so keen. We have been offered the use of oxygen masks as revivers at half-time, but hope they won't be needed.' In the event England won 2–0 with goals from Mortensen and Mannion, and though they hardly justified all the pre-tournament eulogies in the Brazilian press, they were rarely troubled by the South Americans in playing conditions made difficult by a heavy downpour throughout the match. (The team that day was: Williams, Ramsey, Aston, Wright, Hughes, Dickinson, Mannion, Finney, Bentley, Mortensen, Mullen.) The *Daily Mail* match report began on the front page and continued on the back. It finished with the famous last words: 'All things considered England should take the game against the United States in their stride as a preparation for the stiff test against Spain.'

In the four days between the Chile and the USA match in the goldmine town of Belo Horizonte there was not a single report about England in the *Mirror*. The match was expected to be a walkover. In the *Daily Mail* there was not a single piece about England in the build-up to the match, not even on the day itself, other than to announce an unchanged team. Editors, though, certainly sat up and took notice when the cables began to arrive in Fleet Street on the evening of Thursday, 29 June. Most of them refused to believe the score when it appeared on the wires, assuming there had been a typographical or transmission error and that the true score was probably 10–0 or 10–1 to England. Only when the news was announced on the radio was the astonishing truth acknowledged. The following morning, the front page of the *Daily Mail* ran the shock headline 'AMERICA BEATS ENGLAND', reporting that 'A fitter, faster, fighting United States have done the unbelievable! They beat England against all the prophecies 1–0 in the World Cup Tournament. This is the biggest Soccer upset of all time.' But the report contained not a whisper of criticism of Winterbottom; the closest it came to finger-pointing was 'Maybe England should have made changes in the side and included fresher players.'

The American goalscorer, Larry Gaetjens, was chaired from the field amid a riot of firecrackers as the 20,000 locals who had come to admire the skills of the fabled Englishmen reacted with unconfined delight to the demise of their own team's most feared rivals. The American delegation had pre-booked their flight home for the day after their third and final qualifying match, but now it was England, the team everyone expected to be on the pitch at the tournament's final whistle, who were forced to reassess their travel arrangements. England had battered the American goal for most of the match and Williams, the England goalkeeper, claimed after the match that on a normal day England would have been celebrating a 14–0 victory.

It was a dismal day for British sport. Not only had England lost at football to the part-time Americans, by some margin the weakest team in the tournament and only invited to Brazil at the last minute following a spate of withdrawals, but in cricket England had lost their first ever Test at home to the West Indies, while Britain's last hope in the men's singles at Wimbledon was extinguished when Tony Mottram was beaten by Australian Geoff Brown.

For the *Daily Mail*, the World Cup defeat was seen as the greatest humiliation English football had ever suffered. 'BOMBSHELL FOR OUR WORLD CUP HOPES: ENGLAND FALL TO U.S. AMATEURS' ran the backpage headline, while the report read: 'English soccer was humbled as it never has been before in the little stadium here today.'

Overall, though, the reaction in the British papers to what is still regarded as the worst defeat in the country's history was strangely muted. But this was not because those who reported it were not shocked by what they had seen, but because of the extreme difficulties facing reporters trying to cable their dispatches from abroad. Nowadays, reporters plug their mobile phones into their lap-tops and simply press 'Enter', and within seconds the story will be sitting on a sub-editor's screen back in London. Years after the tournament, Frank Butler recounted the tortuous process by which he and his colleagues (there were only six British reporters covering the 1950 World Cup) tried to send their news home from Belo Horizonte. 'We would write our story at the end of the match, wrap it up, tie it to a piece of string, lower it down a wall to a messenger who ran to the other side of ground, then another took it to the cable staff who telephoned it through to their main office in Rio, who then cabled it to London. Frustrated sports writers had the biggest, if saddest, soccer story in years, but couldn't do justice to it for lack of communications.'

Winterbottom, understandably, remembers the day vividly. 'The USA business was a tragedy,' he recalls. 'Where we played was out of the way and the pitch was crude. There was a great high wall around the pitch which made it feel like a bullfighting ring. Our changing rooms were just huts. It was disgraceful. In the match itself, I think we hit the woodwork about six times. It was partly sheer bad luck, but the grass was awful. Their goal came from a forty-yard shot which struck a player's head. I don't think he meant to head it and our goalkeeper was moving the wrong way and it just rolled over the line. From then on the Americans tried all kinds of tactics. They would kick the ball into the stands where the crowd would pass it around. There was time-wasting and a good deal of man-handling of our players. It wasn't rough, but they were using spoiling tactics. It was just one of those matches when you look back and think, What the hell could we have done? The longer it went on and the more dejected we became the more our players started overdoing it, trying to run through the whole team and bring us the goal. It was very, very disappointing. This wasn't a good football team we lost to. We thrashed them several times afterwards. We just had to accept we had been beaten and it shouldn't have been. The USA game was a disaster, but I don't see it as the lowest point of my career. It was bad luck combined with very unhelpful circumstances. It was heartbreaking, and some of the players were absolutely distraught thinking they had let themselves and the country down.'

The match also evoked painful memories for Finney, who,

like Winterbottom, can remember the day as clearly as any in his career. 'It was just one of those games that happens every now and then in football, like Walsall beating Arsenal in the Cup here. You can't explain it. Ninety-nine times out of a hundred you'll beat them, but by the law of averages every now and then you'll get a big upset. It happens to all teams and it happened to us against the States. That said, the pitch was very, very poor and today it would not even be considered for a lower League match let alone a World Cup. It was the same for them, of course, but it did make playing decent football difficult. But I would admit that we did not play that well. We were on a hiding to nothing. They had nothing to lose. They were expected just to make up the numbers but perhaps we were a bit more tense because we knew what was expected of us. Walter was shocked afterwards. We all were. We just stood around getting changed saying over and over again, "How on earth did we manage to lose that one?" '

Still, there was little sense of crisis, only shock, and most of the press felt confident that England would beat Spain and then show the rest of the world the real England in the second stage of the tournament. England, though, despite the recall of Matthews, lost 1–0 to a rough Spanish team in front of 100,000 spectators in the Maracana. But in a display of loyalty and patriotism which would be unthinkable today, the press had nothing but sympathy for the vanquished England team, regardless of the major blow dealt to the nation's footballing reputation. A story on the front page of the *Daily Mirror* reported: 'England were unlucky to lose to Spain yesterday. They gave a fine display of craftsmanship and determination.' Most reports made chummy references to the battling efforts of 'our boys' and 'our lads', and in other instances it was not 'England' who were beaten but 'us'.

The occasion of England's exit prompted several sports editors to run more than just a match report. The *Mirror* carried a comment piece by Tom Phillips which had been written before the Spain match ('I don't intend to change a word, whatever the result,' he told us). His subject was the tendency of Englishmen to whine and find excuses when the national team lost abroad. He claimed that at home England managed to keep a 'sense of proportion', but 'foreign air and customs affect the English peculiarly'. He continued as follows (take a deep breath if you get squeamish at the sight or sound of xenophobia): 'If we are beaten in Italy, members of the English colony there will write to us moaning of the terrible blow England's prestige has suffered. What has happened is this. The Italians (or whatever nation it is), who have never had much to cheer about anyhow, any time, have in their excitable way pulled the legs of every Englishman they could find. And the English, instead of remembering their ability to hit back as they do in real emergencies, in domestic political crises or in war, take, as they say in my part of the country, "the water in". They weep in the corner.'

The day after England's exit the nation's newspapers ran pieces analysing what went wrong. In their final cables from Rio the press called for changes in English football. John Thompson in the *Daily Mirror* demanded that England finally put an end to 'smug complacency' and accept that they had something to learn from foreigners, who, he said, had outstripped England in football ideas and technical ability. Not one of these pieces contained a single word of criticism directed towards Winterbottom. The investigation stopped there, and in the days and weeks that followed, the sports pages turned their attention to cricket. Some of the papers, though, turned their fire on the captain Billy Wright. In a total reversal of what would happen today, when players are forced to come out in support of the manager, Winterbottom told reporters: 'It is both unfair and absurd to make Billy Wright a scapegoat. I still have every confidence in him and believe he is one of the best captains England has ever had.'

'Looking back at it now, I think we were a bit naive and complacent when we arrived in Brazil,' says Finney. 'We had no idea about what we were in for. The temperature was well up in the nineties and in those days we were just not used to travelling to hot countries like most people today. The grass and the hardness of the pitches were also new to us. Everything was alien. We had never been to South America and I think we walked into it a bit wide-eyed. We went to see the opening match between Brazil and Mexico and it was an absolute eye-opener to see how skilful and quick these players were. Another factor was that we were not a settled team at that stage. Lots of our best players had gone and there was a fair amount of chopping and changing by the selectors, so we were a long way from being well established as a group of players like other teams. It must have been very frustrating for Walter, who strongly believed in the benefits of a settled side.'

The vagaries and infighting of the selectors had been major problems in this respect for Winterbottom at the start of his reign, but the all-British nature of the English League made his job doubly difficult. 'The biggest problem for any international side is building confidence,' he says. 'You don't want a side thinking, We're not quite sure about winning. You get that confidence by keeping the same together. The 1974 World Cup finals were a good example: West Germany had six players from Bayern Munich while Holland had six from Ajax. They were players who understood each other instinctively because they played together all the time. When Italy won the 1982 World Cup eleven of their squad were from Juventus, and the Juve coach helped out the national side. With England it was absolutely ridiculous when I was manager. I remember going to see Arsenal play Manchester City, two of the strongest teams of the day, and of the 22 players on the pitch only five were Englishmen. The rest were Scots, Irish or Welsh. What hope was there of me trying to find a unit, a nucleus from just one club? There was no chance of it, and today it is even worse with all the Continental players in the Premier League. This has always been a major problem for England managers. That's where Ramsey was good: he decided on a core group of players and stuck with them. That's where Taylor failed: he was always changing his sides.'

Wednesday, 25 November 1953 – a date painfully etched on the heart of English football. Even those who were born decades later understand its significance when the senior citizens of the football world refer ruefully to that watershed afternoon at a packed Wembley. It was the day that Hungary, the 'Mighty Magyars', rode into the hitherto impregnable fortress of England's football empire and rode out with its most coveted treasure: a reputation as the greatest football team on the planet. No longer could England, the inventors and early masters of the world's most popular game, lay claim to being its finest exponents.

In truth, England's powers had been on the wane for some years – or was it simply that the rest of the world had got so much better? The 1950 World Cup had exposed England's vulnerability on foreign soil, but there remained a widespread conviction that England were indomitable at home. England had lost just two of their 24 games in the three years since the World Cup, 3–2 to Scotland at Wembley in April 1951 and 2–1 to Uruguay, the world champions, in Montevideo in May 1953. Nine of the other games, though, had been drawn, and the great team of the immediate post-war years was but a dim, if glorious, memory. Goalkeeper Frank Swift, whose life would be brought to a tragically early end in the Munich air disaster of 1958, received his last cap against Norway in the 1948/49 season. Neil Franklin, banned by the FA for succumbing to the lure of the dollar in Colombian football, played his last game for England in the 1–0 win over Scotland in 1950. Raich Carter, the brilliant if temperamental inside-forward, was long finished, his last appearance coming in the 1–0 surprise defeat at the hands of Switzerland in Zurich in 1947. George Hardwick, England's first captain after the war, pulled on the white shirt for the last time in the 2–0 win over Scotland in April 1948, while the international career of Tommy Lawton, the greatest centre-forward of the war years, lasted just two matches longer. Stan Mortensen and Wilf Mannion, two of England's greatest ever forwards and veterans of England's failed World Cup bid, were both jettisoned as the selectors experimented with a bewildering number of new players in the search for the perfect formula. Even the great Stan Matthews, a victim of the selectors' suspicion and fickleness throughout his career, found himself in the wilderness for over two seasons. The England team-sheets of the day are conspicuous for their inconsistency; only the names of Merrick, Ramsey, Wright, Dickinson, Finney and Lofthouse appear regularly in the first three years of the decade. Most of the chopping and changing took place in the forward lines where the following, largely forgotten, names of the international scene were given a chance to prove themselves over this period: Hancocks, E. Baily, Hassall, Medley, Metcalfe, Phillips, Pearson, Broadis, Milton, Sewell, T. Thompson, R. Froggatt, Elliott, R. Allen, Berry, Quixall, Wilshaw and Robb.

It was not so much that England were failing to win all their matches, but the manner in which they played was considered utilitarian and unimaginative. Two weeks before the Hungary game, England beat Ireland 3–1, but they came in for heavy criticism from the press (still, though, it was not Winterbottom but the selectors who came under fire).

On the day of the match, however, the press were confident that England would extend their 24-match unbeaten home record against Continental opposition. The *Daily Mail* headline declared: 'PLAYERS OUT TO SLAM HUNGARY – AND CRITICS'. In his preview, Roy Peskett predicted that England's famous 'character' would win the day over Hungarian technique. 'The Hungarians, Olympic Champions, who are rated in some quarters as a "wonder" side, will today face a strong, determined England side,' he wrote. 'Their style will differ a lot from the Hungarian play, but I think it will prevail in one of the most momentous matches played in the Football Association's ninety-year history . . . England should finish two or three goals to the good . . . but the Hungarians will not give in easily.'

Peskett's optimism echoed the mood of most of his contemporaries who joined the 100,000-strong crowd that filed through the turnstiles that afternoon. Millions more were able to see the match from home as the second half was televised live and a full recording was broadcast in the evening. Today, Winterbottom claims that the optimism in the press was entirely wrong-headed. 'They were all saying we were going to beat Hungary, which was ridiculous,' he says. 'I saw them play at the Olympics in Helsinki and watched them win hands down. Six of those players were still in the side when they came to Wembley. Their training methods were far superior to anyone else's. The players were chosen from two clubs in Budapest and they all got together in the week for international training and matches against scratch sides. Every week! Wow! Imagine that here. They also had the good sense to prepare themselves in different ways depending on the opposition. England had a reputation for stamina and being physically strong. So they prepared for facing us by working extra hard on their fitness programme, building up their strength to counter us.

'About five weeks earlier, Sweden drew with Hungary and our press went overboard saying, "Well just wait and see what England will do to them." I saw the papers, and I thought, Oh God! this is ridiculous! because I had seen the quality of their football first hand. Sweden had just kicked long balls forward, grabbed two lucky goals and thrown everyone behind the ball. That was not an option for England.'

What happened that afternoon changed the perception of England's invincibility for ever. This match was the *Titanic* disaster of English football; the supposedly unsinkable was sunk. Never again would English football fans – barring one or two on the Broadmoor wing of the country's following – lay claim to their country's world dominance. It finished 6–3, and by all accounts the visitors might have reached double figures had they not relaxed the pressure in the final third in the knowledge that their mission had already been accomplished (all six Hungarian goals came inside the hour). The following morning, *Daily Mail* readers awoke to see a front page showing a picture of the England team standing to salute the seated Hungarians at the post-match banquet. In what would be an unthinkable editorial line today, the front-page piece was a celebration of Hungarian greatness, rather than a spiteful exposition of England's humiliation. (At the bottom of the report there is a one-paragraph story headed 'CONSOLA-TION' reporting that England beat Hungary 5–4 in a table tennis international at Wembley's Empire Pool.) The eulogies continued on the sports pages of the paper, where Peskett almost gleefully pointed out this was the lesson England had needed to rouse the game's dusty, antediluvian administrators into action. 'Here were the lessons of the value of training a national team. Now perhaps our Soccer will be remodelled not only at national but at club level, to be given the 1953 look instead of the stodgy Victorian touch.'

Finney had injured himself the previous Saturday and was ruled out of the match, but he was there in the crowd working for a national newspaper and was as astonished as everyone else by what he saw. 'It was a tremendous shock to everyone watching,' he recalls. 'The first strange thing we noticed was that the Hungarians came out about twenty minutes before kick-off and started warming up. That was absolutely unheard of in English football at the time. It makes you laugh to think about it now when you realise that limbering up and stretching, especially on cold days, are absolutely essential. We always went out straight from the warmth of the changing room completely cold and stiff. After that club managers started copying the Hungarians. It was just one of the many things about these brilliant Hungarians that made you realise how much more scientific and forward-thinking they were.

'It is not true, though, to say that we were taken completely unawares. Walter drummed it into us that they were the best side he had ever seen. One of the differences between the two sides was that they played and trained together all the time while we hadn't. There was still this idea in English football that you could just take eleven good club players, dump them into white shirts and expect them to perform.'

Winterbottom was not shocked by what he saw, and even claims today that England had been a bit unlucky. 'Our goalkeeper Merrick had a very poor game. Four of their goals came from shots from outside the area. We scored three goals and had more of the play territorially. I think about that match sometimes now, and the Hungarians did play some brilliant football, such as when Puskas dragged the ball back and then shot into the net in virtually the same movement. These kind of skills had never been seen before. They had six players who were genuinely world class. Normally you are lucky if you have two.'

Amazingly, to the modern reader, in all the thousands of words written in the national and local newspapers the day after, there still was not a single significant reference to the manager of the team, Winterbottom. Clearly, the idea that a coach could exert any kind of influence over a team was yet to be acknowledged. To most critics, there were two major problems that needed addressing: the release of players by clubs and the reorganisation of English football at every level with greater emphasis on the development of technique. In the wake of the shattering defeat the FA called an emergency meeting of leading club managers to discuss the way forward. Most commentators claimed that England remained the best in the world for temperament, stamina and knowledge of the game, but that they were being overtaken in terms of technique, training and devotion to skills. There was a general call for the clubs to release players so that the England squad could train for longer spells.

In spite of the Hungarian humiliation at Wembley, England's stock on the international football market was clearly still high when they travelled to Yugoslavia in May 1954 for the start of a two-match tour which would also included a visit to Budapest, in the weeks before the World Cup in Switzerland. England were mobbed on their arrival in Belgrade and cheered all along the route to their hotel. In the match, England outplayed their hosts but squandered a host of chances and lost 1–0. The Yugoslav triumph was greeted with delirium on the terraces; scores of bonfires were lit all over Partisan Stadium at the end of the match.

A week later, on Saturday, 22 May, the eve of the match against Hungary, the *Daily Mail* ran the patriotic headline: 'ENGLAND CHANCE OF REVENGE: HUNGARY WOR-RIED'. With the benefit of hindsight, it is difficult to imagine what on earth Hungary had to worry about, unless it was a fear of scoring fewer than ten goals. Since losing to Austria in May 1950, the 'Mighty Magyars' had won 23 matches, drawn four and lost none. Only a few months earlier they needed just sixty minutes to leave England's formidable reputation lying in pieces and were now, in front of their own fans, facing an uncertain, morale-shaken side with only a handful of genuinely world-class players in Finney, Wright and Dickinson (Manchester United full-back Roger Byrne was considered an outstanding talent but this was only his third senior cap). The England line-up was: Merrick, Staniforth, Byrne, Wright, Owen, Dickinson, P. Harris, Sewell, Jezzard, Broadis, Finney. They lost 7–1, a result which remains the biggest defeat in England's history.

On the Monday, the mood in the papers was one of slight embarrassment and sadness mixed with awe for the Hungarians, rather than one of anger and recrimination. There was a general recognition that England's problems ran far beyond the small number of players who made up the national squad. Yet again, there was not a whisper of criticism directed towards Winterbottom, and most of the post-match analysis was conspicuous for its sense of 'we're all in this together'. The *Daily Mail* featured a large front-page headline announcing 'BIGGEST DEFEAT EVER FOR ENGLISH SOCCER – THE HUNGARIANS ARE FROM ANOTHER PLANET'. The suggestion that England's conquerors were aliens with supernatural powers may not have cut much ice within the scientific community, but it did at least rub home the point to the 'flat-earthers', who continued to believe in England's innate superiority over other nations, that the world was a stranger place than they had imagined.

Winterbottom told reporters on the gloomy flight out of Budapest: 'We were inexperienced and outclassed. None of our lads played below his club form, but it just wasn't good enough. We've no excuses.' But in a thinly concealed attack on the selfishness of those running club football, he added: 'It has been obvious for some time that under our present system we cannot compete against nations who throw overboard everything for the national team.' There was not a reporter on the plane who disagreed with him – at least not in their dispatches the following day.

Johnny Haynes, who was a substitute that day, remembers being amazed by Winterbottom's calmness after the match. 'I never saw him go off his head completely after a match or at half-time,' he recalls. 'Even when we were hammered in Budapest he didn't lay into anyone. We were lucky not to lose by double figures, but he didn't blow his top. He was very down, you could tell, but as a football purist, I think in a funny kind of way he was almost excited to watch the brilliance of the Hungarians. He didn't see it as his fault. The team wasn't down to him – it was the selection committee's team and all the newspaper reporters knew it.'

England's heaviest ever defeat was the last thing they needed in their final match before the fifth World Cup. The event was still some way from becoming the biggest event in the world's sporting calendar, and there was only passing mention of England's preparations in the nation's newspapers in the weeks leading up to it. Short reports speculated about the likely recall of the evergreen Matthews and fretted over the state of Finney's right knee. The *Daily Mail*, a paper with one of the more extensive sports sections, limited its coverage in the build-up to a brief preview explaining the group systems and giving the dates of the matches. Nor, in the event, was there much for the nation's pressmen to report. England's participation lasted just three matches. The opening game against Belgium finished an old-fashioned 4–4, England having been wasteful in front of goal and generous at the back. A pulled muscle ruled Matthews out of the game against their Swiss hosts, but England managed a 2–0 win, the two Wolves forwards Mullen and Wilshaw scoring the goals. In one of the more illogical group systems in the history of the competition, teams only played two of their three rivals in their pool. England finished top of Pool IV having not had to play Italy, but they were beaten 4–2 by Uruguay in the quarter-finals, despite outplaying the reigning champions for much of the game.

Many chose to blame the goalkeeper, Merrick, but the following day's headlines were not exclusively concerned with England's exit. The failure of the national team was no longer news, it seems; their problems had been laid bare for all to see over the preceding year. England's elimination also came on the same day as the quarter-final clash between Hungary and Brazil. The contest, pitching the unquestionable masters of world football against a rising superpower, was predicted to be one of the most memorable in the history of the tournament. And it was, but for none of the reasons expected. The match, won 4–2 by Hungary, was immediately dubbed 'The Battle of Berne' as the players brutalised each other in one of the roughest matches in the history of international football. English referee Arthur Ellis sent off three players, two of them Brazilians, as the match fulfilled its threat to descend into violence. The hostilities were not confined to the pitch for trouble also broke out in the crowd, but the ugliest violence took place behind the scenes as the players battled each other with bottles, boots and chairs in the tunnel and changing area. Back in England, the events were given only marginally less coverage than England's demise.

It seemed almost needless for the press to point out that there were major problems facing the national side. Hungary had already made that startlingly obvious. (Englishmen at least had had the consolation of seeing Scotland being beaten 7–0 by Uruguay, but the humiliation of England's former equals on the international side was also further depressing evidence that the British game as a whole was insular and primitive.) After the World Cup the Football Association made plans to modernise the England set-up. Winterbottom was to concentrate more on the management of the England team than on his other role as the FA's Director of Coaching. He would be given more time to prepare the squad in the build-up to matches, while the International Selection Committee, previously featuring up to ten men and prone to player prejudice and infighting, would be pruned to a small body, mostly of younger men with a keener understanding of modern trends in football. The FA received some rare credit for a radical shake-up of the international set-up which saw the introduction of youth and Under-23 teams designed to establish continuity. The reforms had an immediate impact: England lost just three matches between November 1955 and the end of their World Cup run in 1958. A new generation of players emerged, many of them, like Haynes, Ronnie Clayton, Duncan Edwards and Bobby Robson, via the Under-23s. Six of the players who thrashed France at Wembley in 1957 graduated from the Under-23 side.

England's rehabilitation under Winterbottom's thoughtful and imaginative guidance suffered a crushing setback on 6 February 1958 when the aeroplane carrying Manchester United back home from Belgrade crashed on the ice-bound runway of Munich airport. Twenty-three died, including eight of Matt Busby's 'Babes'. Three of them – Roger Byrne, Duncan Edwards and Tommy Taylor – were key members of the national side and their loss, aside from the human tragedy of their premature deaths, ripped the heart out of England's increasingly impressive side. Byrne was proving to be a full-back of the highest quality, while in Taylor England had found the man to replace the great Lofthouse at centre-forward. In purely football terms, Edwards, who clung on to life for three weeks, was the greatest loss. 'I think that team was developing into something very special,' says Finney. 'Edwards was the most outstanding all-round talent I had ever seen. He had everything. Apart from the terrible sadness we all felt the disaster had a major effect on our chances of success in the World Cup.' There were no players of comparable ability ready to step into the void left by the three United stars. Over the next two seasons England experimented with seven different players at right-back, and it was not until the emergence of Jimmy Greaves at the turn of the decade that England found a goalscorer of Taylor's calibre. Edwards was simply irreplaceable, but in Wolves' Ron Flowers England did at least discover a half-back worthy of the tag 'world-class'.

Byrne, Taylor and Edwards' last appearance for England came in the 4–0 win over France at Wembley on 27 November 1957, but their loss to the national side was not immediately obvious when England played Scotland at Hampden on 19 April 1958 in their first match since the Munich tragedy. England won 4–0 and the *Daily Herald* (which became the *Sun* in 1964) was able to gloat with the headline: 'WHY, IT WAS ONLY 4–0!' And it was around this time that the influence of Winterbottom on the national team was starting to be recognised in the press coverage. His name starts to appear in headlines, and reports begin to refer to England as 'Winterbottom's team'. After the Scotland match, the *Daily Herald* sub-heading read: 'ROLL ON SWEDEN – MR WINTERBOTTOM HAS DONE US PROUD'. There was widespread recognition that much of England's revival was attributable to the efforts of the coach, but the full impact of the loss of the United trio was brought home the next month when England found themselves chasing the shadows of Yugoslavia's blue shirts in the searing heat of Belgrade. On paper, England's line-up looked formidable. Finney, Haynes, Bobby Charlton (making a difficult return to the stadium where the Busby Babes had played their last match before the fateful flight to Munich), Wright, Howe, Clayton and Douglas all took the field, but they were no match for a highly skilled, organised and motivated Yugoslav side that won 5–0 and might have beaten England by an even greater margin had they taken all their chances.

The next day's *Daily Herald* made no attempt to hide its disappointment: 'THIS WAS PLAIN SOCCER SLAUGHTER AT 90 DEGREES IN THE SHADE' ran the headline. Peter Lorenzo's report left his readers in little doubt about his verdict on England's performance and their hopes of winning the World Cup for the first time. He wrote: 'For eleven staggered, crushed Englishmen – and a handful of their stunned countrymen in the stands – it was the funeral pyre of their World Cup dreams . . . On today's form our chances in Sweden have gone up in the smoke of those flaming torches that still smoulder all around me as I write this, the saddest soccer dispatch I have ever had to send from foreign soil.' It was England's heaviest defeat since the 7–1 annihilation by Hungary four years earlier. Winterbottom's rebuilt national side, and the hopes invested in it by an expectant nation, lay in ruins. 'This was the worst performance by an England team I have ever seen. I make no excuses,' said Winterbottom.

The *News of the World*, Britain's best-selling Sunday paper, took the opportunity to lambast the selectors, who reportedly had called in the team's senior players – Finney, Wright and Haynes – to help them in their task of choosing the side. Under the headlines 'THIS MEANS TROUBLE ENGLAND: STOP IT SOCCER' and 'SELECTORS SHOULD MAKE THEIR OWN DECISIONS', Frank Butler wrote: 'The soccer selectors are as good as admitting, "We don't know the answer. You have a go, chums." ' Strangely, there is no suggestion by Butler or any other commentator that Winterbottom should have a greater say in the selection process or that he should take any of the blame. Again, there is not a single reference to Winterbottom in the entire piece.

All Winterbottom's best-laid plans were dashed on the rocks, and he knew it. 'After the Munich disaster we were left with just three established internationals in Finney, Haynes and

Wright,' recalls Winterbottom. 'We had to bring in the whole half-back line from Wolverhampton for a while and we had to start capping players in vital positions just a few months before going to Sweden. At the beginning of the year we had felt confident about our chances of actually winning the World Cup. We couldn't see anyone to challenge us in Europe. Hungary were no longer the team they were and it was not long before that we had thrashed Brazil [a 4–2 win at Wembley in May 1956].'

Despite the obvious difficulties presented to Winterbottom and the selectors by the loss of the United players, the press were in unsympathetic mood in the countdown to the World Cup. The selection of the robust if guileless Derek Kevan at centre-forward ahead of Middlesbrough's Brian Clough, who had scored an astonishing 57 goals in the season just finished, provided the focus of much of the anxiety in the nation's newspapers. The news that Kevan was selected ahead of Charlton for the pre-World Cup friendly against Russia – one of the sides they faced in the group stages – apparently left the *Daily Herald*'s chief soccer writer in need of a stiff drink and a space rocket. 'Pass the vodka! Send me zooming in a Sputnik,' wrote Peter Lorenzo. 'I've just been told the England team to meet Russia on Sunday and I can't believe it.' In the event, England were unrecognisable from the side that folded so easily against the Yugoslavs. The match finished in a 1–1 draw, but by all accounts England would have been worthy winners. Kevan, meanwhile, answered the critics with a goal and a highly impressive all-round performance that had the press corps rubbing their eyes to see if the vodka had been playing tricks with their vision.

The final squad for the World Cup was announced shortly afterwards: Hopkinson and McDonald filled the goalkeeping slots; Banks, Howe, Sillet, Clamp, Clayton, Norman, Slater and Wright formed the backs; and, ignoring the claims of the veteran Lofthouse and the prodigious talent of Clough, the selectors chose A'Court, Brabrook, Broadbent, Charlton, Douglas, Finney, Haynes, Kevan, Robson and Smith as their forwards. The group system for the World Cup finals was an unsatisfactory formula based on global regions rather than seeding, and it pitched England, the strongest team in western Europe, into the same group as three realistic contenders for the Jules Rimet trophy: the USSR, the most powerful team in the east; Brazil, the strongest team in South America and most people's tip for the final; and Austria, who rivalled Hungary as the most formidable side in central Europe.

Fears over Finney's damaged heel proved unfounded, and for England's first match against the Russians in Gothenburg the selectors kept faith with the side that had performed so creditably in Moscow three weeks earlier: McDonald, Howe, Banks, Clamp, Wright, Slater, Douglas, Robson, Kevan, Haynes and Finney. Only the absence of Charlton provoked critical comment in the press. England could not have started their opening match more poorly or finished it more brightly. Two goals down after 65 minutes against a Russian side whose rough-house tactics had surprised and rattled their opponents, England hit back with a goal from Kevan and then equalised five minutes from time with a Finney penalty after Haynes was brought down. And England might even have won had Robson not missed an open goal and had a goal disallowed for handball (to this day, Robson swears it hit his chest). The press were delighted by England's fightback and Kevan was no longer the guileless clodhopper of a few weeks past; he had suddenly become 'the giant-hearted' and 'never-say-die hero'.

Finney had taken such a battering from his Russian marker that it took him ten minutes to get to his hotel bathroom the following morning. He and Winterbottom tried to keep the news of his badly swollen knee a secret, but his conspicuous absence soon alerted the press as to his condition. He was replaced by Liverpool's Alan A'Court for England's next match in Gothenburg against a mighty Brazilian team that boasted the talents of Nilton Santos, Didi, Vava, Zagallo and Gilmar, but not Pele or Garrincha, who were to play in Brazil's next four matches. Again England showed that they were a major force in the tournament, more than holding their own in an entertaining goalless draw that turned out to be the only match the eventual champions failed to win. 'IT'S A GOLDEN DRAW: THOSE SUPERB SEÑORS HELD BY ENGLAND' beamed the back page of the *Daily Herald*. The gloom that had fallen over the English press corps following the Belgrade humiliation had now well and truly lifted. Peter Lorenzo was clearly in high spirits as he cabled home the following message for Herald readers: 'Glory be! England did it! Sing it to the skies ... we're still in the World Cup with a strong fighting chance of winning through to the quarter-finals.' England had survived their two most difficult matches against teams who were many pundits' favourites to win the competition. Only Austria, regarded as the weakest team in the pool, stood in their way of a place in the quarter-finals.

Frank Butler in the *News of the World* berated the selectors for what he saw as a lack of courage and imagination in not selecting Charlton, the rising star of English football. Nor did Winterbottom, this time, escape blame. Having been praised for his efforts in rebuilding the national side after the last World Cup, Winterbottom had now become a more legitimate target. Making it perfectly clear that he felt Winterbottom could have insisted on Charlton's inclusion if he had had the will, Butler added: 'Team-manager Walter Winterbottom, who sits in on all these team selections and has tremendous influence on the final choice, was as calm as ever as he came out of the room smiling quietly to give us the news – which really wasn't news at all.'

A sense of mounting tension between Winterbottom and the press corps becomes evident in the Charlton controversy. The press had barely even referred to him for most of his time in charge, let alone blamed him for poor performances or questionable selections, but after his influence over the team was increased past-1954, his higher profile made him a more visible target on which the press felt entitled to focus their sights. But until the defeat in Belgrade, there was little to complain about; Winterbottom had manifestly done an impressive job in reforming the structure of the national sides at every level while producing a highly successful senior side. During that period it had become increasingly clear that the selectors, more often than not, would defer to the wishes of Winterbottom who, by the time of the 1958 World Cup, had been in his post for twelve years. The sub-text in the reports of the time carried the suggestion that if Winterbottom was entitled to praise for England's achievements, then it was only fair he should receive criticism for the failings. In a clear departure from the earlier policy of sparing Winterbottom when the search for scapegoats was begun, the press now appeared eager to develop a sense of confrontation.

England could only manage a 2–2 draw with Austria, meaning that they had to face the Russians for a third time in a month in a play-off match to reach the last eight. Roared on by a fiercely anti-Soviet Swedish crowd, England outplayed the Russians for much of the game but were unable to capitalise on their superiority and lost 1–0.

England flew home to a barrage of criticism, directed mainly at the selectors but also at Winterbottom. Chelsea chairman Joe Mears, the chief selector, bore the brunt of the recriminations. The morning after their return the *Daily Herald* ran a picture of a smiling Mears next to one of Bobby Charlton, head down and sombre-looking after not being given a single game. Underneath, the paper printed letters from angry fans calling for the removal of Winterbottom. (Letters from the public have always been a convenient way for newspapers to avoid the diplomatic inconvenience of attacking a target directly.) 'I say sack Walter Winterbottom before we really reach rock bottom,' wrote A. Grinstead from Birmingham. Johnny Haynes, who played with badly blistered feet throughout the tournament, says he was unmoved by the criticism on his return home. 'They always expect you to win it and if you don't, the press always have a go and dish out the stick. If we didn't win the whole thing, that simply wasn't good enough in those days. Everyone in England thinks we have a God-given right to win the World Cup.'

The 1958 World Cup is regarded as the time that international football grew up. Thereafter the competition was seen as an accurate barometer of a nation's strength in the world's most popular game. Failure reflected on the whole country. For post-imperial England, still coming to terms with its falling status in the new world order, the failure of its national football team was interpreted as just one more example of the country's decline. The gentlemanly tone that characterised

coverage of England in the immediate post-war years had given
way to something altogether more vicious and vitriolic. Over
the four years that followed Sweden 1958, the relationship
between the press and the England management deteriorated
sharply.

Shortly before setting out for a tour of South America at the
end of the 1958/59 season, England played Italy at Wembley
and drew 2–2. The *Daily Herald* was singularly unimpressed.
The paper had assigned a new reporter, Sam Leitch, to cover
the national side. If it was brutal frankness his editor wanted,
Leitch certainly delivered. Short of including a tirade of sexual
swear words, it is difficult to imagine a reporter writing a more
abusive report. 'Just 48 hours before they fly off on their
20,000-mile tour of the Americas, England plunged into
pathetic depths of tame surrender ... I give the full list of
England flops headed by skipper Billy Wright, whose 101st cap
was his worst.' But it was not until the tour itself that the
gloves well and truly came off. By the time England returned,
the press and the England camp were barely on speaking terms
and the Press Complaints Commission was forced to intervene.

England started well enough – or at least their treatment by
the press did. In their first match against Brazil, Winterbottom's side lost 2–0 in front of 100,000 fans in the Maracana,
but gave a good account of themselves after going behind to
two early goals. By the end of the match, the home side were
being jeered by their own supporters, and the press reports
back in England struck an upbeat note. So far, so good. A
week, though, is a long time in international football, and by
the final whistle of their next match England had become a
team of wretched no-hopers. A team featuring some of the
biggest names of the modern era including Wright, Flowers,
Greaves, Charlton, Haynes, Howe, Armfield and Clayton was
beaten 4–1 by little Peru.

Leitch was unable to contain his disgust at what he had seen.
Rising to near poetic heights of indignation, his cable began:
'Struggling, pathetic shame oozed out of every England
football boot here at the foot of the Andes mountains tonight
as a lightweight, slap-happy side from the ten First Division
teams of Peru thrashed us in a game which could so easily have

ended 8–1. Beside me as I type, people jab at me through the twelve-foot-high steel fence which protects us from the crowd. They beam and ask: Is this really the first national side from England? Here tonight, as in Belo Horizonte nine years ago when America beat us 1–0, the great name of English football was reduced to futile palaver . . . to pathetic indifference . . . to sheer out-of-date fumbling.' England also lost their next match, 2–1 to Mexico, but according to Leitch the earthquake that shook Mexico City during the match was apparently as nothing on the Richter scale next to the seismic shock of England's performance against the little-fancied Central Americans. Leitch was roused to new heights of incandescent contempt for the country's football team, reporting: 'A nerve-tingling earthquake shook the 83,000 fans packed into the fabulous, sun-soaked University Stadium . . . but it was nothing to the shock which rocked and shocked England. Once more the white shirts crashed – and on Empire Day of all days! Beaten in Brazil, pulverised in Peru and now mauled in Mexico.'

The following day the press assault on the England team reached unprecedented levels. While the broadsheet news-papers were predictably more restrained in their critique, their tabloid counterparts poured out the vitriol without restraint. A comparison of newspaper coverage before, during and after the unhappy tour of the Americas shows that those few weeks represented a watershed in the relationship between England and the press. And as the circulation battles among the newspapers intensified, the headlines became more sensation-alist and splenetic, the criticisms less measured and sober.

The post-match pieces following the Mexico defeat sing – or rather yell – from the same songsheet, but the loudest and most discordant notes were struck by the *Daily Herald*'s Leitch who, by the time the party flew out of Mexico City, was beside himself with anger at England's abject displays. If he was frothing at the mouth after the Peru defeat, he was positively fulminating in Mexico City. The back page of the paper called for mass dismissals under the headline 'SCRAP SYSTEM – OR QUIT NOW'. Beneath that were four bullet-point sub-headings which read:

- We are faced everywhere we go with guffaws, giggles and groans.
- I am positive we will never be invited again.
- Players are scared of losing before they lace their boots.
- Even the Yanks are saying this England team is a shambles.

It is unlikely that the report left any of the *Herald*'s readers in any doubt that there were a few technical difficulties with the England set-up: 'On this 18th day of the most disastrous Soccer tour ever undertaken by an England team I AM SICK TO DEATH of using the words "pitiful . . . pathetic . . . dismal . . . outclassed . . . outmanoeuvred . . . outfought." I AM SICK of edgy England players saying to me: "What are you worried about? You love to write this knocking stuff anyway." This tour lies exposed for what is – FIFTH RATE AND UNVARYING IN ITS MEDIOCRITY.' And in a final comment that would have left *Herald* readers wondering what Mr Leitch would have had to say if he was in a really bad mood, he added: 'This inquest is written at 7 a.m. It is not hot-headed sensationalism. It is the truth soberly told about a tour which will torment the history of English sport.' The blunderbuss-style attack left it unclear who exactly was to blame, but the England selectors were clearly in the front rank facing the firing squad. (For the record, the selectors on the tour were Chelsea chairman Joe Mears, Lt-Col Gerry Mitchell of the Army FA, and Harold Shentall of Chesterfield. Other officials included Sir Stanley Rous, the FA secretary, Winterbottom and trainer Harold Shepherdson.)

England beat the USA 8–1 four days after the Mexico game, but there was not a hope that the press would compose their final dispatches on an upbeat or forgiving note. For Leitch, the match merely provided further evidence that the football world had gone completely mad. Under the headline 'OH HOW CRAZY!' he wrote: 'CRAZY? Whoever heard of a full international where the announcer blurted out at the beginning: "There's a traffic jam outside folks. We'll just have to delay the start." CRAZY? Whoever heard of a full international where every player was introduced individually like a boxer from the ring.' Such was the intensity of the press attacks that Mears, the chairman of the International Selection Committee, took the unprecedented step of issuing a public statement calling for the Press Council to intervene and reprimand the troublemakers with the typewriters. Immediately after the match he issued the following statement, which found its way on to the front pages of most of the popular press: 'Accompanying the FA party were journalists who, like some of the players, were experiencing their first long tour. Almost without exception their reports have been inaccurate, misleading, mischievous, and have been a great disservice to English football and footballers. It is our intention to recommend that the Press Council be asked to receive a deputation in order that a repetition of such conduct on future visits abroad may be avoided. Evidence will be available from embassies, consulates, and sports organisations to prove that all our players, even in defeat, have been a credit to their association and their country and have spared no effort in training and in actual matches.'

Winterbottom recalls the tour well. 'I remember we went to Disneyland following a last-minute invitation,' he says. 'Our schedule had said we were meant to be at some other function where one particular journalist assumed we would be. Annoyed that he had missed us he wrote a piece saying, "As I walked around Disneyland with Billy Wright, he told me that England's failures were his fault." It was totally untrue. He hadn't even spoken to him. The press had been gunning for Bill's head all tour and this was the final straw. We wanted to get the Press Council to put a stop to this type of irresponsible journalism. Some of the reporting began to get very nasty around that time and I can even remember some of the more balanced and responsible reporters having a go at their colleagues. There were some good ones like Frank Butler, whose criticism was always constructive and who realised that there were other countries that felt they should be world champions.'

The row escalated on England's return home and became a cause of national debate. The press were up for a fight. On 1 June the front page of the *Herald* carried the bold declaration: 'ON BEHALF OF BRITAIN'S SOCCER FANS

WE SAY: THEY'LL NEVER GAG THE PRESS'. The piece began: 'Thirty million Britons follow Soccer. And they want to read in their newspapers the truth about their favourite footballers. These fans were told bluntly how England's footballers flopped on the tour of the Americas.' Joe Richards, the president of the Football League, reportedly wanted to gag people inside football from talking to the newspapers, radio or television in order to bring the media into line. William McKeag, the solicitor/chairman of Newcastle United, said he felt that action should be taken to curb the viciousness in the press: 'I don't think there is anyone here who does not deplore the wretched stuff that has appeared in the Press this season.' The *Herald* responded to the criticism with sarcastic scorn and insisted there was no preconceived plan or co-ordinated campaign to lambast England, and that reporters faithfully reported what they witnessed out of duty to the truth. The paper invited its readers to write to SOCCER-GAG to air their views on whether they liked their reports 'blunt' or as the 'Soccer bosses' wanted them. 'So you see: the wicked, alarmist press is to blame for all that's wrong in football today,' the front-page piece continued. 'Look at the Big Tour flop. Fifteen Press and BBC reporters accompanied England. Without exception they criticised England. How could they do otherwise? The *Herald* man on the tour was columnist Sam Leitch. He received no instructions to manufacture headlines. He wrote what he saw ... Leitch or any other sports writers on that tour would face the sack if they did not report the facts and explain honestly, professionally and without prejudice. We say the FA and the League must put their own house in order before telling us how to run our business.' Most commentators agreed that the season was too long, that the selectors were a collection of incompetent amateurs out of touch with modern trends in the game, and that greedy and selfish club chairmen and directors, who insisted on a bloated fixture list and refused to sanction the more frequent release of players, were severely damaging the interests of the national team.

There seems to be no single reason for the increased hostility of the press towards the end of the 1950s, but there is a detectable gathering of momentum in the criticisms as the

decade progressed. After the setbacks against Hungary and the
failure in the 1954 World Cup, England gave their critics very
little ammunition with which to attack them. Winterbottom's
reforms brought obvious improvements and between 1955 and
1958 England were undoubtedly a good team. By the time of
England's disastrous tour of the Americas in 1959, a new
mood was abroad in Fleet Street. It was now fourteen years
since the end of the war and the mood of national togetherness
in the difficult years which followed the conflict were spent.
There were no longer any mitigating circumstances to explain
failure – and England did fail in the last two years of the
decade. They won just six games out of 20 and between the
4–1 victory over Denmark in Copenhagen in May 1957 and
the 3–2 triumph over Italy in Rome four years later, they
celebrated victory on non-British soil on just two occasions –
against the amateurs of the United States and the European
minnows Luxembourg.

The great Tommy Lawton was just one of the many
prominent figures voicing their opinions on the decline of the
national side. Lawton, though, felt that it was the players'
preoccupation with money – manifested in the campaign led by
Jimmy Hill for the abolition of the maximum wage – that was
the root cause of the fall in standards. He said at the time:
'People accuse the selectors, team manager and the system. The
main fault is with the players no matter what Jimmy Hill says.
All they think about is, What do I cop and how little can I do?'

But just as the situation appeared to have reached a point of
crisis which would precipitate a radical shake-up in the
England set-up, Winterbottom's team suddenly hit a streak of
outstanding form. In their first six matches of the 1960/61
season, England, inspired by the strike partnership of Jimmy
Greaves and Gerry Hitchens, scored an astonishing forty goals,
beating Northern Ireland 5–2, Luxembourg 9–0, Spain 4–2,
Wales 5–1, Scotland 9–3 and Mexico 8–0. Particularly
impressive were the triumphs over the Spanish – who could
boast the great names of Di Stefano, Suarez, Gento and
Santamaria – and the Scots with such luminaries as Denis Law,
Ian St John, Dave Mackay and Billy McNeil in their ranks. The
rancour in the press was replaced by a mood of optimism. All

was right with the world again. All was forgiven. The headlines no longer referred to Winterbottom, but to Walter. After the demolition of Mexico at Wembley, avenging the defeat of two years earlier, the *Daily Herald* ran the chummy headline: 'EIGHT – BUT WALTER WANTS MORE'. Winterbottom was clearly enjoying his rediscovered popularity. 'We had a great chance to get fifteen or sixteen goals,' he told reporters after the match. 'We've got to get that killer mood.'

England were on a roll and good luck, that precious quality that seems to bestow itself on confident teams, was with them a few days later when a late Greaves goal saw them steal a 3–2 win over Italy in Rome. England's reporters were more impressed than the Italian *tifosi*, who yelled 'Dirty thieves!' at the white shirts as they headed down the tunnel. England's good form and fortune deserted them three days later when they were beaten 3–1 by Austria in Vienna, but the press kept the cork in their bottle of vitriol, reacting to the defeat with a disappointment expressed in fair and moderate terms. After seven wins and a draw from nine games, England had re-established their reputation as a major footballing power and they could now look ahead to the 1962 World Cup finals with optimism.

Hopes that England's streak of good form would be maintained right through to the World Cup finals in Chile were shaken by the departure of Greaves and Hitchens to AC and Inter Milan. The Italian clubs refused to sanction the strikers' release for internationals, thereby blunting England's attacking edge and upsetting the rhythm and unity established by the team over the previous twelve months. Having scored forty goals in six games, England's tally plummeted to just fourteen in seven games, four of which came at home against Luxembourg, a pin-prick principality with a population no larger than a sleepy English market town. In that match England's first goal was greeted with ironic cheers by the Wembley crowd, who then switched their allegiance and cheered every pass made by the amateur Europeans.

It was an inauspicious start to a season which would end in bitter recriminations and the departure of Winterbottom. England played six more games before flying out to the World

Cup, winning three of them, drawing two and losing one. But it was not so much the results as the quality of the performances that drew negative mutterings from the press gallery, the terraces and the nation's armchairs. The 2–0 defeat at the hands of a good Scotland side in April was England's first at Hampden Park in 25 years and was widely seen as evidence that Winterbottom's team were going to struggle at the seventh World Cup. The headline 'THE GREAT ENGLAND FLOP: OUR PRESTIGE AND THOSE PLANS FOR CHILE ARE IN RUINS' certainly left *News of the World* readers in no doubt about the paper's hopes of success.

Jimmy Hill's campaign for the abolition of the players' maximum wage had led many commentators of the day to claim that England's top players were now more interested in playing for their clubs than for their country. Some critics believed the only way to extract 100 per cent effort from England players was to offer them the incentive of cash bonuses for winning. The departures of Greaves, Hitchens, Denis Law and a handful of other British stars to Italy merely reinforced the notion that cash was the great motivator in modern football. It was against this backdrop of suspicion and these accusations of greed that England's players would be judged in Chile.

By 1962, the recognition of Winterbottom's greater influence over the team was being reflected in the more frequent references to him in newspaper dispatches. Barely mentioned in reports a few years earlier, the thoughts and decisions of England's manager had come to be treated with the utmost interest. England was now 'Winterbottom's team' and it was 'Winterbottom' and not 'the selectors', or simply 'England', credited with decisions in selection. On the eve of England's final warm-up match against Peru in Lima, papers reported that 'Winterbottom' was set to gamble by giving a debut to 21-year old right-half Bobby Moore. England won the match 4–0 with a hat-trick from Greaves, providing a timely lift for the squad as they retreated high into the Andes, an hour's drive from Rancagua, to prepare for the group matches against Hungary, Argentina and Bulgaria.

England stayed as the guests of an American copper

company at Coya where their facilities included a cinema, a ten-pin bowling alley and a spectacular golf course carved out of the mountainside. The players slept in wooden bungalows, and in order to make them feel more at home their food was cooked by an old English woman called Bertha Lewis. It was hoped that by hiding them away in the mountains, the players could escape the glare of publicity and focus themselves on the campaign ahead without the noise and distractions of a hotel in a busy city. After the tournament, however, many players complained that the isolation tactics had made them feel homesick and that they had felt cut off from the growing sense of drama that attended the build-up to the World Cup. There were also reports that cliques and factions emerged within the squad, further destabilising morale.

Winterbottom had assembled an experienced squad with eleven of the twenty players capped ten times or more. The focus of the team was Fulham's Haynes, an immensely talented player with a devastating, defence-splitting pass. But England's over-reliance on their captain for their creativity was well-known to their opponents. Asked how his team would play against England, Hungary's coach Baroti told reporters: 'Simple. Number ten takes the corners, number ten takes the throw-ins, number ten does everything. So what do we do? We put a man on number ten. Goodbye England.' And that is exactly what happened when England were beaten 2–1, their poverty of attacking ideas exposed just as Baroti had predicted. Haynes, looking jaded anyhow, was marked out of the game and England rarely threatened a mediocre Hungarian team, who were but a pale shadow of the great team of the early 1950s (Puskas, incidentally, was now playing for his adoptive Spain). After months, even years of preparation, England's World Cup campaign could not have started more flatly.

They had travelled 8,000 miles to get there, dozens of players had been tried and discarded as Winterbottom searched for his perfect formula, hundreds of thousands of words had been written about their warm-up matches and chances. The World Cup had become a major event. A nation expected. But when England finally emerged from their mountain retreat and took the winding road to the match venue to face the Hungarians, they found just a scattering of locals dotted around the picturesque Rancagua stadium. The crowd, no larger than the average gate for an English Third Division match, had no great interest in the outcome of the match, and players later talked of the difficulty of motivating themselves in the eerie atmosphere. 'I really enjoyed the 1958 World Cup, but not the one in 1962. The quarters and training facilities were okay but we had long treks to the matches and the crowds were very small,' recalls England's captain Johnny Haynes, who moved to Edinburgh to live with his Scottish wife after retiring from the game. 'For our first game against Hungary we had about 3,000 people. It just didn't feel like an international and it was difficult to get a sense of the importance of the occasion in such an atmosphere. When we played Argentina it was better because they all came over the border, but apart from that it wasn't very good. We weren't very happy out there.'

England's lack of inspiration sparked a barrage of criticism in the following day's papers as reporters predicted another World Cup humiliation for the one-time masters of world football. Even if they still managed to advance from their group, it was now virtually certain they would face the might of favourites and holders Brazil in the quarter-finals. The *Daily Mail* headline was unequivocal in its evaluation of the performance against Hungary: 'ENGLAND DO THEIR WORST: ENERGY NIL, COURAGE NIL, PRIDE NIL'. The match reporter, J.L. Manning, wrote: 'It is the story of a mountain of opportunity being tackled by mice – a timid effort instead of a roaring start ... England were not beaten by a very good Hungarian team but by their own lack of fight.'

'Lack of fight' was not a problem in the other opening matches. The eight games played over the first two days produced an orgy of violence unprecedented in the history of the tournament. Thirty-four players suffered injuries in those games, three of them broken legs. (One name on the casualty list was that of Pele, the greatest player in the world, but his wound was self-inflicted as he pulled a muscle attempting a physiologically impossible shot on goal.) The Argentinians were singled out as the worst offenders after their opening match against Bulgaria. Sixty-nine free-kicks were awarded in the match, and one Bulgarian showed reporters his broken nose and the stud scrapes down both his legs, complaining as he hobbled off to hospital, 'They are worse than boxers.' Reacting with alarm to the brutality of the opening exchanges, one Chilean newspaper ran a front-page headline reading, simply, 'WORLD WAR!' The level of violence so disturbed the organisers and FIFA that the sixteen managers of the finalists were summoned to a meeting where they were urged to order their players to bring an end to the warring lest the image of the competition suffer irreparable damage. It was even suggested that teams would be sent home if they persisted to flout the rules governing fair play.

The worst of the violence flared in Chile's match against Italy. In that match English referee Ken Aston ordered off the Italian Ferrini, who stood his ground for ten minutes before being escorted from the pitch by armed police. Chileans were reportedly incensed by the comments of Italian journalists who had heavily criticised the organisation of the tournament, claiming that the competition should never have been awarded to the inexperienced South Americans in the first place, not least because a devastating earthquake had destroyed much of the country's infrastructure. The dismissal of Ferrini sparked all-out war between the two sides as the match descended into one of the most violent in the history of international football, worse even than the 'Battle of Berne' between Hungary and Brazil in 1954, 'The Battle of Bordeaux' in 1938 between Brazil and Czechoslovakia and the famous 'Battle of Highbury' between England and Italy in 1933.

A sense that England's World Cup was over barely before it had started ran through the nation's column inches after the Hungary defeat and Argentina's win over Bulgaria. But in keeping with England's extraordinary inconsistency in World Cups, they rallied against the brutal and highly fancied Argentinians in their next match. The untried Peacock, of Second Division Middlesbrough and a controversial inclusion in the party, replaced the ineffective Hitchens up front and it was his threat that led to England's opening goal in the 3–1 victory. His header cannoned off the crossbar, Navarro handled and Flowers converted from the penalty spot. England were a team transformed, with the young Moore superb at right-half and Wilson and Armfield, both forwards converted into full-backs, an inspiration both in defence and attack. Haynes and Charlton combined well in the heart of the midfield, constantly punching holes in the Argentinian defence. Armfield set up England's second goal when his powerful shot rebounded off the bar and Charlton tucked the ball home. Blackburn winger Brian Douglas sealed the win with the best goal of the game when he wrong-footed the defence with a feinted pass and found the back of the net with a crisp, low drive. England were back on track and Frank Butler, in the *News of the World*, felt moved enough by England's imaginative and fighting display to write that he had never seen England play better abroad.

England's final group opponents were Bulgaria, who quickly established a reputation as the weakest side in the tournament after losing 1–0 to Argentina and 6–1 to Hungary. The English press described the Eastern Europeans as being no better than a weak Second Division team. England, though, were at their most frustratingly lacklustre as they laboured to a 0–0 draw. Both teams were jeered off the pitch and Bulgaria, who had no chance of qualifying, were later accused by the conspiracy theorists in the South American press of making no effort out of revenge for Argentina's violent antics in the opening match. Winterbottom had opted to field his strongest possible team, even though many players were clearly in need of a rest. For this the England manager came in for heavy criticism, but it was the players' apparent lack of urgency which was most galling to their followers. A win would have meant that they avoided Brazil – the team everyone feared with a line-up that comprised the illustrious names of Gilmar, Djalma Santos, Mauro, Nilton Santos, Zito, Zozimo, Garrincha, Didi, Vava, Amarildo and Zagallo – in the quarter-finals. In the event, England played their best match of the tournament against the Brazilians but lost 3–1. Garrincha, 'the black Matthews' on the wing, was outstanding and scored Brazil's third goal with a dipping 25-yard drive which the Brazilian press had poetically dubbed his 'autumn leaf' shot.

The response in the press to England's failure varied from paper to paper, but by and large the popular press were damning, occasionally hysterical, in their verdicts and vociferous in their calls for root-and-branch change in English football. The broadsheets, predictably, were more measured, even indifferent, in their reaction to England's fourth consecutive failure in the World Cup finals. The *Guardian*'s reporting of England's World Cup was sobriety itself. The paper's reports for the matches themselves were just three to four hundred words long and appear to have been taken from one of the news agencies as no reporter is credited for their composition. Nor did the paper run any stories concerning England between the matches themselves, or any commentary or 'colour' pieces analysing the team's performances. 'BRAZIL BEAT ENGLAND WITH NO GREAT DIFFICULTY' was the paper's dry headline following the quarter-final. A measure of the significance of England's World Cup campaign relative to other sports news is reflected in the fact that the report of the match was given less space on the page than the County Championship Roses clash between Yorkshire and Lancashire. Even the Inter-counties Athletics championship at the British Games at White City was granted more column inches on the sports pages that day.

Meanwhile, feelings were running considerably higher among the reporters of the popular press. On 17 June, a week after England's elimination the *News of the World*'s veteran football reporter Frank Butler wrote an angry commentary piece laying the blame for England's poor performance squarely at the door of the Football League and the 'greedy' directors of the clubs whose selfishness, he claimed, had stunted the national side's development since the end of the war. 'The trouble with English football is that the tinkers and tailors, having made their pile of cash, get the ambition to be on the board of the local football club, without a clue about the game. But the nouveau riche of soccer still want to run the game. They are the little tin gods who are always prepared to put club before country and self before all.' Only at the end of the piece does Butler point a finger at Winterbottom, and even then it is more of a wagging than a jabbing digit. He wrote: 'Walter Winterbottom, as team manager, must accept a certain amount of criticism because the boss stands or falls on the results produced by the men under him.' J.L. Manning, in the *Daily Mail*, said success could only be found on the world stage by pooling the talents of all four of the home countries, adding: 'I have no relish for psychoanalysing our professional footballers, harassing Walter Winterbottom, counting the ages of our elderly selectors, arguing over team changes, or even debating tactics. At worst these are personal and gossipy and at best they are superficial.'

Haynes claims the real cause of England's failure in Chile, as well as in other World Cups, was the fatigue of the players caused by a bloated domestic fixture list. 'The big problem is that we were all tired after a long season. At Fulham we had a long Cup run to the semi-final and a lot of replays and I was definitely tired when we arrived in Chile. The conditions, being locked away in the mountains, didn't help and that also took away a lot of our edge.' But whatever the reasons for England's lack of success in World Cup competition, a lack it certainly was. The bare facts of England's performances in the World Cup since condescending to enter the tournament twelve years earlier made for chilling reading: they had won just three out of fourteen games, against Chile in 1950, Switzerland in 1954 and Argentina in 1962.

The Brazil match proved to be Winterbottom's last in charge. He resigned without fuss midway through that summer, reportedly upset that Denis Follows, and not him, was appointed earlier in the year to succeed Sir Stanley Rous as secretary of the FA. 'It was well known that I wanted to progress to being secretary and I was not happy with the way it was handled,' recalls Winterbottom. His departure was neither mourned nor celebrated in the nation's papers. The general verdict was that Winterbottom had made the best of a bad job. It was not his fault that he could not choose his own side, even though it seems to have been widely accepted that by the end of his time in charge the selectors were more prepared to yield to his will. Nor was it his fault that the chairmen and directors of the League clubs were unwilling to sanction the more frequent release of their players; Winterbottom had constantly, if always diplomatically, insisted that the national team would benefit considerably if they were able to train and play together as often as possible. Nor was it Winterbottom's fault that football in the rest of the world had improved rapidly during his sixteen years in charge, or that so many Englishmen felt that their countrymen were, by nature and tradition, a superior breed of footballer. Plenty of England managers since have failed to endear themselves as human beings to the press corps, but Winterbottom the man appeared to have made few, if any, personal enemies during his marathon period in office.

The valedictory pieces that followed his departure were noticeable for the universal appreciation of his courteousness, coolness under pressure, his intelligence, his loyalty to his players, his organisational and diplomatic skills and his willingness to embrace new ideas. The worst criticism of him was that he was felt to be almost too nice for the job and that a more inspirational, even frightening, character might have been more successful firing up players before crucial matches. It is a view echoed by Haynes, who says: 'If you could criticise Walter for anything it was that he was a bit too quiet and didn't get himself worked up if things weren't going well. He never created a sense of fear and urgency in the players. It just wasn't in his nature.' Critics also suggested that his gentle integrity was a weakness in that it made him unable to force through the changes that were necessary if England was to re-establish itself as a major force in world football. Others said that his cerebral team-talks often left some of his players scratching their heads and staring vacantly out of the room. But in spite of the carping, England's overall record under Winterbottom is by any standard an impressive one: played 137, won 78, drew 32, lost 27. However, the World Cup failures provided the statistics to damn him; like Revie and Taylor in later years, Winterbottom rarely won the matches that mattered.

For Finney, who played under Winterbottom more than any other player except Billy Wright, England's first manager was never given the praise he deserved for leading England at a time of enormous change in the game. 'Walter Winterbottom was a man way ahead of his time in many ways,' says Finney, who occasionally over the years ran into his former manager at Wembley. 'At the time people had lost a bit of respect for English football. We had fallen behind while everyone else was embracing new ideas. Walter was one of the few people who understood that English football needed to change in order to keep up. He had great respect abroad, which is strange when you consider that English coaching methods, what there were of them, were not that admired in his time. I thought the most impressive thing about him was his knowledge of the opposition. At the time it was much more difficult to get information on players from abroad. There weren't the media services like there are today. But before a match he would sit us down and go through the opposition one by one and tell you everything about his strengths and weaknesses. He seemed to grow into the job, and after they started to hand him more responsibility he was much more his own man.'

Haynes was also an admirer of Winterbottom and insists that he could have achieved much more had he not been hamstrung by the selectors. 'He knew his football inside out. He was incredibly thorough in his preparation and always knew his opposition. The only problem for Walter was having to answer to a group of selectors, which didn't make his job very easy. He didn't actually pick the team, although of course he had a say. The players weren't happy about it, except the ones in the team, but it was a totally unsatisfactory way of doing things and made life very difficult for the manager. When Ramsey came along and insisted on picking his own team, England were obviously much better for it.

'I never played for any other England manager, so I have nothing to compare him to, but he was always one step ahead of the rest in terms of understanding the importance of coaching and moving with the times. He knew English football needed to be shaken up and his biggest contribution was in reforming the whole international set-up as well as people's attitudes to tactics and coaching. He wasn't what you'd call "one of the boys" and he always kept his distance, but we all looked up to him. He was perfect. Off the pitch he didn't interfere too much and always treated us like adults and never told us when we had to go to bed, like some managers.'

It is commonplace to read nowadays that Winterbottom was heavily criticised throughout his time in charge, but after trawling through the newspapers of the day, it is difficult to support this view. Perhaps the truth is that by the more restrained editorial standards of his day the criticism of Winterbottom *was* heavy, but compared to the often vicious and personalised hatchet-jobs carried out by the press in more recent years, England's first manager escaped with a mere rap on the knuckles. Never was he caricatured as a root vegetable or depicted with a noose around his neck or pictured next to a mock-up of a steaming pile of manure. His wife was never spat at in the street, his children were never mocked in the playground, and never were details of his private life splashed across the front pages. If it was 'heavy criticism' that Winterbottom endured, then it is difficult to think of a phrase that accurately describes the experiences of subsequent England managers.

On 2 August, the day after the announcement of Winterbottom's resignation, the *Herald* ran a back-page splash with a mock job advertisement: 'Situation Vacant. WANTED: manager for international football team, must be qualified coach, able to handle players, directors, officials, impervious to criticism, hours 24 daily, starting salary according to ability, rising to £2,500 approx. if we win the World Cup, apply to FA, 22 Lancaster Gate, W2.' Under the headline 'WHO WANTS IT ... AT THIS PRICE?' Lorenzo warned that leading contenders for the post would be put off by the relatively small salary, believed to be around £2,000 (Winterbottom, incidentally, claimed he earned the same as a local chief of police). There was a widespread fear that the niggardliness of the Football Association would cost England the chance of landing the likes of Ramsey, Wolves' Stan Cullis, Spurs' Bill Nicholson or Aston Villa's Joe Mercer. Lorenzo wrote in the *Herald*: 'The Walter Winterbottom era is over. Now the big question is not who takes over from Walter as

England team manager . . . but who WANTS the job under the same terms? Why should these men of Soccer stature who have made their mark on and off the field step into an even hotter, certainly less rewarding managerial seat?'

2 Knighted Then Slighted

Sir Alf Ramsey 1963–1973

W INTERBOTTOM'S RESIGNATION allowed the critics to call for a widespread overhaul of the England set-up. Some said the job should be split between two people with one concentrating on training and another on the administration that went with the post. Most commentators seemed to agree that the new man should be paid at least £3,000, the same as the FA secretary and considerably more than Winterbottom. Inevitably, there were also widespread calls for the abolition of the International Selection Committee. After several weeks of speculation, Jimmy Adamson of Burnley was widely tipped to become England's second manager, sparking fears in the press that, as he did not carry the same weight of authority as figures like Cullis, Ramsey and Nicholson, the selectors would remain in a position of power and influence. In the event, Adamson, who served as Winterbottom's right-hand man in Chile, turned down the post as he was reluctant to leave the north-west of England.

By the end of the year, the FA were able to announce that they had landed one of the most respected coaches in the business: Alf Ramsey. The former Spurs and England full-back had astounded English football when he inspired unfashionable Ipswich to the League title in 1962 on a shoestring budget and with a team of players who might have been household names in Suffolk and north Essex, but virtually nowhere else. Ramsey made it clear that he would only take the job on the strict condition that he, and only he, would choose the England team. At a stroke he transformed the England manager's job for ever. The abolition of the International Selection Committee made obvious sense, but from that moment on there would be no hiding-place for the man in charge. Critics could still blame the general state of the domestic game and take pot shots at club directors and FA administrators, but the England manager was now a sitting duck for the powerful guns of the nation's press.

Ramsey, though, either as player or manager, was never short of conviction when it came to his own ability. With a confidence that surprised everyone at the time and would beggar belief today, the poker-faced new England boss dramatically raised the stakes when he leant across the table in one of his early press conferences and announced to the pressmen seated before him: 'England will win the 1966 World Cup.' In that one sentence Ramsey created the yardstick by which his time in charge would be measured. Should he fail to help England fulfil his astonishingly bold prediction, then Ramsey would never have been allowed to forget what would have been seen as a foolish conceit.

But then he did not care much for the opinions of the men in the press box. From the outset, Ramsey was recognised as a man whose attitude towards reporters was at best cold, and at worse rude and hostile. When England did, as he predicted, win the World Cup for the first time in their history, Ramsey felt even less need to put on an appearance of co-operation. His disdain for the Fourth Estate was not well received in the offices of Fleet Street, and when, in the second period of his reign, results began to go against England, he found there were few men at the typewriters prepared to show sympathy. It is perhaps stretching the truth to say that the press forced him out of his job, but it seems fair to say that he would have stood a greater chance of survival had he not given his critics the opportunity to get their own back.

In what with the benefit of hindsight resonates with ominously accurate clairvoyance, Bob Pennington of the *News of the World* warned that Ramsey would have to improve his PR skills or risk a potentially fatal battering in the press. On 23 December, he wrote in his column: 'A note of warning. He must improve his public relations. Recently I heard Ramsey parry a reporter's question by asking: "What do you want me to do: write your column for you?" Alf is a reserved man who has never really understood the value of Press co-operation. He must overcome this, for despite all his new power he is more vulnerable than at any time in his career.' The dictatorship which Ramsey rightly insisted on as the only condition of acceptance has cut away the safety net from the English managership. Temperamentally, too, Ramsey is even more exposed than his predecessor. There was a personal warmth and humility about Winterbottom that tempered every lash of criticism. Ramsey, the player who walked by himself, is a colder character. Urbane, meticulous in his dress and speech, appearing at times to carry his dignity heavily – but not like Winterbottom a man to natter with cosily into the wee small hours.'

And to understand Ramsey the manager it is necessary to try to understand Ramsey the man, a task that even the most patient and enthusiastic of psychiatrists might think twice about taking on. For Ramsey was nothing if not an enigma who by turns infuriated and inspired. Charming or diplomatic he was not, as any press reporter of the day would be quick to point out. To the outside world, he was taciturn, gruff, aloof, stubborn, self-righteous, patriotic to the point of xenophobia, almost disturbingly immaculate in his appearance, and breathtakingly rude on occasion. In short, his public character neatly fitted the foreigner's caricature of an Englishman at his coldest, most reserved and uptight.

As far as his players were concerned, however, Ramsey could do no wrong. He was a players' manager who, like them, had played football at the highest level (as a full-back under Winterbottom between 1949 and 1953. 'Nothing could disturb this footballer with the perfect balance and poise,' said Billy Wright.) Martin Peters, one of Ramsey's favourites and scorer of the 'other' goal in the World Cup final, still will not hear a word of criticism of the man who engineered English football's finest hour. 'For him the players were the most important thing,' recalls the former West Ham, Tottenham and Norwich midfielder. 'The press were of little or no interest to him. He was incredibly loyal and never publicly criticised us. Of course, he would criticise us to our faces, but it was always behind closed doors and when he went out to speak to the media he would never repeat to them what he had said to us. He gave us everything and we gave him everything back. We had total respect for him. Alf was his own man. He had his vision of what he wanted and he would not be swayed from his purpose. He didn't care what anyone else thought. He was completely single-minded and so the criticism he received didn't bother him, or at least it didn't appear to bother him.'

Jimmy Armfield, one of the few stars of England's 1962 World Cup campaign, played under Ramsey in the early part of his reign. He has nothing but positive memories of Ramsey as a man or a manager. 'He was incredibly loyal,' says Armfield, who is best known to younger football followers as the expert voice on BBC Radio Five's match commentaries. 'Maybe he wasn't the best communicator by a long way, but for us as players, when he spoke we listened. We'd hang on to every word. He was a very private man, always very calm on the surface but often boiling underneath. At training sessions he would never be shouting. He would just come over and have a quiet word in your ear and then he would walk away and let you get on with it.'

The public image of Ramsey as a man belonging to a bygone era is brought into even sharper focus by the context in which he rose to international prominence. It was the 'swinging sixties', when men grew their hair below the collar and women wore their hem lines just an inch or so below their panty-lines, when ties and suits were traded for floral shirts and Afghan coats, and when footballers first began to be lauded like stars of pop and film. The picture of England's golden-haired captain Bobby Moore holding aloft the Jules Rimet trophy at Wembley in the sunshine of late afternoon on 30 July 1966 evokes a whole reel of other 1960s images: of mini-skirts, of Minis, of the Beatles, of a society which had let its hair down after the austerity and hard work of the post-war years. But when the camera cuts to Ramsey, an entirely different world is brought to mind. As England's jubilant players and fans jump, skip, cry and embrace all over the Wembley turf, Ramsey remains seated on the bench poker-faced, elbows on knees, chin on clenched hands, as if deliberating his next move in a game of chess. Time has not staled the awkwardness of the scene. Even as the final whistle heralds England's first ever triumph in the World Cup after 120 minutes of gut-wrenching anxiety, Ramsey looks as if he is watching a dull programme on television.

What he was feeling, though, is another matter – and this is the point about Ramsey. He was private to an almost hermit-like extent. That is the way it always was, and still is, with Ramsey, who has spent the last third of his life hidden away in the same semi-detached home he bought when he moved to Ipswich in the 1950s. But ask any player who worked with Ramsey and they will tell you that his outward composure should never be mistaken for a lack of passion. He positively boiled with the emotion, they say, but he always kept the lid firmly on. One of those emotions raging behind his granite-hewn features and Sphinx-like demeanour, which so accurately conveyed his unshakeable faith in his own convictions, was a fierce love of his country. 'Alf is the most patriotic man I have ever met,' says Geoff Hurst. Shortly after taking over as manager of the national team, Ramsey declared: 'I believe in England, and Englishmen, as well as English football.'

Peters believes Ramsey's emotional self-discipline was one of the keys to his success as a manager. 'He was always very calm, even in moments of great crisis or celebration, and that rubbed off on the rest of us. It was reassuring and gave us confidence. He was not a screamer or a ranter. He was a man of strong passions but he was also very disciplined and kept a lot to himself. But he could relax, and behind closed doors he could be one of the boys. Because as an ex-player he understood the importance of communicating with players on their own level. He was a players' manager.'

After Bobby Moore had walked the 39 steps to receive the trophy from the Queen, Ramsey refused the overtures of dozens of photographers, and his own players, to join in the team photograph. With obvious reluctance he did pose for one picture in which he is captured staring rather awkwardly at the golden figure as if it was a ticking-bomb. Not until he was back in the dressing-room did England's manager show any type of emotion, and even then it was expressed with old-fashioned courtesy as he approached every member of the squad, shook them by the hand and congratulated them on their efforts. 'It was the players' day,' he said later. 'I just sat there enjoying their reaction. I wanted just to sit there and watch so that I could remember what I was seeing.'

On that afternoon, Ramsey became the most famous manager in world football. It was some achievement for the man whose application for a job at Dagenham's Ford motor plant was rejected, and whose earliest ambition was to be a successful grocer. People often say that you can take the man out of Yorkshire or Dagenham or wherever but you can never take the Yorkshire or Dagenham or wherever out of the man. Ramsey, though, had a damned good go at taking the Dagenham out of himself. (In a radio interview he was once asked where his parents lived and replied: 'Dagenham ... I believe.') The son of Herbert, a hay and straw dealer, and Florence, Ramsey grew up in the flat, proudly working-class hinterlands of the Thames estuary. But it was not something he liked to be reminded of in his later years. Elocution lessons had squeezed his vowels into an accent that was more Mayfair than Mile End, more Prince Charles than Alf Garnett. Contemporary observers recorded how listening to Ramsey address a press conference or a television interviewer was a painful experience. 'He is more careful of his aspirates than his answers,' wrote Arthur Hopcraft in the *Observer*. Ramsey's struggle with words also perhaps explains the tension that was often generated in his famously prickly press conferences. His painful battle with the polysyllables often had journalists, who get paid for communicating clearly and intelligibly, squirming in their seats and rolling their eyes. (Ramsey, as he was the first to admit, was also a bad loser, which did little to improve his public manner when in front of the microphones.)

For Tottenham's Alan Mullery, a key figure in Ramsey's midfield in the latter period of his reign, the England manager's awkwardly polished manner was no more than the outward proof of a fierce and admirable determination to make the most of himself. 'After a couple of beers he would drop his aitches, which was always quite funny,' says Mullery. 'He very rarely let the mask slip or dropped his guard. You never saw him in a casual outfit. Wherever he went he always had a shirt and tie on. He was always playing the part and he played it extremely well. He wanted to better himself and improve his elocution. He wanted to be a gentleman – and he was a natural gent – and he liked it that way. It wasn't strange for me because when I first met him he was talking like that anyway. I think his old Tottenham team-mates like Eddie Baily used to take the mickey out of him and say, "Come off it, Alf!" But we would never dream of doing that. To us, the players, he was just a brilliant feller regardless of how he spoke or looked.'

As early as 1952, when still a player, Ramsey's preoccupation with bettering himself – off the pitch as well as on – was apparent. He said: 'I have found that serious reading has helped me develop a command of words so essential when you suddenly find yourself called upon to make a speech. People, remember, are inclined to forget that speechmaking may not be your strong point. With this in mind, I always try to put on some sort of show when asked to say a few words.' This eagerness to put Dagenham behind him explains a lot about Alf Ramsey and his restless ambition. As a player and as a manager he was constantly striving for something better. His diction, littered with tortuous phrases, revealed a man who did not want to sound inferior or less talented than anyone else in the room. There is a parallel in his playing career. Ramsey was not the most gifted of athletes. He was neither fast nor especially skilful, but he worked on his game with an application that lifted him out of mediocrity to become one of the greatest full-backs of his day. Precision in his passing, composure under pressure (he rarely missed a penalty), a near perfect positional sense and intelligence characterised his footballing style, making him a formidable opponent. In *Alf Ramsey: The Anatomy of a Football Manager*, a compelling portrait of the man, Max Marquis wrote: 'If his accent had moved to Kensington . . . his footballing philosophy remained in Dagenham – a tough community where hard work and enterprise were essential to survival, if not success.'

Like most successful footballers, Ramsey began playing the

game before he can remember. After years of kicking a ball around with his two elder brothers on scrubland in the East End, he represented Dagenham Schools and then a local Sunday League team called Five Elms. It was then that he was spotted by a scout and signed for Portsmouth, but the outbreak of the Second World War prevented him from playing for them. He joined the Army in 1940 and became a quartermaster with the Duke of Cornwall's Light Infantry, attached to an anti-aircraft unit. He caught the eye while playing for his battalion against Southampton (despite his team losing 12–0) and was signed by the south coast club. Ramsey quickly impressed his employers with his insatiable appetite for improvement, and was often seen doing hours of extra practice after training as he strove to perfect his passing and crossing. His first full season (1946/47) with the Saints, then in Division Two, ended with his surprise call-up for England's end-of-season tour of Europe. A virtual unknown, Ramsey found himself sharing the same dressing-room with the legendary likes of Lawton, Mannion and Finney. Jackie Milburn recalled that Alf was interested in little else but football.

He soon moved to Tottenham, where he fell under the influence of Arthur Rowe, the manager of the great Spurs team of the 1950s and the founder of the London club's success over subsequent decades. Rowe is best remembered as the English pioneer of the 'push-and-run' technique, a simple but highly effective strategy based on quick, short passing and rapid movement off the ball. At a time when the word 'tactics' went down in the dressing-room about as well as a beery belch at a Buckingham Palace garden party, Rowe's approach to the game was, indeed, revolutionary. Rowe and his scientific methods made an enormous impact on Ramsey, bolstering the young player's conviction that hard work and a scientific application of simple ideas could bring as much success as raw natural talent. Ramsey's ability to squeeze the maximum out of limited natural resources would prove to be one of the hallmarks of his success as a manager with Ipswich and England. Likewise, his legendary dedication to the job in hand became a feature of his managerial career. (When Ipswich threw a party to celebrate promotion to the First Division, one man was conspicuous by his absence at the post-match celebrations: the manager. After enquiries, Ipswich chairman John Cobbold found Ramsey taking notes on the sidelines at a match between Ipswich Boys and Norwich Boys.)

Ramsey, the last of whose 32 caps came in England's famous 6–3 defeat at the hands of Hungary at Wembley, went to manage Ipswich in 1955. He had no formal coaching qualifications, just a host of strong convictions, belief in his abilities and an appetite for hard work. In his first full season, the sleepy Suffolk club won the Third Division championship, and after four seasons in the Second, Ramsey led Ipswich, a team of unknowns and supposed has beens, into the top flight. One of them, winger Jimmy Leadbetter, looked almost comically old and was once described by a reporter as looking like 'Steptoe's illegitimate father.'

In the close season following their promotion, Ramsey bought just one player, Dixie Moran, for £12,000, and the whole of his team was valued at not much more than £30,000; by way of contrast, Tottenham, who became the first club to do the Double the previous season, were worth ten times that figure. During his seven years at Ipswich Ramsey spent a total of just £29,000 on new players. No one gave them a prayer of making an impact in the top flight, and they were widely predicted to go straight back down to the Second Division. The first sign that Ipswich were a force to be reckoned with came when they beat Tottenham at Portman Road in October (they also won the return match 3–1 at White Hart Lane).

At the end of their first year in the First Division, Ipswich, to everyone's astonishment except Ramsey's, won the 1961/62 championship with virtually the same hybrid team of journeymen and veterans that had won promotion. One of the keys to their success was that no one could quite take Ipswich seriously. Ipswich? Champions? It just didn't sound right, and perhaps the opposition, especially the bigger clubs, under-estimated them. (It is a view borne out by events the following season, when Ipswich struggled against relegation for much of the campaign as their opponents treated them with the respect champions deserved.) Fleet Street dubbed them 'Ramsey's Rustics', and they were indeed from another world altogether than their more cosmopolitan rivals. The title-winning Ipswich team were on a relatively proletarian £25 per week compared to the £100 or so earned by their *nouveaux riches* colleagues at the glamour clubs, following Jimmy Hill's successful campaign to abolish the players' maximum wage.

Ramsey was the architect of their success. With his unshakeable conviction that anything was possible given thorough planning, sound organisation and a red-blooded will to win, Ramsey came up with a strategy he thought best suited to maximising the limited talent at his disposal. It was simple. He used two wingers, Ray Stephenson on the right and Leadbetter in a withdrawn role on the left, in a kind of 4–2–4 formation which was still a fairly radical system in England at the time. Leadbetter was the fulcrum of Ipswich's attacks, spreading the passes while his fellow forwards Ray Crawford and Ted Phillips ran themselves into the ground trying to find space in front of him, and the rest of the team ran themselves into the ground winning possession and keeping out the opposition.

On the back of Ipswich's stunning triumph Ramsey rocketed to national prominence at just the right time – for himself and, as it would turn out, for England. With the football world still open-mouthed at the meteoric rise of Ipswich from sleepy backwater minnows to champions of the world's toughest league, the FA did not need to look much further for a replacement for Winterbottom than the man who took them there (once, of course, the original target, Jimmy Adamson, had declined to take up the position). In October 1962 the FA approached Ipswich chairman John Cobbold for permission to talk to Ramsey. Cobbold, a patriot and an old-fashioned gentleman to the toes of his bespoke brogues, provided his consent. Ramsey, surprisingly, took a whole month to consider the FA's offer – surprising not just because he was a man of driving ambition, but also because Ipswich were at that time battling for their very survival in the top flight and most managers would have jumped at the chance of deserting a sinking ship that might easily have dragged their reputations with it. Ipswich's rivals had quickly grown wise to Ramsey's championship-winning tactics and they also made sure that they would not fall into the trap of underestimating them, as they had done the previous season. Moreover, Ipswich had no money to buy their way out of trouble, and the long-term future looked even bleaker as their youth and scouting policies were not nearly so advanced as their rivals. Talented footballers were thick on the ground in the dense conurbations of northern England, Greater London and the Midlands; in Suffolk, there were lots of pigs, sheep and cows. Ramsey would not have needed to hire a management consultant to tell him that Ipswich were facing a difficult future without a major and rapid injection of capital, or an accountant to tell him that his personal finances would be improved by the move. Nor can the famously thick-skinned Ramsey have been worried about the prospect of the hail of darts that would inevitably shower down on him from the press gallery.

But it seems the biggest sticking point for Ramsey was the prospect of being beholden to the whims of the selectors. For after weeks of negotiations he finally accepted the FA's offer, on the proviso that he and not a committee would select the team. Ramsey did not start in his new job in earnest until the spring of 1963 allowing Ipswich to find a successor. The club eventually appointed former Newcastle legend Jackie Milburn, who later made some less than complimentary comments about his predecessor. Ramsey allegedly had told Milburn that Ipswich were in deep trouble and that they would struggle to survive the drop. When finally the team was relegated, Ramsey publicly stated that Milburn had inherited a very good team and implied that their demise was Milburn's fault. Milburn, a mild-mannered and much liked character, was incensed, claiming among other things that 'Alf Ramsey gave me neither help nor encouragement'.

The first occasion on which Ramsey entered the England dressing room was at half-time in the European Championship qualifier against France in Paris on 27 February 1963. He was not officially in charge yet but England were being hopelessly outplayed and were losing. He told the players: 'You can still win this.' His confidence, though, proved misplaced as England slumped to a 5–2 defeat which ended their hopes of reaching the finals. It also meant that Ramsey would have no chance of seeing his players taking part in meaningful competition before the World Cup finals themselves over three years later. England's international standing appeared to have reached a new low, and a dreadful night was rounded off when the return flight from Le Bourget to London airport was delayed by four hours after the plane collided with a luggage tractor. When the squad finally stepped off the plane, Ramsey spent the next hour staring at the luggage carousel before realising that his bags had been lost.

Predictably, there were few Englishmen who were impressed by the showing in the French capital. In the letters to the sports pages of the *Daily Mirror* on the Saturday G.F. Roberts of Audeley Avenue, Torquay, did at least attempt to see the funny side, albeit with a pun that would have shamed the authors of jokes inside Christmas crackers: 'France with de Gaulle very annoying. But France with five-de-goals — shocking.' Mr P. Collins of Birmingham made no effort to tickle his fellow *Mirror* readers: 'I was disappointed and disgusted at the pathetic performance put up by England. If this is a sample of our 1966 World Cup team we may as well not enter.' Many people blamed the rout on goalkeeper Ron Springett, who was forced to tell reporters that, contrary to reports, he was not suffering from poor eyesight. There were the usual calls for more England training sessions, but even though England's next match, against Scotland, was not for another five weeks, Ramsey was forced to concede, 'I fear there is little chance of a get-together before then.' England's latest flop also sparked, for the umpteenth time, widespread calls for the hard-liners in the Football League to be more accommodating in their attitude towards the national side. Some, like the *Daily Mirror*'s Peter Wilson, 'The man they can't gag', even suggested that England should be disbanded: 'If English football is so deeply rooted in the moss-encrusted idea that domestic competition must take precedence over international tournaments, then in all seriousness I say that we should pull out of the international scene.'

After the France game Ramsey began his new job in earnest, though clearly the stock of the England manager still had some distance to rise in the eyes of the FA. Ramsey was given a small, screened off cubicle in a room at headquarters in Lancaster Gate to go about his business (his office facilities were later to be upgraded when he was given a whole room of his own measuring precisely thirteen feet by eight feet). It was a strange new world for Ramsey, a tracksuit manager so used to close contact with his players, whose success at Ipswich depended so much on generating a sense of community. Ramsey had spent his entire working life outdoors, first as a player and then as a club manager; now he was an office-bound commuter catching the train each morning from Ipswich to Liverpool Street station before taking the Underground to Lancaster Gate and heading into his tiny third-floor office. There he drew up and updated detailed dossiers on about a hundred of the country's best players. On Saturdays he would attend matches, mostly in the First Division, but he was also seen at Second and occasionally at Third Division matches.

Ramsey's first full match in charge was against Scotland at Wembley on 6 April 1963. The team that day, showing five changes from the Paris defeat, was: Banks, Armfield, Byrne, Moore, Norman, Flowers, Douglas, Greaves, Smith, Melia and Bobby Charlton. 'After the France flop, England dare not fail against Scotland if they are to retain their fast-fading reputation abroad,' wrote Ken Jones in the *Daily Mirror*, but England, did fail, going down 2–1 to a Scottish side brimming with the talents of Law, Baxter, White, St John and Mackay. 'ENGLAND WERE A TEAM OF TIRED GHOSTS' ran the headline in Monday's *Mirror*, but there was no criticism of Ramsey in the press, only hope that he might be able to sort out the apparent mess the England team had become. Six months later, the papers were crowing as England strung together a sequence of impressive results and Ramsey became the darling of Fleet Street. After holding world champions Brazil to a 1–1 draw at Wembley in May, England returned from a highly successful summer tour having beaten Czechoslovakia 4–2, East Germany 2–1 and Switzerland 8–1. On his return, Ramsey repeated his bold declaration that England would win the World Cup. At a press conference on 21 August he said: 'I say it again. I think England will win the

World Cup in 1966. We have the ability, strength, character and, perhaps above all, the players with the right temperament. Such thoughts must be put to the public, and particularly to the players, so that confidence can be built up.' His words were seized upon by the British and foreign press, delighted to have a rod with which to beat him if his players failed to deliver.

In the autumn Wales were thumped 4–0 in Cardiff and Northern Ireland by the old-fashioned margin of 8–3, making it five wins on the hoof with an average of over five goals per game. Glowing reviews appeared in the papers which only six months earlier had claimed that England would be forever mired in mediocrity. The impression (or illusion to some) that England had regained superpower status was reinforced by a 2–1 win over a Rest of the World team at Wembley in a spectacle to celebrate the centenary of the Football League. 'England are back in the First Division of international football,' wrote Bob Pennington in the *News of the World*. Fernando Riera, the manager of the world XI which starred Di Stefano, Gento, Law, Puskas, Eusebio, Baxter and Masopust, said: 'I have always been impressed by the depth of your football. Now it is back on top.' However, some wise old hacks who had seen England flatter to deceive in the past were less convinced of England's imminent domination of world football. The *News of the World*'s veteran chief sports writer Frank Butler (the journalist most admired by Winterbottom) struck a note of caution when he wrote: 'For heaven's sake, let's get back to reality and plan an England team that might win the 1966 World Cup instead of deciding that the rest of the world lie shattered in the dust.'

Ramsey's star, though, was in the ascendant, and he was even accused of being expansive and affable in his press conferences. The only voice of criticism directed at him in the first year or so of his tenure came from north of the border. Like Samuel Johnson, Ramsey came from that particular school of English thought that the best thing about Scotland was the road out of it. The England manager made no effort to disguise his disdain for the Auld Enemy. On one occasion, when the England team arrived in Glasgow, a cheery local journalist approached Ramsey and said: 'Welcome to Scotland,

Sir Alf!' Stony-faced, he replied: 'You must be joking.' The traditional war of words between the two countries intensified after England were beaten at Hampden Park in April 1964. Alan Gilzean, a future star of Tottenham but then with Dundee, scored the only goal of the game with a header from a corner. Afterwards, Ramsey sneered: 'Scotland scored with the type of goal you don't expect in this class of football.' A few weeks later, Bob Kelly, the chairman of Celtic and outgoing president of the Scottish FA, launched an unambiguous attack on Ramsey claiming the England manager was squeezing all the flair and individuality out of his players. 'They are like puppets,' he said. 'Ramsey pulls the strings and the players dance for him. I think he has theorised them out of the game. They mustn't think for themselves. They mustn't deviate from the plan. They have been so brainwashed by tactics and talks that their individual talent has been thrust into the background.'

Kelly's comments came not as a direct response to Ramsey's post-match jibes but three weeks later, when England struggled to a 2–1 victory over a poor Uruguay side who had lost 3-0 against Northern Ireland a few days earlier. England were jeered and slow-clapped by the 55,000 crowd inside Wembley. Ramsey offered no excuses, telling reporters after the match: 'After this type of soul-destroying football my players do not feel they have been in a match.' They may have been sniggering at England's display over the border, but no brickbats were hurled at Ramsey, who was still enjoying the benefit of the statutory honeymoon period bestowed on all new managers. Peter Lorenzo of the *Daily Herald*, however, took the opportunity of England's lacklustre display to question whether England could afford to persevere with Bobby Charlton. 'How long can England afford the luxury of waiting, almost praying that all his potential will pay consistent dividends.'

Two weeks later, reporters were again wearing their 'England-are-great-after-all' hats when Ramsey's side triumphed 4–3 in Lisbon over a powerful Portugal side boasting seven Benfica players and the formidable names of Augusto, Simoes, Eusebio and Torres. And as Ramsey and his players basked in the glow of a famous victory, Kelly's comments seemed nothing more than the froth-at-the-mouth rantings of an instinctively anti-English Scotsman. (Six years later Kelly would have the pleasure of hearing a large proportion of English football followers laying exactly the same charges in reverse at Ramsey's door.)

On 22 May 1964 England set off in high spirits on a summer tour to Dublin and New York, and then on to Rio de Janeiro for the 'Little World Cup' where they would meet Brazil, Portugal and Argentina. But they left behind a miserable figure in the form of Tottenham's promising young midfielder Alan Mullery, who was forced to withdraw from the squad after ricking his back while shaving. 'Apparently he had turned around to pick up the shaving brush when his legs gave way,' his wife June told reporters.

First stop was Dublin, where England continued to belie their reputation as poor travellers by chalking up their fifth successive win on foreign soil with a 3–1 victory. West Ham's John 'Budgie' Byrne, who hit a hat-trick in Lisbon, scored another against the Irish and Arsenal's George Eastham and Tottenham's Jimmy Greaves sealed an impressive win. All the noises in the following day's press struck an upbeat note, with the *Daily Herald* crowing: 'Ramsey's raiders continue their triumphant march across Europe. No other European nation has a record like it.' Three days later England arrived in New York to play a United States team containing three Germans, three Argentinians, two Hungarians, one Englishman and one British Honduran. England had beaten the States 6–3 and 8–1 since the shock World Cup defeat of 1950 in Belo Horizonte, but Ramsey, who played in the match, told reporters that he wanted to exorcise his personal ghosts of the experience with an emphatic victory, adding, just in case no one realised, 'I am not a light-hearted man. I take things very seriously.' Ramsey got the thrashing he wanted as England, without Greaves or Moore, matched their post-war record 10–0 win over Portugal in 1947. Only 5,000 people were there to see it, including fifty sailors from a Liverpool liner. The *Daily Herald* reported that England had made about 'as much of a head-turning impact in this sky-scraping city as a Negro in Harlem'.

The New York trip, though, proved to be a defining moment in Ramsey's relationship with his players. Shortly before

England had flown out to Lisbon in May, Moore, Eastham, Hurst, Byrne, Charlton, Banks and Wilson had slipped out of the hotel for a night on the town. When they returned they found their passports had been placed on their beds. Nothing was said the next day, but as the players prepared to leave the changing room for their first training session after arriving in Portugal Ramsey ordered 'the lads' to stay behind. 'They know who they are,' he said. He told them that if he had had seven other players to fill their boots he would have sent them home. Moore was unimpressed, and in New York ten days later he and a group of others ignored Ramsey's threats and again went out for a drink. Ramsey was furious and confronted Moore, telling him that any drinking would be done as a squad and under his supervision. England's glamorous pin-up boy captain told his Victorian-minded manager that the players were unhappy with the boot-camp discipline. The confrontation strained their relationship for years afterwards, and it would not be until the immediate build-up to the World Cup finals that the strong bond between these two very different sons of east London would be forged once and for all. At one point, Ramsey even dropped Moore for the demonstrably less gifted Norman Hunter.

The former quartermaster was a strict disciplinarian, and did not want anyone stepping out of line on his parade ground; shortly after taking over, Ramsey had said: 'Even when England had great players like Stan Matthews and Tom Finney, I believe the team would have been even better with a rigid plan. Any plan must be adapted to the strengths and weaknesses of the players.' After his run-ins with Moore (and Greaves who, like Moore, didn't mind a pint and had the sort of troublesome, rebellious streak Ramsey found difficult to cope with) he was quick to lay down the law to newcomers to the squad. Allan Clarke recalled an incident on his first England tour when Ramsey heard him laughing and joking at the back of the aeroplane. The England manager walked down the aisle and said to the young Leeds United striker, 'Are you enjoying yourself, Allan?' Clarke replied, 'Very much so, thanks, Sir Alf, and then sat dumbstruck as Ramsey retorted, 'Well, you don't fucking enjoy yourself with me.'

Fewer than 24 hours after arriving in Rio de Janeiro, after a twelve-hour flight from New York, England were to face the world champions in front of 180,000 fans in the Maracana Stadium. England, who went into the match on the back of ten wins in eleven starts, held their own for an hour and even threatened a famous victory before Pele produced one of his greatest ever performances and swept Brazil to a crushing 5–1 triumph. 'IT'S BLACK MAGIC' proclaimed the back page of the *Daily Mirror*. Pele scored one goal and helped engineer the other four, and afterwards Moore told reporters: 'Take Pele away from them and we are every bit as good. If he had been born in Bethnal Green the score would have been England 5 Brazil 1.' Brazilian selector Dr Hilton Gosling paid England a double-edged compliment, saying: 'This is the best England team I have ever seen.' Pele's performance bolstered his reputation as the greatest footballer on the planet, but a few days later he was in disgrace when he felled Argentina's Messiano with a ferocious head-butt as Brazil crashed to a 3–0 defeat against their bitter South American rivals. A mass brawl ensued before Messiano was carried from the field with blood pouring from his broken nose.

England could plead a string of excuses: jet-lag, the searing heat, and the fact that they were kept waiting for an hour in the changing-room because the Brazilian coach was 'unavoidably' delayed in traffic. But Ramsey admitted that the match had showed 'there is still a tremendous gap between us and them . . . but not one that can't be bridged'. A 1–1 draw with Portugal in São Paulo and a 1–0 defeat at the hands of Argentina back in Rio meant England finished last in the Little World Cup. The tour had been a disturbing eye-opener for England's players. On one rest day a group of them had returned from Copacabana beach amazed by the skills of thousands of ball-juggling youngsters. 'They make even Margot Fonteyn look clumsy,' said Byrne.

Ramsey immediately went to work on rebuilding England the following season, making the defence his first priority. As a former defender himself, Ramsey was aware of the importance of laying solid foundations, and it was during this period that Banks, Cohen, Wilson, Jack Charlton, Moore and

Stiles were established as his first-choice six at the back of the team. Jack Charlton and Norbert 'Nobby' Stiles both made their debuts in the 2–2 draw with Scotland at Wembley on 10 April 1965 – to the amazement of many and the despair of others. Both received letters telling them they were the worst players in England. Neither player could be accused of making football a pretty spectacle to watch, but Ramsey was convinced that he needed a couple of 'enforcers' and brushed aside the inevitable criticism from the more aesthetic wing of England's following. Years later, Moore, one of the most cultured players ever to pull on an England shirt, insisted that both players' contributions to England's successful World Cup campaign were as significant as anyone else's. 'When you see a little bloke like Stiles haring around the field, sleeves up and elbows pumping, it made the rest of the team realise what they could do if they put in the same amount of effort. As for Jack Charlton, he rarely lost anything in the air or on the ground and was much better coming forward that many people were prepared to give him credit for.'

Ramsey was nothing like as sure about his choice of personnel further upfield, and in that one season alone he tried fifteen different forwards; in all, Ramsey tried 25 forwards before the World Cup finals. Even then it was not until the quarter-finals that he settled on a front-line he would stick with. With the benefit of hindsight it seemed as if Ramsey was almost deliberately building his team from the back. On England's summer tour at the end of the season he also gave a debut to a flame-haired nineteen-year-old prodigy from Blackpool called Alan Ball. Ramsey's vision of a World Cup-winning team was slowly coming into focus, and things were going well enough on the field. England finished the 1964/65 season unbeaten, winning five of their nine matches, but they won few admirers along the way as a creeping sense of disillusionment with Ramsey's increasingly functional and artisan team began to emerge. The relationship between Ramsey and the press – 'a relationship which has been as uncomfortable as trying to make love to a porcupine,' as Max Marquis wrote in his book on the England manager – grew colder.

Ramsey's audacious prophecy on taking charge of the

national side that England would win the World Cup in 1966 hung over him like a dark cloud from the moment the words first left his mouth right up until Swiss referee Gottfried Dienst put the whistle to his lips for a final time on that golden afternoon of 30 July 1966. Certainly at the start of the 1965/66 season it seemed as if there was more chance of the Queen Mother joining a hippy colony than an England captain climbing the 39 steps at Wembley to receive the Jules Rimet trophy from her daughter. In their first match of the autumn on 2 October England were held to a goalless draw in Wales and were then beaten 3–2 at Wembley by Austria, a country that had not been able to consider itself a force in world football since the 1930s. It wasn't just that England were not proving themselves to be world-beaters, they weren't even Austria-beaters. Ramsey was struggling to find the right formula, but seven weeks after his team were booed off at Wembley he took a gamble when England flew to Madrid to play Spain, the European champions, who had never lost to England outside England. Ramsey opted for a then radical formation of 4–3–3 and dispensed with orthodox wingers.

England football teams had traditionally lined up in a 3–2–5 formation but, inspired by the World Cup-winning Brazilians, the national side had switched to 4–2–4 after 1958. Ramsey had tried the 4–3–3 formation for the first time in England's 1–0 win over West Germany in Nuremberg during the summer tour, and had retained it for the 2–1 win over Sweden in Gothenburg a few days later. But despite its success, and perhaps mindful of the critics who deplored the emphasis on defence and rued the disappearance of crowd-thrilling wingers in the mould of Finney and Matthews, Ramsey had abandoned the system at the start of the season. The success of a 4–2–4 system, however, depended on having good wingers who could meet the demands of modern football by fulfilling the twin roles of attacking and then dropping back to help out the defence when needed (the modern trend of wing-backs places the emphasis the other way round, where players in that position occasionally forage up front but remain essentially defenders). The idea of the 4–3–3 filled many traditionalists with horror, though it was as nothing compared to the heavily defensive *catenaccio* sweeper system which was emerging in Italian football at around the same period.

After the setback against Wales and the shock of defeat by a mediocre Austrian side, Ramsey was forced to experiment again with 4–3–3. The three in midfield were Ball, Stiles and Eastham, while the forwards were Roger Hunt, Joe Baker and Bobby Charlton. England won 2–0, and they so outclassed their hosts that even Spanish reporters were forced to admit that with better finishing the visitors might have won by at least three times as many goals. Ramsey's 'wingless wonders' were born. 'It was after the Spain game that I realised England could win the World Cup with this system,' Ramsey said later, but he had not given up on orthodox wingers and would persevere with at least one of them right through to the final group match of the World Cup finals. Ramsey's famous 'wingless wonders' were not born out of his determination to play 4–3–3, but out of necessity: he simply could not find wingers good enough to justify persisting with a more traditional 4–2–4 system.

Wingers, though, were not his only problem. The question of who to play as strikers was presenting him with a even greater dilemma. In theory, Jimmy Greaves should have been the first name down on the England team-sheet. By the time Ramsey took charge of the team Greaves had established a reputation as one of the world's deadliest strikers since the war. Greaves, though, was a rebel in Ramsey's eyes, a cheeky maverick who loved a night out and whose languid brilliance and the way he appeared to drift in and out of the game gave the impression that he wasn't trying or didn't care. Those who played against Greaves knew this was not true, that his drifting out of the match was a deliberate part of his game plan, allowing him to go unnoticed for long periods only to pounce at the crucial moment. His strike rate of 44 goals in 57 games for England, second only to Nat Lofthouse's 30 in 33 games, provides the statistical evidence of his remarkable talents. It has often been said that Ramsey only admired raw, natural talent if it came dripping in sweat; Greaves did not give this impression, and Ramsey's suspicions about the stocky Londoner's commitment led him to start experimenting with more demonstrably industrious players like Liverpool's Roger Hunt and West Ham's Geoff Hurst. As far as Ramsey was concerned, the collective work ethic took precedence over individual brilliance and therefore Greaves was expendable. If England were to win the World Cup, it would be a team achievement.

Ramsey continued to ring the changes during the 1965/66 season, leading to accusations that he did not know his own mind and fears that it was too late to establish a settled side before the finals. Geoff Hurst, who had been transformed by West Ham manager Ron Greenwood from a journeyman midfielder into a bullish, all-action centre-forward, was called up for the match against Poland on 5 January 1966. He did not play in the match (which ended 1–1) after failing to impress in training ('I was overawed by the company and felt unworthy of being there,' he recalls), but after a quiet word from Ramsey, Hurst began to throw himself about on the training ground and made his debut in England's next match against West Germany at Wembley on 23 February. Greaves was still recovering from a serious bout of jaundice, and Byrne, Hurst's West Ham team-mate, was injured. It was not the most artful line-up in England's history: Leeds United hard man Norman 'bite yer legs' Hunter was chosen to partner Jack Charlton in central defence, while Moore was moved into midfield alongside Stiles and Ball; up front, alongside Bobby Charlton, the one truly creative and exciting ball player in the line-up, were Hunt and Hurst, neither of whom had ever been accused of being blessed with Brazilian-style ball skills. Ramsey's critics were unimpressed by his growing obsession with putting graft before grace, and though England won 1–0 thanks to a scrappy Stiles goal, the 75,000-strong Wembley crowd booed them off the pitch. 'They may be moaning now,' Ramsey told his players in the changing-room, 'but if we beat West Germany 1–0 playing like that in the World Cup final, they'll all be going mad.'

Ramsey persevered with his 4–3–3 formation at the beginning of April, when England met Scotland in a full-blooded encounter at Hampden Park which England won by the odd goal in seven courtesy of Hurst, Hunt (two) and

Bobby Charlton. 'GAY ENGLAND ATTACK STUNS SCOTS!' beamed the back page of the *News of the World*. It was the first time in fifteen games that England had scored more than two goals, and Ramsey was in almost flippant mood with the press afterwards. 'So much has been said about the team and the damage I have done to the players,' he said. 'What were they called? Oh yes! Ramsey's Robots. I have taken a tremendous hammering, as have the players. Please excuse my grin today. I am pleased because I am a good winner and an awfully bad loser.' Ramsey, though, was still not happy, and for England's final match at Wembley before the World Cup, against Yugoslavia, he called up a third West Ham player, Martin Peters, a midfielder he described as being 'ten years ahead of his time'. England won 2–0 and Peters, who had developed a near telepathic understanding with Hurst at West Ham, impressed Ramsey with his intelligent reading of the game, neat passing and, of course, his willingness to run for ninety minutes.

At the end of the season the England players were sent home with orders from their manager to rest for two weeks before the squad of 28 reassembled for an intensive eighteen-day training session at Lilleshall, deep in the Shropshire countryside. When the players arrived, Ramsey and his trainer Les Cocker spelt out the rules. No one would leave the grounds, and there were to be no visitors. Two afternoons per week were set aside for press conferences, but they were to be the only intrusions from the outside world. Ramsey told the players they were going to be pushed to their mental and physical limits and invited anyone to leave there and then if they were not prepared to stomach his Spartan regime. Each day was organised with military precision. Cocker was a hard taskmaster whose gruelling fitness programmes had helped turn Don Revie's Leeds United into one of the most formidably well-drilled and physically robust outfits in the country. Cocker shared Ramsey's belief in rigorous fitness, but many felt his energy-sapping sessions were the reason behind England's occasionally lacklustre performances. Ramsey's own training sessions were followed by lunch and then non-contact sports in the afternoon like tennis, badminton, basketball and indoor cricket. (The basketball sessions quickly became highly physical affairs when the hyper-competitive Stiles was involved. Several players later recalled how Stiles was as aggressive on the basketball court as he was on the football pitch, winding and bruising several of his colleagues with characteristically manic challenges.) The players took a bath in the late afternoon, followed by an early dinner. The evenings were spent playing cards and board games or watching films (Ramsey preferred Westerns, but was said to be open-minded). Alcohol was banned, and after a cup of Ovaltine or hot chocolate the players were dispatched to bed long before midnight. No detail of the preparation was ignored. There were daily medical checks, weigh-ins and a collective purge of athlete's foot. Such was the meticulousness of Ramsey's planning that the players were even given lessons in how to cut their toe-nails for fear that a poor clipping technique could lead to a septic toe.

At first the players were unhappy with the boot-camp regime – not least the drinkers like Moore, Greaves and Jack Charlton, who felt that as fully grown adults they should be allowed to decide for themselves what was good or bad for them. England's country retreat was quickly dubbed 'Stalag Lilleshall' and 'Colditz', and discontent began to rumble throughout the squad. It was not long before a plot was hatched by a hardcore of rebels to break the curfew and go for a night out in the local pub despite Ramsey's insistence that anyone caught going for a drink would be expelled from the squad for ever. (Over the eighteen days, only one day was given over to relaxation but it was supervised Soviet-style by the management, and when they went for a drink in a local golf club Ramsey bought the beers – in half-pint measures.) When Ramsey got wind of 'The Great Escape', the squad was summoned to be reminded that anyone caught off the premises would not figure in the World Cup finals. 'Alf wanted to push us to the utmost limit of human endurance,' Jack Charlton recalled. 'It was a test of character as much as a physical training programme.' The isolation and Spartan regime generated a sense of 'cabin fever' in Ramsey's tightly run ship.

After a while Jack Charlton and Nobby Stiles, the two most

aggressive characters in the squad, began to clash on the field, at first verbally and then physically. 'The situation threatened to get ugly,' says Hurst, who watched the two hard men provoke each other to breaking point. Under the relentless and exhausting pressure of the strict daily regime, the very morale and unity of the squad seemed to be on the verge of collapse. But when the running row between Stiles and Charlton finally spilt over on the training ground, Ramsey turned the explosive situation to his, and the squad's, advantage. Stiles and Charlton were pulled apart and Ramsey took his players aside, admonishing no one and pointing out how both players had been right to react in the way that they had. It was as if Ramsey was almost encouraging his other players to match the same intensity and emotional pitch. After the World Cup the players looked back on this response as an astute piece of psychological conditioning, channelling the growing tension among the squad into something positive. Ramsey had the players just how he wanted them: fired up and bitching. The tension remained, but now it was working to England's ultimate benefit. United by their isolation and the severity of the regime, the squad came to feel like a tight-knit club, regiment or family, with all the feelings of loyalty and togetherness and all the simmering tensions that are found in those institutions.

When the squad dispersed before their final warm-up tour, Ramsey broke the news to Peter Thompson, Gordon Milne, Keith Newton, Bobby Tambling and John Byrne that they were not in the final party ('The worst moment of my career as England manager,' Ramsey told reporters). The tour involved softish games against Finland, Norway and Denmark followed by what one player later described as 'a right bastard of a game' against Poland. Ramsey rotated his players during the tour, sparking fears and accusations in the press that he still did not know his best team. Ramsey did not say so at the time for fear of blunting his players' competitive edge, but he later insisted that by the time the squad left Lilleshall he knew his starting eleven for the opening match of the World Cup finals against Uruguay. 'In the past, England have been too reliant on players who later became injured or lost form,' he told reporters. 'I have said it many times since taking over as manager: I want a squad, not a team, with players ready for first-team action when I call them.'

In the first game against Finland in Helsinki on 26 June, Peters and Jack Charlton scored their first goals for England in a comfortable 3–0 win. Greaves, though, was the star of the show in the next match against Norway in Oslo. Proving his full recovery from the jaundice that first took the edge off his performances and then ruled him out of football altogether, England's best centre-forward since Tommy Lawton scored four as Ramsey's team cantered to a 6–1 win. Proving the all-round quality of his marksmanship, Greaves notched up those four goals with a header, a dazzling individual effort, a classic piece of predatory poaching and an expert piece of finishing. Neither Greaves nor England hit the same heights against Denmark a few days later in Copenhagen, but a 2–0 win, achieved without much fuss, at least maintained England's winning ways.

For their final match, Ramsey had deliberately chosen as tough a test as possible: Poland in Poland. If Ramsey wanted to test his players under the severest of conditions he certainly got what he wanted – and more. Originally, the match was to be played in Warsaw, but on arrival they were told by the Polish Soviet authorities that the match would now be played in Katowice, a grim industrial city lying in the heart of the flat coalfields of Silesia down by the Czechoslovakian border. England flew to Krakow and then took a bus for a journey that they were told would take just over an hour. On a vehicle that was barely roadworthy, let alone comfortable, Ramsey and his squad found themselves on a seven-hour odyssey through the bleak Polish countryside. The players were growing steadily more irritated, and in an effort to try to lighten the mood of the thunder-faced Ramsey, the Polish interpreter asked the England manager what he planned to do later that night. 'Get to bloody Katowice, I hope,' Ramsey snapped back. The match was as tough as the journey to get there, but England, perhaps worked into a froth of fury by their travel arrangements, were in the mood for a battle – especially Stiles and Jack Charlton, who relished the physical confrontation with their tough opponents in the intimidating atmosphere generated by the partisan 80,000 crowd. The match was settled in England's favour thanks to a stunning strike by Hunt.

The squad returned to glowing reviews in the nation's press. 'READY TO LICK THE WORLD NOW!' was the beamingly optimistic headline on the back page of the *Daily Mirror*. 'Tackling with the aggression of street fighters,' wrote the paper's chief football reporter, Ken Jones, 'I cannot recall an England team playing with such ferocity, with such utter belief in their right to win. This was the sort of professionalism that has so often been lacking in British sides in the past.' Now Ramsey could turn his thoughts exclusively to England's first internationals in a major competition since February 1963.

England's players were allowed to return home to their families for two days before reassembling at the weekend at their base, Hendon Hall Hotel, ahead of the opening match against Uruguay on Monday, 11 July. Meanwhile, England's rivals began arriving by the planeload. From Europe came West Germany, considered as outsiders by the bookies; Portugal, boasting the talents of Torres and Eusebio, who many considered to be the greatest footballer in the world at the time, better even than Pele; and Italy, who in their final warm-up games had beaten Bulgaria 6–1, Mexico 5–0 and Argentina 3 0. Those three were seen as England's biggest threat from their own continent, but it was the South Americans that troubled the England camp the most, especially Brazil, bidding for a third consecutive triumph, and the volatile Argentinians, whose mixture of outrageous skill with a willingness to 'put the shoe in' made them especially dangerous to the European sides who always felt they would have the upper hand in physical confrontations. Brazil were the tournament favourites at 7–4 (England were second at 9–2). As always, Brazilian football had focused all its efforts on preparing the national side. In the six weeks before the finals they had played twelve friendlies, winning nine and drawing three of them. There were 44 players in the squad, which was split into four teams, each of which set off on its own separate tour before a final 22 were brought together a couple of weeks before arriving in England.

The arrival of North Korea, an unknown quantity in world football, provoked a great deal of interest in the media. In a special World Cup edition, the *News of the World* claimed that the Asians would be the fittest team in the competition. 'The average height of their players is 5'6" though smoking hasn't stunted their growth,' said the paper. 'Every member of their initial forty footballers, who have trained together for the past eighteen months, is a non-smoking, non-drinking, fitness fanatic.'

One problem for England was Bobby Moore's long-running dispute with West Ham. England's captain was out of contract with the club and therefore not officially an FA-registered player. As FIFA were technically obliged to bar him from England's squad, Ramsey summoned Hammers' manager Ron Greenwood to Hendon Hall, where he was put into a room with England's captain. They emerged moments later with Moore clutching a contract to cover him for July, and Ramsey was thus allowed to include Moore in the line-up for the opening match submitted to FIFA, which read: Banks, Cohen, Wilson, Stiles, J. Charlton, Moore, Ball, Greaves, B. Charlton, Hunt, Connelly. After all the speculation and experimentation with 4–3–3, the England manager kept faith with Greaves and opted to play a winger in Manchester United's John Connelly in a traditional 4–2–4 formation. Announcing his line-up to the press, Ramsey said: 'If I could start all over again at this stage I don't think I would change anything. The best men have been chosen and a way of playing best suited to them decided upon.'

Uruguay arrived with a reputation for an impregnable defence: they had qualified having conceded just two goals in four games. A long opening ceremony featuring the bands of the Grenadier and Coldstream Guards preceded the match, before the Queen was introduced to the players. But to the disappointment of the hundreds of millions tuning in around the world, that was pretty well where the entertainment ended. The match, later described by Jack Charlton as the most frustrating he had ever played in, finished goalless as England tried without success to find a way through the South Americans' heavily-packed and well-drilled defence. It was the first match in which England had failed to score at the Empire Stadium for 28 years. 'THE WORLD CUP KICKS OFF WITH A LET-DOWN' bemoaned the front page of the *Daily Mirror*.

In order to distract the players and stop self-doubt creeping into their minds, the very next day Ramsey whisked the players off to Pinewood studios to watch the filming of the latest James Bond movie, *Thunderball*, where they met Sean Connery, Yul Brynner, Britt Ekland and a number of other stars. A day later the squad returned to Wembley to watch group rivals Mexico and France play and were heartened by the toothless display of both teams. 'RELAX, THESE TWO ARE EASY' the *Daily Mirror* assured its readers the following morning. England, though, were able to take greater heart from the growing chaos in the Brazilian camp where the players, increasingly unhappy with their management team, were threatening revolt. The troubles off the pitch had clearly affected the team's performance, and when they lost 3–1 at Goodison Park to a Hungarian side inspired by the brilliance of Florian Albert, it left the world champions needing to beat the powerful Portuguese by three clear goals to reach the last eight.

Ramsey made two changes for England's next match, against Mexico on 16 July. Connelly was replaced on the wing by Southampton's Terry Paine, while Alan Ball was dropped to make way for Martin Peters. Once again, though, England found themselves facing a seemingly immovable object in the form of a Mexican defensive wall featuring as many as eight outfield players at a time. England's frustration and that of their fans was growing by the minute before one moment of inspiration by Bobby Charlton finally kick-started England's World Cup campaign. The balding Manchester United star received the ball on the edge of the centre circle and swept upfield before unleashing a 30-yard thunderbolt that was still gathering pace when it thumped into the back of the net. The Korean linesman flagged for offside as Greaves stole into position, but the Italian referee Carlo Lobello overruled him. After 127 minutes England had scored their first goal of the World Cup finals. Thirteen minutes from time they added a second when Liverpool's Hunt struck from close range to net his thirteenth England goal in fifteen appearances.

England now had three points from four and needed just a draw against an unfancied French team which had lost much of its potency since the retirement of Jus Fontaine and Raymond Kopa. Not everyone, though, was impressed by England's display against Mexico. 'Unless there is a dramatic injection of imagination in midfield and of vigorous initiative in attack, the dreams that have been cherished over three years of preparation are likely to dissolve miserably,' wrote Hugh McIlvanney in the *Observer*. But McIlvanney conceded that England's ambitions to play entertaining, attacking football were made virtually impossible by the negativity of their opponents. 'On the evidence of this performance Mexico have about as much right to be in the World Cup as the Isle of Man has to be on the Security Council,' he added.

The news from the other groups around the country over the next few days provided a boost for all Englishmen: Brazil and Italy were out. The reigning world champions were beaten 3–1 by a Portuguese side who were growing in confidence and quality by the game. Nor did Brazil's mother country, who had already qualified, show them much maternal love: Pele was crippled by a series of brutal challenges in the first half. Italy, meanwhile, were the victims of the biggest upset of the finals, beaten 1–0 by North Korea at Ayresome Park.

The England players were keen to see off France by playing with a more attacking line-up, but Ramsey, ever the pragmatist, was in no mood to take any risks by playing expansive football, even though the French needed to win by two clear goals to go through. 'If we need eleven men in defence to keep out the French, then we will have eleven men back in defence,' he said before the match. England did win the match, but not without a fight and not without controversy. Ramsey made one change, handing Liverpool's Ian Callaghan his second cap in place of the unfortunate if ineffectual Paine in the troublesome wing position. France's hopes suffered an early setback when one of their best players, Robert Herbin, twisted his knee and could barely run for the remainder of the match. England took the lead in highly dubious circumstances when Hunt prodded home from a blatantly offside position after Jack Charlton's header had rebounded off the post. The

Japanese referee, Yamasaki, waved away a posse of cursing Frenchmen, and what was already a poor spectacle grew even uglier on the eye. The biggest talking point of the match, and one of the most contentious moments in the finals, came four minutes from time when Stiles, playing as always as if possessed by the Furies, crunched Jacques Simon right under the nose of the referee with a challenge so late that it beggared belief. From the ensuing play England scored their second goal, when Hunt headed in Callaghan's cross. Back at the halfway line, Simon lay rolling and screaming in agony before being stretchered away to leave the Frenchmen effectively with just nine fit players.

England were into the last eight, and were firm favourites to win the tournament, but they had made precious few friends along the way – especially across La Manche. France's scorn for England's World Cup progress was pithily expressed in a cartoon in the prestigious sports newspaper *L'Equipe* shortly afterwards. The cartoon depicted Bobby Charlton driving in a Rolls-Royce while referees in bobby uniforms cleared his route by holding back the opposition. The caption read, 'Let us pass, please'. Predictably, Stiles' barbaric challenge provoked a storm of outrage, not just in France or elsewhere abroad but also in England. Several members of the press, who had never been convinced of Nobby's footballing prowess anyway, called for his removal from the team and the FA put pressure on Ramsey to drop him. Ramsey, though, was unmoveable in his support for Stiles, a stance which some saw as evidence of his loyalty to his players, others as proof of the manager's pig-headedness. 'If Stiles doesn't play, England doesn't,' Ramsey told his employers. And there the affair ended, although the press still reserved its right to remark upon England's poverty of ideas after the France game. 'ENGLAND'S SPARK IS STILL MISSING' read the headline in the *Daily Mirror*. 'This time there can be no excuse,' wrote Ken Jones. 'There were no barricades in front of them smothering every attempt at a build-up.'

The France match proved to be a highly significant moment in the career of Greaves and, arguably, in the final outcome of the tournament. Greaves, who had been largely ineffective against the brickwall defences he encountered in the group matches, suffered a badly gashed leg and would take no part in the quarter-final against Argentina. Hurst, who had watched all the matches from the stands and whose frustration nearly saw him come to blows with an over-critical England fan, was called into the side. The France match also proved to be the end of the road for wingers after Ramsey's unsuccessful experiments with Connelly, Paine and Callaghan. From now on England's formation would be strictly 4–3–3 with Peters, Ball and Stiles forming the midfield.

Argentina arrived at Wembley on 23 July with their reputation as a highly talented side with an appetite for brutality enhanced after a ferocious goalless contest with West Germany. 'I regard Argentina as the most militant and aggressive side I have seen in this World Cup,' Ken Jones warned *Daily Mirror* readers. The emotional temperature in both camps and among the public was now reaching boiling point. It was knockout time, and the two heaviest of the heavyweights left in the tournament were in the mood for it. In the tunnel, the towering Argentinian captain Antonio Rattin, the millionaire aristocrat with the gilded boots and the iron elbows, snarled and jabbed his fingers at his own players. Rattin turned out to be the central character of the drama that unfolded, sparking (or perhaps exacerbating) a sense of mutual hostility between the footballing nations of Europe and South America that continues to this day. Several England players admitted at the end of their careers that the match was the roughest they ever played in. 'Most teams have one hardman, perhaps two,' said Hurst, 'but this Argentinian team had about eight or nine.'

The off-the-ball kicks and elbows started almost immediately, but not content with taking out his aggression on the opposition, Rattin, from the outset, harangued German referee Rudolf Kreitlein. The Argentine skipper was booked for a challenge on Bobby Charlton before committing further fouls on Hurst (twice), Ball and another on Charlton. He was lucky to be on the pitch at all when Kreitlein booked Luis Artime for dissent in the 36th minute. Rattin exploded. As the official retreated towards the centre of the pitch, Rattin pursued him, shouting, gesticulating and pulling his captain's armband.

Kreitlein had had enough. His face a picture of barely contained rage, the little balding German threw his right arm in the direction of the stands. Rattin, the first man ever to be ordered off at Wembley, refused to move. For eight minutes the Argentinian stood his ground protesting violently with the official. While Rattin, Kreitlein, FIFA officials and a handful of bemused bobbies tried to settle the dispute, the rest of the Argentinians walked off the pitch in an apparent threat to withdraw from the match.

Finally, though, Rattin walked and the match resumed, but Argentina continued to frustrate their 'hosts' with a mixture of dazzling football, comic play-acting and bone-shuddering challenges. The South Americans put men behind the ball hoping to catch England on the counter-attack, or perhaps hold out to the end of extra time when the outcome of the match would be settled on the toss of a coin. Both Charltons managed to get booked when Bobby raced to the aid of his elder brother who was lifted off the ground by an Argentinian kick as he lay on the turf. England, though, finally broke the deadlock after 75 minutes when Peters swung over a perfect left-wing cross for his West Ham team-mate Hurst to head in. (Afterwards, Hurst admitted that the goal would probably never have come had Rattin still been on the pitch as the giant Argentinian had been getting the better of him in the air, by fair means or foul.)

The final whistle, however, did not signal the end of the hostilities. As Kreitlein was escorted off the pitch by a bevy of bobbies, Argentina's players, with nothing more to lose than more of their dignity, gave vent to their feelings to England's players and the match officials. One spat on a FIFA official, another urinated in the tunnel, and another rubbed his finger and thumb together – suggesting bribery – in the face of England doctor Alan Bass. A chair was thrown through the glass door of the England dressing room as the Argentinians tried to break in for a fight. Moments earlier, Ramsey, in a rare expression of emotion, ran on to the pitch and tried to stop Cohen from swapping shirts with an Argentinian. 'I played under Alf for eight years and that was the only time I ever saw him lose his rag,' says Martin Peters.

Ramsey later called the Argentinians 'animals' as the fall-out from the match developed into a full-blown diplomatic incident; later still he issued a terse apology after he received a letter of rebuke from FIFA, who said his remarks did 'not foster good international relations'. No one else, certainly in England, thought that Ramsey had spoken anything but the truth. Max Marquis wrote in *Anatomy of a Football Manager*: 'I think it only right that Ramsey should apologise for using the word "animals" – not to FIFA, but to the RSPCA.' For the South Americans, the sending off of Rattin and the comments of Ramsey were the final straws of the World Cup finals, which they claimed were rigged from the outset to favour the Europeans, and especially England. It turned out that Argentina had been smarting from the outset after having been barred from practising at Wembley on the eve of the match because groundstaff wanted to prepare for an evening digs meeting. 'Calling the Argentinians "animals" caused outrage in Latin America,' said Pele, years later. 'From then on South American teams were determined to make England teams suffer.' The referees, they claimed, had been instructed to be lenient on the traditionally tougher-tackling Europeans while being tough on any perceived transgression by Brazil, Argentina, Mexico or Uruguay. For a few months after the tournament there was talk of a Latin American boycott of the next World Cup. The threats slowly faded away, but the experiences of the South Americans in England were neither forgiven nor forgotten.

Two days after the match, the front page of the *Daily Mirror* carried a picture of a smiling Rattin taking a photograph of a Scots Guardsman outside Buckingham Palace. He told the reporter he was unrepentant about his behaviour, adding as a parting shot: 'England will win the World Cup because the referees are on their side.' FIFA's reaction to the incident was to fine Argentina the maximum, if laughable, figure of £83 and ban three of their players for four matches: Rattin, Onega for spitting in the face of FIFA official Harry Cavan, and Roberto Ferreiro for assaulting Kreitlein after the match. The nation's sports writers, meanwhile, were in a frothy lather over the Argentinians' behaviour, and it is painful to imagine how they might have reacted had England lost. 'LATIN LUNACY PLUNGES SOCCER INTO CHAOS!' bellowed the back page of the *Daily Mirror*. Peter Wilson called for Argentina to be banned for four years, including the 1970 World Cup. He wrote: 'This is sporting anarchy, Soccer in chaos, warfare for nationalistic aggrandisement run riot. THIS IS SHAMEFUL.'

Fair play and good football made a welcome return for England's first ever World Cup semi-final, against Portugal, which, much to the disgust of football fans in the north (and the suspicion of the French and South American conspiracy theorists) had been switched from Goodison Park to Wembley on the grounds of ticket demand. Portugal arrived with no mean reputation for violence themselves after the world watched them kick the great Pele black and blue in their highly charged group match. Ramsey kept faith with the team that had battled and scrapped their way to the disturbingly narrow victory over Argentina (several England players joined Hurst in admitting that had Rattin kept his cool and stayed on the pitch it might well have been the South Americans and not the English lining up to face Eusebio and Co.). As England whiled away their three days before the match at their hotel and shopping in Hendon, they were able to reflect on the fact that Portugal had beaten England only once and had never even managed so much as a draw in England itself.

Amazingly, the semi-final was the first of England's matches to be sold out. Some 76,000 had watched the opening game against Uruguay, 85,000 the Mexico game and 92,500 – 500 short of a full house – the France and Argentina games. England players down the years had complained (and continued to until recent years) about the lack of support they received from Wembley crowds, just as England's cricketers have been known to moan about the reserve of the spectators at Lord's, but against Portugal the Wembley hordes, perhaps finally believing that England had a chance of winning the trophy, rose to the occasion and created an atmosphere more familiar to the country's notoriously raucous club grounds.

The match was a spectacle to savour from the first whistle. The football flowed from both teams. The match would be remembered as a great spectacle of entertaining and fairly contested football (it took 23 minutes for the referee to award a foul, and 56 for him to award one against the Portuguese), making it all the more ironic that Nobby Stiles was widely acknowledged to be the man of the match. Perhaps lifted by the rare sound of the capacity crowd chanting his name into the evening sky as he emerged from the tunnel, Stiles responded with his greatest performance in an England shirt. Detailed to follow Eusebio wherever he went, the Manchester United spoiler barely allowed the Mozambique-born former European footballer of the year a threatening kick all match. Bobby Charlton was enjoying himself too, and after they had both retired, Jack claimed it was his brother's best ever performance for England. Bobby put England in front on 30 minutes with a firm shot from the edge of the area, and the game continued to flow after the break with England perhaps marginally the better side. The country seemed assured of seeing England in the final when, with twelve minutes to go, Charlton put them 2–0 up with one of the great goals in the history of the World Cup. Hurst laid the ball back from the by-line and Charlton, bursting from midfield like a runaway train struck as sweet and powerful a shot as Wembley had ever seen, one that was still gathering pace when it crashed on to the stanchion in the roof of the net. As he trotted back to his own half, modestly acknowledging the wild applause of the crowd and the congratulations of his colleagues, a couple of Portuguese players felt moved enough by what they had seen to offer him their hands in humble acknowledgement of his masterful strike.

That, however, was not the end of the excitement. With nine minutes left on the clock Torres, with Banks stranded, headed goalwards and Jack Charlton, on the line, instinctively thrust out a hand to stop the ball's inevitable progress into the net. A penalty was awarded, but in line with the rules of the day Charlton was not sent off, or even booked. Eusebio, 'the black panther' as he was dubbed by the press, stepped up and smashed the ball to the right of Banks. Portugal were back in the match, and just three minutes later they were inches away from equalising when Simoes bore down on goal with just Banks to beat, only for Stiles to come hurtling out of the night to block his shot.

After the match, Ramsey walked into the dressing room and said to his players: 'Gentlemen, you know I don't normally talk about individual players, but I think you will agree that Nobby has produced a truly professional performance.' England were in the World Cup final, thanks in part to the man with the thick-rimmed ice-cube glasses (he wore contact lenses on the pitch) whose football career might never have happened after he was knocked over by a bus as a small boy.

Ramsey struggled to keep a lid on his joy when he faced reporters after the match. 'This must be our greatest win since I became manager,' he beamed. 'I have known nothing like this.' Of the full-throated, boisterous crowd, he said: 'They have been really great. One might think that Liverpool must have transferred some of their supporters down here.' The England manager's doubters were finally won over, and over the next few days the papers were full of glowing profiles of the man who had made so little effort to endear himself to their authors. 'With Wembley standing in acclaim for England, Alf Ramsey rose from his touchline seat on Tuesday and went quietly to the tunnel in the wake of his triumphant team,' wrote Ken Jones. 'Nothing, it seems, can crack the mask that hides the real Ramsey from a nation that at last has respect for him . . . Out of abuse, Ramsey has won a nation's respect.'

Predictably, the build-up to the final against West Germany gave rise to plenty of bellicose, *Dad's Army*-style headlines in the nation's popular press. It was only just over twenty years since the two countries had ended their hostilities on the battlefield, and with football lending itself easily to the vocabulary of warfare, Fleet Street's sub-editors had a field day. The German television commentator Werner Schneider was not the only one of his countrymen to be disturbed by what he read and heard in those days leading up the final. 'It is said that the Germans are the most militaristic people but it is not so,' he said. 'The British are. Even winning at football is treated like a victory in battle.'

Franz Beckenbauer, a virtually unknown twenty-year-old from Bayern Munich, had been the star of Germany's progress to the final. Four goals in five games and a composure belying his age had earned him a string of glowing reviews. But after picking up his second booking in the dour 2–1 win over the Soviet Union in the other semi-final he was technically ruled out of the final. However, just as Brazil's brilliant winger Garrincha had been given a special reprieve by FIFA in Chile four years earlier, so too the young German was shown leniency by world football's governing body. Ramsey, though, was unmoved by FIFA's act of clemency, predicting (rightly as it turned out) that Beckenbauer would be deployed to track Bobby Charlton. As a precaution, Stiles was told to do exactly the same to Beckenbauer if he assumed a more attacking role.

The Germans had proved in the previous three World Cups that they were a footballing nation to be taken seriously. To general astonishment they had beaten the outstanding Hungarians to win the event in 1954, and had showed by reaching the semi-finals in Sweden and the last eight in Chile that there had been nothing fortuitous about their triumph in Switzerland. But they had one major psychological problem: they had never beaten England. England, or Ramsey, had only one major problem: who would partner Hunt up front, Greaves or Hurst? Greaves, whose gashed leg had healed, was the people's favourite and indisputably one of the greatest goalscorers of all time. Hurst, though, had seized his opportunity, running himself into the ground in England's matches against Argentina and Portugal with the kind of sweat-soaked determination his manager so admired in players. In the end, Ramsey decided against disrupting a winning team. Greaves, according to his room-mate and close friend Bobby Moore, was inconsolable. 'Jimmy was absolutely devastated,' Moore recalled in later years. 'I think it was from that moment that his career began to go downhill. He never quite got over it.'

In fact both sides were unchanged from the semi-finals for what turned out to be one of the most dramatic matches in the history of the World Cup. 'No more gripping finale could have been offered as a product of the scriptwriter's art,' said the FA's official report of the finals. 'If it had been fiction instead of fact it would have been regarded incredulously.' England found themselves a goal down after just twelve minutes when Ray Wilson's weak clearing header allowed Helmut Haller to sweep the ball past Banks. It was the first goal England had conceded in open play in over 700 minutes of action, but they were back on level terms five minutes later when Moore caught the German defence unprepared with a quickly taken free-kick to Hurst, who rose unmarked to head in. England had the better of the second half and scored what seemed the winner when the indefatigable Ball chased what seemed a lost cause and won a corner from which Peters swept the ball into the net after Hurst's shot had been blocked. Wembley exploded in delight and the crowd were running through a medley of patriotic songs before disaster struck as the match headed into time added on. Jack Charlton was dubiously adjudged to have fouled Held just outside the area, and from Emmerich's free-kick Weber pounced from close range. Wembley fell silent and the heads of the England players slumped in disbelief. Almost immediately, Swiss referee Gottfried Dienst blew his whistle to mark the end of full time. The players of both sides slid to the ground, exhausted by their efforts and by the prospect of a further 30 minutes of energy-sapping struggle. Ramsey marched on to the pitch and delivered a simple message: 'You have beaten them once. Now go out and do it again.'

There followed one of the most controversial incidents in the history of international football. It all happened in the blink of an eye. Midway through the first period of extra time, Hurst unleashed a powerful shot that cannoned down off the crossbar and on to the ground. Roger Hunt, following up, had the chance to make sure of the goal but instead threw his arms in the air in celebration. England claimed the ball had crossed the line, the Germans protested that it hadn't; even if an observer had been sitting in the goal it is unlikely that he would be able to say for certain whether the ball had crossed the white line. Dienst jogged over to the touchline and consulted the Russian linesman, Tofik Bakhramov, who, with one nod of the head, became one of the most celebrated figures in the history of English football. A fractious hush had descended on Wembley, but it was broken by an almighty roar as Dienst signalled that a goal had been scored.

The FA's official report into the World Cup published in

1967 claimed that television proved conclusively that the ball had crossed the line. 'There is nothing controversial now about England's third goal, the one which would have been debated as long as football is played if the human eye had been left to confirm or disprove the decision of the Swiss referee, Mr Gottfried Dienst, or the Russian linesman, Mr Tofik Bakhramov,' it claimed. 'The probing motion picture cameras established unquestionably the validity of the goal.' Despite the wishful thinking of the author of the FA report, the goal has continued to be debated to the present day, but scientists at Oxford University claimed in 1996 that their calculations proved the ball did not cross the line. 'Maybe these fellows were right when they said God was an Englishman,' wrote Hugh McIlvanney in the next day's *Observer*.

Hurst, though, was not finished, and with spectators starting to invade the pitch and BBC commentator Kenneth Wolstenholme declaring that 'they think it's all over', the exhausted West Ham striker mustered one last burst of energy and stormed downfield to crash a left-footed volley inside the near post. 'It was the most sweetly struck shot of my life,' Hurst would say at the end of his career. Dienst blew his whistle for the final time and Wembley erupted in a riot of red, white and blue joy. England were world champions, although it would be difficult to believe it by looking at the preternaturally impassive Ramsey on the bench.

After the immediate post-match celebrations the victorious squad set off on an eight-mile coach ride across the capital to the Royal Garden Hotel on Kensington High Street, cheered all along the route by jubilant Londoners who had not waved their Union Jacks so vigorously since VE Day 21 years earlier. Outside the hotel a huge crowd had formed to salute their heroes. The players appeared on the balcony, Buckingham Palace-style, to acknowledge the well-wishers before the party began in earnest. There was one conspicuous absentee at the post-match banquet attended by Prime Minister Harold Wilson and his Cabinet colleague Jim Callaghan. Jimmy Greaves was so shaken by his omission that he could not bear to impose his depression on his joyful colleagues. He went to the pub instead. After almost two months without a serious drink inside him, Jack Charlton, like most of his team-mates, had only one ambition that evening. He left a note in the top pocket of his jacket which read: 'If found please return this body to room 501, Royal Garden Hotel'. Early the following morning, the giant Leeds defender found himself sitting in someone's front garden in north London talking to an old lady who had known his mother in Northumberland.

World Cup glory, it seemed, did little to thaw Ramsey's frostiness towards the gentlemen of the press. The following day he was approached by two reporters who had steadfastly supported him while some of their colleagues were ladling out the vitriol. But on asking for a short interview, they were told, 'Sorry, it's my day off.' But what did Ramsey care? He made no attempt to humour the press in the worst of times, and now that he had engineered England's finest moment in nearly a century of international football he was above criticism – at least for the time being.

All the papers, broadsheet as well as tabloid, splashed England's triumph over front page and back on the Sunday and Monday. The *Daily Mirror* carried a picture of Peters, Moore and Hurst wearing ties and grinning from ear to ear, having a pillow fight in their hotel room. Next to it was a picture of a stony-faced Ramsey holding a glass of wine at a champagne lunch in a TV studio. He is talking to FA secretary Denis Follows who is holding a briefcase containing the Jules Rimet trophy. Ramsey told the reporter: 'I am sorry for appearing unemotional. It is not intentional. But it is important that somebody remained sane in the England party. That was me.' 'THE WORLD IS AT ALF'S FEET' declared the back page of Monday's *Daily Mirror*. Underneath there was a cartoon showing a man in his armchair staring blankly at a giant portrait of the England manager on his mantelpiece, with his wife saying: 'I know what you think of him, but don't you think it's a little big?' In his report, Ken Jones wrote: 'His reputation as a master manager will go untouched by time, unaffected by any failure he may meet in the future.'

Ramsey, who would be knighted in the New Year's Honours list, had indeed reached the pinnacle of international football. According to Alan Mullery, his new status did not affect his attitude to his players. 'I remember after he got his knighthood we were travelling to Cardiff to play Wales and I used to sit in the front next to him because I was a terrible traveller.' So I said, "what do we call you now?" and he said "A wanker, just like you always have." He could be very funny when he was in a good mood.'

Ramsey's relations with the press corps worsened after the immediate rush of joy following England's World Cup triumph faded the short memories of journalists and football fans alike. Many journalists found that Ramsey became even more aloof, uncooperative and downright awkward after 1966, although it should be said that the England manager always professed astonishment when these accusations were put to him. Winning the biggest prize in world football gave Ramsey even greater cause to believe that he didn't need to try to make friends and influence them. His success spoke for itself. He was beyond reproach. Press conferences became increasingly tense affairs, and at one of them he told reporters: 'You need me, I don't need you.'

The pressure was now on to show that 1966 had not been a fluke achieved only by virtue of home advantage, favourable refereeing decisions, the unforeseen (and, in some instances, unfortunate) demise of their main rivals and as much sweat as it was possible for the human body to shed. England were the world champions; now they had to start playing like world champions. The problem for Ramsey was that now that he had touched the very heights, the only way was down. Nothing short of high-quality football underlining the global supremacy the World Cup triumph was supposed to have proved would satisfy his critics. The statistics show that between the start of the 1966 season and the end of the 1970 season England were relatively successful. Of their 33 games in that period nineteen were won, ten were drawn and only four were lost. The only trouble was that England rarely turned on the style and thrilled onlookers in the way that Brazil had since the late 1950s. England became increasingly workmanlike as Ramsey stuck with his 4–3–3 formation and then slowly transformed it into an even more defence-minded 4–4–2 by the time of the 1970 World Cup in Mexico.

Ramsey was often criticised for his apparent reluctance to play wingers, but no one could accuse him of not trying. Right up until the quarter-finals of 1966 he played with a wide man, but as his supporters point out, Paine, Connelly and Callaghan were simply not good enough to trouble world-class defenders. The bare truth was that England lacked great wingers of the class of Jairzinho, Garrincha, Johnstone, Finney or Matthews. And Ramsey was a pragmatic man who was not going to persevere with a player in that position for sentimental or traditional reasons if he felt by doing so England stood less chance of winning. He began to show a marked favouritism for the hard men and the grafters over the ball players and the entertainers. England were functional, not fun, to watch. His team began to assume an abrasiveness every bit as rankling as his attitude to the press (in particular, his persistence with Stiles and his admiration for Hunter, another whole-hearted but often brutal player who made few personal contributions to Pele's vision of 'the beautiful game', became focuses of criticism). 'England winning the World Cup in 1966 was the worst thing to happen in British football because it killed attacking football and the art of goalscoring,' Denis Law would say many years later. 'Ramsey himself cannot be blamed. It was the coaches who slavishly followed his example. 1966 was the start of a long and bad period for English football. Once Ramsey's 4–3–3 system had been copied up by most club sides over the next couple of seasons, English football became boring, negative and unimaginative.'

Ramsey believed that his squad for Mexico was stronger than the one he had assembled four years earlier, but by the start of 1970 there were very few commentators predicting that England would succeed in defending their title. In January the draw was made, and England found themselves in a tough group with favourites Brazil, Czechoslovakia and Romania. Ramsey would famously tell reporters that 'England had nothing to learn from Brazil', but he openly conceded that retaining their crown would be difficult in the alien conditions of Mexico with its stifling heat, oxygen-sapping altitude and hostile crowds. Furthermore, as Ramsey continually reminded his squad, opponents would now want to beat England more than ever as they were not just representatives of the sport's mother country, but also its modern-day world champions. 'I have impressed upon the players that every team we meet will be more intent upon stopping us than winning the World Cup themselves,' said Ramsey on the eve of England's flight to Mexico. 'I made this clear last November before we met Holland in Amsterdam because I wanted to make sure that none of my players – even six months before we left for Mexico – had any false illusions about the task ahead of them.'

But it was Ramsey's choice of players and his cautious formations in the build-up to Mexico that were causing the most concern. After a highly unconvincing 1–0 win over a mediocre Portugal side at Wembley in December 1969, Jimmy Hill took the England manager to task in the *News of the World*. 'I BLAME SIR ALF: WORLD CUP BOSS GETS NO PASS MARKS FOR THIS TEAM'. Ramsey had dropped Ball, Moore and Hurst in order to experiment with Francis Lee, Ian Moore and Mick Jones, but the new trio had an ineffective match in which they looked guileless and witless. 'While I think Sir Alf is a master at motivating players to give their all, the seed of doubt has been sown in my mind concerning his understanding of modern forward play,' wrote Hill. 'SHAKE 'EM UP, RAMSEY!' bellowed the back page of the same paper after England had been held to a 1–1 draw in Cardiff in April 1970. When England drew 0–0 with Scotland at Hampden a week later – the first goalless draw in the fixture since the first ever international in 1872 – anxieties mounted over England's evident toothlessness in attack and their lack of imagination in midfield.

No one, though, could accuse England of being ill prepared for the attempted defence of their world crown. The squad flew to Mexico City, 29 days before their opening match against Romania in order to spend two weeks acclimatising before playing friendlies in Colombia and Ecuador. But the doubts remained. 'They travel with the best wishes of everyone back home,' wrote Reg Drury in the *News of the World*. 'But with the confidence of precious few. I haven't encountered many football folk who honestly believe England will become the first European nation to win a World Cup in Latin America.'

The six players left out of Ramsey's final party were Peter Shilton, Bob McNab, David Sadler, Ralph Coates, Brian Kidd and Peter Thompson, also one of the unfortunates to be jettisoned at the final count in 1966). Ramsey kept faith with the backbone of the team that had won the Cup four years earlier: Banks, Moore, Peters, both Charltons, Ball, Stiles and Hurst were all on board, while new faces included Mullery, Francis Lee, Terry Cooper and Brian Labone and the extravagantly talented if erratic Peter Osgood. Ramsey's loyalty to the old guard, particularly Stiles, led to accusations of favouritism and an unwillingness to gamble on young talent. Alan Mullery, though, insists that while he was unshakeably loyal to his players, Ramsey was also brutal and unsentimental. 'He was a very pragmatic man and there was never any favouritism in spite of what some critics have said. I remember after one game at Wembley, not long after 1966, Geoff Hurst said to him: "Well, see you next time then, Alf." To which Alf said, with a completely straight face: "That of course will depend on whether you are selected, Geoffrey." '

After two weeks of acclimatising in Mexico, England flew to Bogotá where their final preparations were thrown into disarray when Moore, the golden boy of world football, was arrested on charges of stealing a cheap bracelet from a boutique while out shopping with Bobby Charlton. Moore spent four days in jail and the charges, which were immediately suspected to be bogus and designed to unsettle the morale of the world champions, were widely denounced, not least in Colombia, a country which had grown used to kidnapping and the extortion of money from the rich and famous. After four days of heavy diplomatic pressure on the Colombian authorities, England's captain was released from captivity with the relaxed air of someone emerging from a long lunch in a smart restaurant. His dignified response to the squalid episode earned him universal praise.

England beat Colombia 4–0 and Ecuador 2–0 in their first ever encounters with both countries before heading back to their hotel near Guadalajara, Mexico's second largest city, the capital of Jalisco state in the western central area of this vast Central American country. England were to stay in the Hilton

Hotel in the centre of town in what turned out to be a disastrous piece of planning. The public had free access to the hotel and England's players soon found themselves hounded by day, as they tried to relax around the swimming pool, and at night by noisy gangs of local youths who would gather outside blaring music and beeping the horns of their cars and motor bikes. Ramsey made a public appeal to England fans not to besiege the hotel, saying: 'This could upset our preparations. I'm calling on the fans to show some self-restraint and leave players to concentrate on the job they have come to do.' Ramsey's pleas fell on deaf ears, and as England fans arrived in the city the squad found themselves effectively under house arrest as they retreated to their rooms, the only place they could guarantee solitude. After the tournament the players admitted that their enforced isolation and the feelings of claustrophobia it brought on had a bad effect on their spirits. Ramsey also appealed to the hotel authorities and local police to try to improve the security arrangements, but his requests were met with little more than a Mexican shrug of the shoulders.

England's other preparations were extremely meticulous. To counter dehydration, the players were ordered to drink at least two bottles of Coke with every meal while drinking-water, fruit and local produce were strictly off the menu. A refrigerated container packed with frozen beefburgers, saus-ages, fish fingers and tomato ketchup was flown in from England, much to the dismay of the locals who saw England's dining arrangements as a snub. Even orange juice was flown over – the equivalent of the Mexicans bringing over their own toad-in-the-hole to England – and the party even brought their own bus complete with Cockney bus driver. The players were ordered to scrub their hands like prep school boys before meals, prompting Moore, when asked by Sir Alf whether he had been to the bathroom, to retort, 'Why haven't they got knives and forks?' England's near-paranoid meticulousness in their off-pitch arrangements did at least ensure that the squad were able to report a clean bill of health in the early part of the tournament. The only casualty was trainer Les Cocker, who was laid up for two days after ricking his back lugging

England's kit bag. (England, however, did not give off the image of a super-fit and well-drilled unit of world beaters when their flight arrived in Mexico City. West Bromwich Albion striker Jeff Astle had drunk heavily on the long flight in order to overcome his fear of flying, and when he staggered off the plane, his tie at three o'clock, local photographers could not believe their luck at the chance of casting the world champions in an unflattering light.)

Back in England, not everyone was getting behind England. The difficulties Ramsey encountered trying to persuade clubs to release their players for the national side were highlighted by some astonishing comments from controversial Football League secretary Alan Hardaker on the eve of the tournament. 'We're all going overboard about the importance of the World Cup,' he said. 'It's not the be-all and end-all of football. What possible difference can it make to our football?' When it was put to him that there had been a massive boom in gates after England's 1966 triumph, Hardaker replied: 'That's what everybody said – but it just wasn't true. It was the weather which made the difference, good weather always does. Winning the trophy didn't make a ha'p'orth of difference.'

Ramsey appeared to be on good enough terms with the press corps to turn out for them in a knockabout match against his own players, but there were clear divisions of opinion among reporters about the qualities of the England manager which had emerged and then hardened in the build-up to Mexico. For some, the only man to have won the World Cup for England was above reproach; to others, leaving aside their feelings for him as a man, he was a coach of limited imagination and adventure who had sacrificed exciting football on the altar of efficiency. Foreign journalists had a particular dislike for him. In 1970 one approached him and said, 'Hello, Sir Alf, do you remember me?' Ramsey replied, 'Yes, you're a pest,' and carried on his way. When a Mexican journalist, on another occasion, asked him why he talked so little, Ramsey said, 'Empty drums make the most noise.' To many of his critics, this lack of tact could not be dismissed merely as a personal character trait of little consequence to the fortunes of the national side. Firstly, they said, Ramsey was the senior ambassador or figure-head of English football who had a responsibility to cast English football – and, indeed, England – in a favourable light when abroad. Secondly, it was often pointed out that every time Ramsey snapped at or brushed aside a foreigner, it only increased the will of the opposition to beat his teams. On England's 1969 summer tour of Central and South America, Ramsey had put on a diplomatic performance which by all accounts made Prince Philip look like Henry Kissinger. The local press, hurt by Ramsey's apparent contempt for them and their country, did not forget it, and when England returned a year later to defend their crown they entered a hostile environment that did little to make the squad feel at ease.

Before England's match against Brazil, for example, the players were kept awake all night by a crowd of jeering, music-blaring locals outside their hotel. It might have happened anyway, but the Mexican police did virtually nothing to help, despite the endless appeals of the England management. The match kicked off at noon, and by the time the players had to get up most of them had managed only an hour's sleep, while some had not slept at all. By contrast, England's rivals went out of their way to ingratiate themselves with the locals, who in turn would make their life easier by seeing to their every need and cheering them on the pitch. (England were booed in their opening match, and when the Union Jack emerged at the opening ceremony.) As world champions, a certain hostility was to be expected, though Brazil were given a warm welcome both in Chile and England. With the benefit of hindsight, a charm offensive can only have helped England's cause. A few gifts to the local kids, a visit to the hospital and a few judiciously placed compliments about the hospitality of the natives in front of the world's media, and England may not have instantly become angels, but at least they would not have been cast as demons.

Ramsey's uneasy relationship with the British press deteriorated sharply when he gave the names in the final squad to a small group of journalists to help with their deadlines, a few hours before he told the players themselves. One reporter allegedly leaked the news to a player that he was in the squad. Ramsey was furious. An unnamed international of the day later revealed in the press that 'from then on Alf never trusted another journo and the knives were out'. Ralph Finn, one of the leading soccer writers of the day, who had followed Ramsey from his earliest days at Ipswich and beyond Mexico 1970, later recorded how he noticed Ramsey growing ever more distant from the press, and even said: 'I hated the thought that this man, now manager of England, could make me feel like a grubby little boy.' 'THE HEAT IS ON ALF' claimed the headline in the *News of the World*. 'Nobody else involved in the competition – manager, player or referee – will be under as much pressure as Ramsey,' wrote Reg Drury. 'Or subjected to such a fierce personal spotlight. Ramsey is not a popular man. His dedication to England's cause is so unswerving that he often refuses to spare time for the diplomacy which would improve his own image both at home and abroad.'

On 31 May, the day of the tournament's opening match between Mexico and the Soviet Union, the front page of the *News of the World* claimed the World Cup was on the brink of chaos. 'WORLD CUP FRENZY ERUPTS' declared the headline, while the report claimed: 'Violence, intimidation, dishonesty and hysteria are threatening to turn the competition on which the eyes of the world are focused into a shambles.' Fears of violence were raised after Mexican police battled with fans angry at being unable to obtain tickets; the threats of intimidation emerged after a South American guerrilla organisation called the Tuparos were reported to be plotting the kidnapping of Germany's Uwe Seeler; 'dishonesty', the report claimed, took the form of an epidemic of racketeering, petty crime and ticket forgery; while the warnings of 'hysteria' claimed that 'excitable locals' would storm the pitch at the slightest provocation. The following day, Norman Giller of the *Daily Express* reported that the opening ceremony and the match that followed in the giant concrete bowl of the Aztec Stadium in Mexico City generated the most intimidating atmosphere he had ever witnessed. The appearance of the English and Soviet flags prompted a deafening cacophony of jeers and whistles. 'It was the beginning of a hate war,' wrote Giller. 'England must be prepared for the malice mania. This was the Mexican reaction to Sir Alf's alleged coldness.'

England's first group match was on 2 June in Guadalajara's Jalisco Stadium, 5,069 feet above sea level, against a tough Romanian team who had twice held England to a draw in the previous two years. It was a brutally contested match, settled by a single goal from Hurst, which left the England players in little doubt about their popularity with the locals. Every time an England player was fouled – roughly every four minutes – the crowd cheered. The match was also a useful if disturbing reminder that, as Ramsey continually pointed out, the opposition were more motivated than ever to see England beaten. To their credit the English players kept their cool in the blistering heat and against a Romanian side evidently more intent on maiming than winning. 'ENGLAND SHAME THE THUGS!' cheered the following day's *Daily Express*. Moore, cool as you like, had what most commentators agreed was one of his best games for England. Even the hostile local press felt moved enough by his brilliance to salute him as the 'King of Football'. Ramsey allowed his players a night out to celebrate their victory but imposed an eleven o'clock curfew, which most of his weary, bruised and dehydrated players were happy to respect. 'He was a very strict disciplinarian,' recalls Mullery. 'He would stroll into the players at about ten o'clock on tour and say, "It's now ten o'clock, I think it's time for bed," and everybody to a man would get up and go to bed. None of us normally went to bed before twelve, but when he said it we would just do it. That was the end of the matter. There were a lot of players in the squad who liked a night on the town, but by the time I joined the set-up no one took liberties with him.'

England's next match, against Brazil five days later, was one of the most eagerly anticipated in the history of the competition, and a record worldwide television audience for a football match running into billions would tune in to see the competition's favourites challenge the holders. The match promised a fascinating contrast of styles, with the world's greatest attack facing the world's greatest defence. England, of course, did not have the best night's sleep before their biggest match since the 1966 World Cup final, and their cause was not helped by the demands of the television companies which dictated that the match would kick-off in the searing heat of midday. In addition, England faced a Brazilian team which many consider to be the greatest of all time. The team sheet read: Felix, Carlos Alberto, Brito, Piazza, Everaldo, Paulo Cesar, Clodoaldo, Rivelino, Jairzinho, Tostão and Pele. England lined up as follows: Banks, Wright, Cooper, Moore, Labone, Mullery, Ball, B. Charlton, Peters, Hurst, Lee.

The match more than lived up to its billing. A classic encounter was settled in Brazil's favour by a goal from Jairzinho, but England were the equals, if not the superiors, of their opponents for much of the match. After England's defeat, Ramsey told reporters: 'The best team did not win today.' They might have been celebrating a famous victory had substitute Jeff Astle not snatched at his shot with just Felix to beat, and had Ball's shot against the crossbar in the dying minutes been just an inch or so lower. The highlight of the match, however, was not a shot or a goal, but Banks' remarkable save from Pele's header that brought an audible gasp from the crowd, and still today is generally recognised as being the greatest stop of all time. 'I could not believe what I saw,' said Pele directly after the match. 'At that moment I hated Banks more than any other footballer in the world, but when I cooled down I could only applaud him in my heart. It was the greatest save I have ever seen.' Afterwards, most commentators agreed that they had just witnessed a dress rehearsal of the final itself, and when that prediction failed to become reality the match was remembered by some as 'the moral final'. (Certainly, it seems fair to suggest that England would not have collapsed like Italy, despite Brazil's breath-taking display in their 4–1 win.) The following day the papers reported that England had ground to a standstill. Pubs and picture-houses were virtually empty, and the politicians giving local lectures in the run-up to the General Election addressed near-empty town halls. Churches, though, according to a front-page piece in the *Daily Express*, generally reported 'no effect on the size of their congregations'. The back page was in agony. 'O, BALL! O, ASTLE! O, ENGLAND!' wailed the headline. (Another heading further down read: 'GAY GERMANS MARCH ON'.)

England were nothing like as impressive in their final group match against a Czechoslovakian side who had no chance of qualifying after losing to both Romania and Brazil. It was, by all accounts, a dreadful spectacle, with England content to bang long balls into the box. The match was settled by an Allan Clarke penalty after a Czech defender was dubiously deemed to have handled the ball. 'It was a sterile game with England playing so badly that it hurt to watch,' wrote Ralph Finn in his book *World Cup 1970*. 'England got the bird. They deserved a whole aviary. Compared with the magic of Brazil we served up dross. You can see better on Hackney Marshes or Wimbledon Common. If this satisfies the England manager all I can say is that it doesn't take a lot to please him.' Ouch. But no matter. England were into the quarter-finals where they would face their old sparring partners West Germany, on 14 June in Leon.

Perhaps the most telling moment of the encounter came the day before, when Gordon Banks drank or ate something that quickly brought on a raging temperature and confined him to bed. Chelsea's inexperienced Peter Bonetti replaced him between the posts. The Germans had scored ten goals in their three group games and were bursting to avenge their famous defeat four years earlier. Both line-ups featured five players from that Wembley afternoon, but the form book ran with England who had lost just once in nine encounters with the Germans. But vengeance did not look like it would be West Germany's when England romped into a 2–0 lead after 50 minutes thanks to a stunning strike from Mullery and a second from Peters. England were in total control, and Ramsey decided to take off both Bobby Charlton and Peters to rest them for the semi-final. Little can Charlton have suspected at the moment he trotted from the field that he had just kicked his last ball in international football. There followed one of the most extraordinary reversals of fortune in the history of the World Cup as Germany fought back to level the match with goals from Beckenbauer and Seeler before Gerd Muller sealed a remarkable win with a goal in the first period of extra time. Bonetti came in for heavy criticism after the match, and perhaps the fairest comment about his performance would be to say that England would probably have won had Banks not been felled by a rogue virus. Ramsey, though, refused to blame Bonetti or any of his players. At the final whistle he looked as impassive as he had done when England had beaten the Germans in equally dramatic circumstances four years earlier. Now, just as then, he took the time to shake the hand of each squad member and thank them for their efforts. But his face, as so often, was not telling the story of what he was feeling inside. 'I have never seen Alf so devastated,' recalls Alan Mullery. 'He honestly thought his 1970 squad was better than that of 1966. We played extremely well against Brazil and Pele said to me after the match that the only team they really feared was England. We went back to the hotel and he bought us all a drink and we just sat around the pool barely saying anything. Alf was totally blown away and just started reminiscing about old times. It was sad.'

The freakish nature of the match and the misfortune to befall Banks almost certainly saved Ramsey a battering in the press, but inevitably there were questions raised about his future. Prime Minister Harold Wilson and Edward Heath, his opposite number in the upcoming General Election, sent cables to the team, commiserating with the manner of their exit and congratulating them on their performances. In the TV studio back in London Malcolm Allison said of Ramsey: 'He is a great manager of bad teams, but when he has a good team he does not know what to do.' The headline on the front page of the *Daily Express* read: 'SIR ALF: I'M STILL PROUD OF THEM – NOW FOR THE INQUEST'. A small piece at the bottom of the page reported: 'In Britain, once more the publicans bemoaned a fantastic drop in trade. Despite warm weather the pubs were almost empty. Cinemas too reported a big drop in business. An AA spokesman said the roads were virtually dead two hours before kick-off.' The back page had a simple message: 'CHUCKED AWAY'.

The next day, as England prepared to fly home, John Morgan, sports editor of the *Daily Express*, urged critics to spare Ramsey. 'It's up to the League clubs to give him the flair he needs. It's a bit sickening to hear the knockers demanding Ramsey's head for the happenings in Mexico.' According to several of the papers unnamed FA officials wanted him out because they had not come to terms with their loss of power since Ramsey took the job on the condition that the International Selection Committee would be disbanded. Thunderface had stolen their thunder. Ramsey brushed off speculation about his future, saying: 'At the moment there is no reason why I should not continue as England manager.' On arriving back at London, Ramsey told reporters: 'We must now look ahead to the next World Cup in Munich where our chances of winning I would say are very good indeed. Now please don't misinterpret that quote to make it seem as if I said we *will* win the World Cup. I know you are going to ask me if I will be in charge for Munich. That is the way I'm thinking right now. But who knows? We'll just have to wait and see.'

The Mexico failure marked the end of an era for English football. England's reign as world champions was over, and the core of that team slowly began to disintegrate as new, younger names fought their way into contention. The main criticism of England's performance in Mexico was that by playing 4–4–2 Ramsey had sent out a negative message to his rivals which implied that England, despite being world champions, did not have the confidence to take the game to the opposition. Critics suggested that Ramsey's judgement was at fault in sending out just two forwards in the 100-degree Mexican heat to chase around four defenders to find space. Bobby Charlton and Martin Peters were also felt to be off-form, and that Ramsey only retained them out of loyalty while ignoring the pressing claims of Colin Bell and Peter Osgood, two players at the peak of their game and, on their day, capable of troubling the best defences in the world. The players, however, refused to hear any criticism of their manager and returned his unwavering loyalty by mounting a blanket defence of him when they faced the press on their return. Mullery told reporters: 'If we had not made a couple of stupid defensive errors we would have been through to the semi-finals and everyone would have been raving about him. It would be Lord Alf by now.'

In the press there were more calls for him to stay than to go, though some of the supportive pieces were clearly written with gritted teeth by reporters trying to be objective despite their personal irritation at Ramsey's high-handed treatment of them in Mexico. Under the headline 'RAMSEY – THE MAN ALONE', Frank Butler called for Ramsey to stay but urged him to brush up on his diplomacy for the sake of the national team. 'When England failed in Mexico the little dogs started yapping. Having slapped Sir Alf Ramsey on the back when England won the World Cup, they now want his head on the block.' Butler pointed out Ramsey was a 'flop' at public relations and that he almost seemed to get a perverse thrill out of being rude and provocative to the press, but he added: 'Against the liabilities his assets are integrity and loyalty to his players, and what is better than integrity and loyalty? Ramsey must remain England's soccer supremo, but if he is supposed to be making friends and influencing people, England would do well to employ a good public relations man – unless we want to remain the world's most disliked team. It's all right to be hated when you are the champions, but bad business when you're among the also-rans.'

The England football team were about to enter the worst period of their history, and it would be another ten years before the country again graced the finals of either of the two major international competitions. But at first there seemed little reason for followers of English football to suspect that the national team were at the start of a steep decline. England won six out of seven of their matches in the 1970/71 season, and would lose only twice between November 1970 and June 1973, when they lost a World Cup qualifier to Poland in Katowice. But the bare statistics hide the fact that during that period England had become even more robotic and workman-like than ever. When England lost 3–1 at Wembley to West Germany, their new bogey team, in April 1972, effectively ending their hopes of reaching the European Championship finals, Ramsey's growing band of critics, hovering like birds of prey for the right time to strike, decided to swoop. From then on the criticism of Ramsey in the newspapers and among the public grew steadily more intense, and when England failed to beat Poland at Wembley eighteen months later, killing their hopes of reaching the 1974 World Cup finals, Ramsey's position was effectively untenable. He may have won the World Cup for England and been made a knight of the realm for his efforts, but Ramsey had made enemies within the FA as well as in the press, and when the results began to go the same way as England's entertainment value, he looked around for support but found no one there. 'The man who liked to stand alone' they used to call him in the press and that's exactly how he stood on the night of 17 October 1973 after watching England lay siege to the Polish goal only to be held to a 1–1 draw.

Ramsey was accused of many things in the latter part of his reign. Critics lambasted him for not blooding young talents like Kevin Keegan, Mike Channon, Trevor Brooking and Dave Watson, relying instead on trusted veterans like Peters, Ball and Hunter. Ramsey also began to chop and change his line-ups, prompting his detractors to claim that he did not know his own mind. 'If Ramsey knows what his squad for Europe is going to be, the man's either crackers or a genius,' said Brian Clough, then a rising young star in the managerial firmament. He was also accused of not exploiting the new law permitting substitutions, while the oldest charge of all, that his excessive caution and obsession with not losing blunted England's attacking edge, intensified in the final years of his tenure.

With only a handful of loyal supporters left in the press and the FA worried about the lack of revenue caused by England's failure to qualify for the World Cup finals, Ramsey could only hope that the public backing he received from his players and the fact that he had won the World Cup would keep him in the post. He tried to head off his increasingly inevitable dismissal by presenting his own plans for change, which included demands for more time with players and more internationals, and in the last squad he selected, for a friendly against Portugal on 3 April 1974, he finally bowed to public pressure and called up a batch of England's most talented youngsters. Despite this, on 1 May he was summoned to Lancaster Gate and informed by FA chairman Sir Andrew Stephen and secretary Ted Croker that his services were no longer required. The man knighted for leading England to World Cup glory was told to clear his drawers. Ramsey was given a £15,000 golden handshake which amounted to less than his yearly salary – a farewell gift he felt was insulting. 'He was treated very, very shabbily by the FA,' says Mullery. 'We were all very upset by the way the FA dumped him so unceremoniously. He was paid a pittance, which was a disgrace.' Ramsey never forgave the FA. Shortly after his death it was announced that he had asked for his memorial service to be held in Ipswich and not in London. The decision was widely interpreted in the media as being a final snub to the FA.

Looking back on Ramsey's dramatic demise from darling to demon, Martin Peters, who played his last match for England against Scotland the month after Ramsey's dismissal, believes that better relations with the media might have saved him. 'He really didn't care about the press. He had his views on what team he wanted to play and how he would approach a game tactically and he didn't give a damn if other people didn't agree with him. He was very much his own man. But he paid for it in the end when we didn't qualify. He had very few friends left in the press box and he found himself isolated and without support, except from the players. We were all very upset by the way he was treated by the press and then by the FA. The simple truth is that on a normal day we would have beaten Poland 6–0. We created so many chances, it was just a freak match you get every now and then. Poland ended up coming third in Germany, so who knows what would have happened if we had got just the one bit of luck we needed at Wembley. We were all desperately disappointed when Alf went, and the way he went. But it might all have been very different if the press had mounted a campaign to make sure he stayed.' According to Mullery, Ramsey did not understand that the press had the power to undermine his position. 'It was different with the press in those days. When we went to Mexico, there was just one reporter from each paper and that was it. Now you get hundreds of pressmen just from England. A press conference in those days wasn't what it is now. He would just walk into a room or a hotel lobby where there would be a huddle of press boys and just say, "This is the team for tomorrow" and then turn on his heels and walk out. That was it. He wasn't a press man. He did it his way and no one else's. He wasn't interested in what the press thought.'

Ramsey continues to divide opinion today. There are broadly two camps, with the press in one and the players in another. There are a handful of players, such as Greaves, Rodney Marsh and Charlie George, who felt that they suffered from Ramsey's gravitation towards grafters. (Marsh tells a story of how in his first of only nine caps, Ramsey shouted from the touchline, 'Rodney, I'm pulling you off at half time' to which he replied 'Oh, thanks very much, Sir Alf. At QPR all we get is a cup of tea and an orange.') But players who have criticised him are very much the exception. Almost to a man, those who played under him do not just say he was a good manager, but a great one. Alan Mullery, a man with plenty of strong opinions, will not hear a bad word said about Ramsey. 'He was brilliant. Very, very clever tactically. He treated players like men and despite what people say he never showed any favouritism. There was never any long-drawn tactical analysis of the opposition. He just said "Go out and play your natural game." He picked the team and the formation he wanted and then let us get on with it. He devised systems, most notably 4–3–3 and then 4–4–2, because he thought they were the systems most likely to see England win. He didn't care what anyone else thought of his systems.

'To be honest I never really saw Alf coach. It may sound strange, but at training we would just have a game, sort of first eleven against a second eleven or eight against eight, and he would just stand on the touchline watching, saying virtually nothing. If there was a free-kick we would organise ourselves. Occasionally he might pop his head in and say, "I think you should do so and so," but he just used to let the senior players get on with running the show. There was very little analysis of the opposition. Alf often had a problem getting the foreigners' names right, so we just didn't talk about the other teams.

'I remember when we went to Brazil in 1969 and I had the job of marking Pele, the greatest player of all time, in front of 150,000 fans in the Maracana. I was feeling a bit nervous and obviously looking it, because Alf came over and said, "What's the problem?" and I told him that I was a bit worried about Pele, and he said very calmly, "Look, if you weren't good enough to mark him you would be back home watching this on TV. You're here because you're good enough to do it, so don't worry about it. Now get out there and make sure he doesn't get a kick." He was very good at making you feel confident without ever laying on the praise too thick.

'I can't think of any football weaknesses. But if he had a problem it was that he never, ever trusted the media. The press boys could never get a story out of him. That's where it all stemmed from. He gave them nothing and made their jobs very difficult so there was bound to be resentment. But he gave his players and England everything, so what did it matter?

'Above all, though, he was such a loyal man, and that's why we loved him. I have worked with some great managers, like Bill Nicholson at Tottenham, one of the all-time great managers, but Alf was as good as any of them without question. He won the World Cup for England, and how many people can say that?'

3 High Treason and Low Farce
Don Revie 1974–1977

THEY USED TO CALL HIM 'The Don'. He was the godfather of a powerful, well-drilled posse of ruthless hitmen who were not averse to dishing out intimidation to get what they wanted. He was the head of a close-knit family who looked after each other on and off the pitch, who, when the mood took them, could turn on the style for the outside world. There were rivals, of course, in Merseyside, Manchester and London, but in the brutal gang warfare that often was English football in the late 1960s and early 1970s, Leeds United were the bosses. No one messed with them while Revie was in charge.

It has often been said that Leeds' reputation as a dirty, cynical team who kicked their opponents in the tunnel as well as all over the pitch was created and exaggerated by Fleet Street hacks with a bias towards the London teams. Revie and his players complained that their reputation for the rough stuff and Italian-style 'professionalism' meant that opposition teams would try to get their retaliation in first, fighting fire with fire. But with players like Jack Charlton, Norman 'bite-yer-legs' Hunter and Billy Bremner, it is not difficult to see why opponents would take one look at the team-sheet and immediately pull a second pair of shin pads out of the kit bag. Allan Clarke certainly believes the violence of many of Leeds' games was started by the opposition. 'When I was at Fulham and Leicester before joining Leeds in 1969 I had first-hand experience of what other teams used to say before playing them. We would sit in the dressing-room and everyone was saying, "Come on, let's tuck into them before they have a go at us," and we would go out and try and dish it out. Leeds obviously weren't having any of it, and the reason why this reputation stuck was because they were better than anyone else at looking after themselves if they wanted to.

'When I went to Leeds, the attitude was: We're better than them and we'll play them off the park – but if they want a scrap then we'll kick them off. Either way, Leeds would win. There was also a bit of a musketeer's attitude at Leeds where we would all look out for each other. If Billy [Bremner], for example, got chopped, you could bet your life that within a couple of minutes the lad who did it would be on the floor himself. We had the same attitude as the British Lions rugby team when they won in South Africa in 1974. We were all in it together. 'But I think it's unfair to single out Leeds as a dirty team. Football was generally harder then and there were a lot of hard teams and hard players. It's just that Leeds were the most successful and we were always in the public eye. When you're successful everyone hates you. It was the same at Liverpool in the late 1970s, and at Manchester United today.'

What is indisputable is that Revie transformed Leeds, rooted in the heart of traditional rugby league territory, from a peripheral force in English football languishing at the foot of the Second Division and struggling to attract five-figure gates into arguably the most formidable club side in Europe. Only their own outrageous ambition denied them greater glory. Come the end of the season, Leeds would often find themselves battling for honours on three, occasionally four, fronts: in the League, in Europe, the League Cup and the FA Cup, in which often marathon replays would stretch the players' famous resilience and stamina to breaking point. Bremner often liked to recall that on a handful of occasions Revie insisted on him playing when he could barely walk, let alone run, because the mere presence on the pitch of one his celebrated players was felt to be worth more than the fitness of a lesser player.

When the FA went in search of a successor to Ramsey, they did not head straight up the A1 to approach the most successful English manager of his generation and one of the great club managers of all time. Instead, they turned to former Manchester City boss Joe Mercer to act as a caretaker during the Home Championship and England's summer tour to eastern Europe. But when Revie accepted the FA's eventual offer on 4 July 1974, there was little argument with the appointment in the following day's papers, only doubts about whether he could come to terms with leaving his beloved Leeds. Fewer than three years later, Revie's reputation lay in ruins after he deserted England in the middle of a World Cup qualifying campaign and headed off to manage the United Arab Emirates for more money than any international manager had ever been offered. His desertion, which he revealed to a newspaper before his employers (for a tidy sum thought to be as much as £10,000), caused a national uproar. 'The Don' became 'Don Readies' or 'the traitor'. Only in Leeds, where he now has a road and a stand named after him, did his aura remain undiminished.

Revie was born on 10 July 1927, the son of an often unemployed joiner, into a poor though not destitute family living within kicking distance of Middlesbrough's Ayresome Park. At the age of twelve he was bought by a local team, the Middlesbrough Swifts, for five shillings. It proved to be a defining moment in his career, as he fell under the spell of the manager Bill Sanderson, a train driver by profession who had a trainspotter's interest in the tactical minutiae of the game. Sanderson held regular meetings in the front room of his council house during which the game was analysed *ad nauseam*. Showing more dedication to the job than managers of most First Division teams, Sanderson would regularly spy on the opposition before returning home to prepare exhaustive dossiers on the players he had just seen. Sanderson made the young Revie aware that stronger teams could be overcome by thorough planning.

Revie worked as an apprentice bricklayer after leaving school at the age of fourteen, before joining Leicester City where he made his debut at the age of sixteen and quickly showed that he compensated for a lack of pace with a good football brain. Lured by the temptation of playing under the legendary figure of Raich Carter, Revie then joined Hull City, but his most successful period as a player came at Manchester City in the mid-1950s when he shot to prominence for what became known as the 'Revie Plan', a system copied from the great Hungarian side of the day which involved him playing in a deep-lying centre-forward role and using his considerable passing skills to release the front runners. The success of the system helped City reach successive finals of the FA Cup in 1955 and 1956, and saw Revie voted Player of the Year. Revie won six England caps before joining Sunderland, and finally, in 1958, Leeds for £14,000 in what proved to be the crucial moment in both Revie's career as well as the history of the Yorkshire club.

Leeds were going through a turbulent period when Revie arrived. In his second season Leeds were relegated to Division Two, and they were spiralling towards the Third with gates down to 8,000 and the club in financial crisis when, in a move that seemed to smack of desperation at the time, the Yorkshire club appointed the ageing midfielder as player/manager. Revie immediately sought the advice of Manchester United's Matt Busby, who told him: 'Be loyal and honest to them, never lie, and they will do anything for you in return.' Revie immediately set about trying to foster a sense of community at the directionless club, taking time to talk to and involve even the most humble of employees and playing on a sense of pride. He was keen to involve the players' families to enforce the sense of togetherness, handing out gifts, complimentary tickets and even bunches of flowers to the wives and girlfriends. Every Thursday he personally administered soapy massages to his players. Shortly after taking over he changed the Leeds strip to all white, copying the famous strip of Real Madrid, and announcing that one day Leeds would match the achievements of the all-conquering Spanish giants – a claim that was sniggered at in the press.

Leeds quickly developed a bone-shuddering sense of purpose and a win-at-all-costs attitude that prompted accusations of brutality, professional fouls, badgering referees, over acting and feigning injury. Revie had two good players on his books in Billy Bremner and Jack Charlton as well as some talented youngsters in Norman Hunter, Terry Cooper, Gary Sprake and Jimmy Greenhoff. They were joined over the next few seasons by Peter Lorimer, Eddie Gray, a black South African winger Albert Johannesson, Johnny Giles and, in 1969, by Allan

Clarke for a then British transfer record of £165,000. Revie and chairman Harry Reynolds went out of their way to ensure that the families of the new arrivals were found accommodation and, in some cases, jobs. 'There was nothing he wouldn't do for us. From top to bottom of the club, everybody admired him. He was a father figure to everyone,' says Clarke. 'He used to go up to Scotland or wherever to watch a youngster and meet his parents, and when the kid turned up a year later Don would always remember the first names of everyone in the family. He gave the impression he really cared, and parents were happy to let their kid sign for the club.'

In 1962 Revie was accused of trying to bribe the opposition by buying off Bury manager Bob Stokoe for £500. It was not the last time that Revie would be accused of trying to fix matches, and Stokoe never withdrew his allegations. 'I lost all respect for Revie after that,' said Stokoe. Similar accusations were made in the *Sunday People* ten years later after Leeds had lost their final League game of the season against Wolves to miss out on the League title. Three Wolves players claimed they were offered £1,000 to relax their efforts; two of the players said the bribes had been made while on the pitch. The FA and CID investigated but the Director of Public Prosecutions found insufficient evidence and the case was closed. Five years later, when the nation's newspapers were treading over themselves to run derogatory stories about Revie following his desertion to the Middle East, the *Daily Mirror* repeated the *People*'s allegations, claiming it had all the names and sources missing from the original story. The *Mirror* said former Leeds player Mike O'Grady, who had moved to Wolves, had been approached by Revie to act as a go-between. O'Grady, the paper claimed, agreed to tell his story because he had been appalled by Revie's act of desertion, but he later denied that any money had changed hands. The truth of what happened has never been established.

Leeds almost won the Double in their first season back in the top flight, 1964/65, losing the FA Cup final after extra time to Liverpool 2–1 and the League title on goal difference to Manchester United. Over the next ten years they would never finish lower than fourth in the League, and their record in all competitions over that period is remarkable as much for its near misses as its triumphs. They won the League title in 1969 (with a record 67 points and without losing in their last 28 matches) and again in 1974, and were runners-up in 1965, 1966, 1970, 1971 and 1972. They won the League Cup in 1968 (their first trophy), the FA Cup in 1972, and were runners-up in the latter competition in 1965, 1970 and 1973. In Europe they won the European Fairs Cup (now the UEFA Cup) in 1968, were runners-up the year before, and were runners-up in the Cup-Winners' Cup in 1973. 'We want to win everything there is to win and we will not rest until Leeds are acknowledged around the world as one of the greatest teams of all time,' said Bremner.

But Revie's and his players' all-consuming ambition proved a handicap as Leeds became exhausted in their relentless pursuit of perfection. Rather than targeting the League and the European Cup, the team went all out to win everything on offer. The most dramatic instance of this came in 1969/70 when Leeds were on course for a stunning Treble: League, FA Cup and European Cup. An already punishing schedule of fixtures was not helped by the abbreviation of the League season to help Alf Ramsey prepare England for the World Cup. Towards the end of March, Leeds were ten games from completing the treble, but six of them had to be played in two weeks. Matters got worse when Leeds needed two replays to beat Manchester United in the semi-finals of the FA Cup. Injuries piled up, the players grew more exhausted by the match, and in the end the championship was lost to Everton and the famous FA Cup final to Chelsea in a replay at Old Trafford. Before the replay Leeds lost the European semi-final to Celtic, 2–1 on aggregate, after drawing 1–1 at Hampden Park. 'Perhaps we would have won more if we had concentrated our efforts on just two competitions, but it was never on,' says Clarke. 'We wanted to win it all, and you never heard anyone complain about being tired or wanting a rest. In my first season at Leeds I played 70 games, but no one in the club ever said we were overstretching ourselves. I remember after the replay against Chelsea we all got on to the coach feeling knackered and a bit deflated having nothing to show for a brilliant season, and the gaffer walked on and said, "Right, we'll start pre-season training a bit earlier – and this time we'll sweat blood." It was the same after we lost that FA Cup final in 1973. Straight after, the manager said we were to report back a week early for pre-season training, and it worked because we were unbeaten in our first 29 games.'

When Revie left in July 1974 to take over England, he was a living legend. Revie actually rang FA secretary Ted Croker to register his interest in taking over the England job. 'I made the first move,' he said at his first press conference. 'They did not contact me. I fancied being England manager.' After receiving Revie's phone call, Dick Wragg, the chairman of the International Committee, sped north to negotiate terms with Leeds for the release of their manager. Revie had spent fifteen years at the club, but he cleared his desk and his locker within two days. The hastiness of his departure struck many at the club as strange after all his strenuous efforts to create a family atmosphere at Leeds. Trainer Syd Owen said, years later: 'He didn't make sure all the coaches and physios who had served him had been made more secure with contracts. He just cleared his desk and left.' (Brian Clough, an outspoken critic of both Leeds and Revie over the years, was taken on as his successor, but lasted just 44 stormy days. Revie's ghost still haunted Elland Road, and even the formidable figure of Clough was unable to exorcise it. His relationship with the players got off to a dreadful start when he told them they should throw away all their medals and cups because they had won them cheating.)

After the Cold War waged between Ramsey and the press, Revie began by launching a diplomatic offensive on Fleet Street, laying on drinks and snacks at England get-togethers and making himself readily available for interview. Morale in the England squad and in the wider public was at a low ebb following England's failure to qualify for the World Cup finals for the first time in their history. Revie was quick to make an impression. He succeeded in persuading Alan Hardaker, his old adversary at the Football League, that Saturday's League programme should be postponed when England had an international on the Wednesday, thereby giving him nearly a week to prepare his team. He assembled an amazing 81 players for his first training session and saw to it that the players would be financially rewarded with bonuses of £100 for a draw and £200 for a win, arguing that the players deserved a slice of the huge revenue generated for the FA by England internationals. He also struck a sponsorship deal with Admiral, the kit-makers, and both deals were later cited as examples of Revie's obsession with money. 'When I ask players to pull on an England shirt I expect them to do it for the pride of playing for their country,' he said at the time. 'But football is a short career and the rewards should be proportionate to the amount of money the national association collects as a result of their efforts.' In an apparent attempt to head off criticism that his controversial new payment system for the players devalued the England shirt, Revie revealed his puritanical and sanctimonious streak in an article for the *Evening Standard*: 'Some players don't realise how lucky they are. They should go down on their hands and knees every night and thank God they are doing something which they love and are being well paid for at the same time.' He also had eccentric ways. His team-mates at Manchester City recalled their shock years earlier when they once entered his hotel room to discover him in his pyjamas kneeling at the foot of his bed saying his prayers. But, like so many areas of his life, there were contradictions in Revie's apparent religious devotion, and while manager of Leeds he constantly tried to have matches postponed to Sunday. He was also notoriously superstitious, and was said to have a phobia about ornamental elephants. His belief that birds also brought bad luck led him to have the cockerel removed from the Leeds badge, and, believing that a curse had been laid on Elland Road, he once called in a gypsy from Scarborough to have the bad spirits exorcised.

For his first match in charge, a European Championship qualifier against Czechoslovakia on 30 October 1974, Revie insisted that songsheets of *Land of Hope and Glory* were distributed at Wembley in a bid to stir up a frenzy of patriotism after years of sliding morale among England's following. England won the match 3–0 at the start of a highly successful first season in charge for Revie. England were unbeaten in their first nine matches under the new manager, the highlights being a 5–1 demolition of Scotland and a 2–0 win over world champions West Germany.

Not everyone, though, was happy with the new regime, and the first rumblings of discontent could be heard at the end of the season. Kevin Keegan, a future captain and coach of England, walked out on the squad after being dropped for the match against Wales. In words that would return to haunt him two years later, Revie said at the time: 'I don't want any players at the World Cup who go running for the airport just because they are left out for one match.' Keegan was soon persuaded to return, but there were also reports of the squad escaping the claustrophobic atmosphere of their hotel get-togethers for clandestine drinking sessions. Meanwhile, Alan Ball, a player Revie went to great lengths to try to sign for Leeds, never forgave Revie after he was summarily dropped after captaining the side for six games, to be replaced by QPR's Gerry Francis. Ball launched an all-out assault on Revie, accusing him of favouring players who towed the squad line rather than picking the best team available. 'Some of the players are donkeys. Give them a sugar lump and they will run all day and play bingo and carpet bowls all night,' said Ball in a reference to Revie's much-ridiculed games evenings.

Ball admits that even 25 years later he still does not understand why Revie did not have the courtesy to tell him that he was going to be dropped. 'He gave me the greatest honour of my career when he asked me to captain England and I'll always be grateful to him for that. But I couldn't believe it when he didn't tell me personally that I was dropped from the team. I knew I didn't have long left at the top of the game, but still, all he had to do was pick up the phone and say, "Well, thanks for your efforts down the years but I feel it's time for a younger player." But he didn't. I found out from a journalist who called to ask me for my reaction.' Ball recalls that he and his England colleagues were bemused by Revie's chronic indecision in his team selection. 'With Alf Ramsey, it was more difficult to get out of his side than in, but it was completely different with Don Revie. Even the Leeds players in the squad were scratching their heads to explain what was going on. No one could understand it.' Another source of bemusement to the players was Revie's insistence on handing out detailed dossiers to each player about their opposite man on the eve of a match. 'We used to go to bed clutching these fat dossiers the night before playing teams like Cyprus,' says Ball. 'Before, we barely even talked about the opposition, even if it was Germany. The players couldn't quite take it seriously, the idea of reading up every last detail on some Cypriot bloke we never heard of. We were England; we thought they should have been worrying about us.'

Goalkeeper Peter Shilton and Kevin Beattie, a highly talented young defender making waves at Ipswich, also publicly expressed their discontent with the Revie regime, as the England boss found himself under fire for constantly changing his line-ups, a policy which baffled those who remembered his determination to stick with a settled team at Leeds even if it meant putting injured players on to the field. ('You can now buy England caps at Woolworth's' was a popular joke with comedians of the day. In total, Revie gave caps to 60 players during his three years in charge.)

But not all the players griped. Mick Channon, a rare regular under Revie, remembers the carpet bowls Ball spoke disparagingly of. 'It was just a bit of fun. I think I enjoyed the sessions more than anyone else because Don made me bookmaker and I always managed to take a few quid off everyone.' Channon believes the organised games evenings were just Revie's way of trying to recreate the same family atmosphere he had at Leeds. 'He was incredibly enthusiastic when he got to see us. He obviously missed being involved with players on a daily basis. When we arrived for a rare get-together he was so full of energy. We were all a bit bored of training because that's what we did all week long with our clubs, and I think some of the players found it difficult to be as enthusiastic as he was with all his dossiers and carpet bowls.'

Gerry Francis' promising England career barely seemed to have started when it was ended after he suffered a severe injury at the start of the 1976/77 season that kept him out of the game for two years. Francis, who has twice been interviewed for the England manager's job, believes key injuries and

Revie's poor judgement in dropping Ball, were responsible for the poor run of form that followed his first year in charge. 'I think Revie made a mistake with Alan Ball who still had a lot to offer. He was my childhood hero and I played alongside him and Colin Bell in a three-man midfield and it worked really well in Revie's first year. But then the manager decided to drop Alan Ball and shortly afterwards he lost Colin and myself and the whole of his midfield was gone in a couple of matches. It was after that that Revie started to chop and change his line-up and the important results dried up.'

Francis has enjoyed a successful career in management with Bristol Rovers, QPR (twice) and Tottenham, but he refuses to pass judgement on the performance of former England managers on the grounds that he has never experienced the job himself. 'No one knows what international management is like until they've done it. It's like a man talking about having a baby. I wouldn't know what I'm talking about,' he says. 'I've been interviewed for the job on two occasions, once while I was at QPR after Graham Taylor left and once while I was at Tottenham after Terry Venables left. But I didn't want the job. It was lovely to be asked and I'm as patriotic as they come but at the time I was more interested in club football and the day-to-day involvement of that. I said all along that I didn't want the job on each occasion but they still interviewed me. You have to be careful as well because if you start saying publicly that you are interested in the job, it's not going to go down well with the club and the fans.

'It's not that important but what did surprise me in the interviews was the amount of money they were offering. It was significantly less than what you get as a club manager of a Premier Division club or even most First Division clubs. I would have had to take a salary cut of about 50 per cent if I became England manager. Maybe its changed in the last few years but I remember thinking at the time that as the job was the ultimate in English football it should be the best paid manager's job in the country. I don't know what Don Revie was earning but he did at least see that some of the money generated by England games went back to the squad and not just straight into the FA coffers.'

At the end of his first season in charge, in May 1975, Revie came under fire after England were held to a 0–0 draw by Northern Ireland in Belfast. It was the first match to be played in the Ulster capital for four years, since the outbreak of the Troubles, and England were expected to win by a street. The headline in the following day's *News of the World* read 'ENGLAND – THEY'RE JUST IRISH JOKES', but Revie was angered by the hostile reaction from the press. 'People cannot expect us just because we put on a white shirt to come over here and perform miracles. We have no divine right to win,' he said, adding that England were yet to concede a single goal in six games under his management. Four days later, England were held to a 2–2 draw by Wales at Wembley, sparking a fresh wave of negative reviews. Revie expressed his irritation at the criticism, but he was warned he could expect a lot worse if there were more poor results. 'The criticism of the man himself has been mild,' wrote Reg Drury in the *News of the World*. 'Yet the belief that Revie is a Soccer Messiah is no longer as strong it was when he agreed to take the England job last summer.'

England, though, hammered Scotland 5–1 at Wembley the following Saturday in what was probably the side's best performance under Revie. Afterwards, the England boss told reporters: 'The job has gone better than I hoped. Everybody from the players to the FA staff have supported me. It takes nine months to get to know everyone really well. I've travelled thousands of miles and haven't seen much of the wife and family, but they knew what to expect when I took the job.' He admitted he was still a long way from establishing a side capable of mounting a serious challenge for the World Cup: 'We're not ready yet. It will take another nine months before I even begin to think about the squad for Argentina. But I think we have managed to recapture some pride for England.'

Criticism of Revie intensified at the start of the next season when a 2–1 defeat at the hands of Czechoslovakia in Bratislava on 30 October and a 1–1 draw with Portugal in Lisbon the following November ended England's hopes of qualifying for the finals of the European Championships. Revie found he even had enemies within the FA. Sir Harold Thompson, the newly appointed FA chairman, was, according to many of his contemporaries, a prickly and arrogant character who seemed bent on undermining and humiliating Revie. In one exchange the cigar-smoking former Professor of Chemistry, who taught Margaret Thatcher at Oxford and was called 'Atom Bomb Harry' by his students, said to England's football manager: 'When I get to know you better, Revie, I shall call you Don.' Revie replied: 'When I get to know you better, Thompson, I shall call you Sir Harold.' Lord Harewood, the president of the FA at the time, said he was appalled by Thompson's condescending treatment of Revie: 'His interest in seeing Don exposed as an unsuccessful force was, in my view, greater than his interest in seeing England win. Don was very badly treated.'

Alan Odell, the secretary of the International Committee who organised England's tours abroad for 23 years, knew both Revie and Thompson well. 'Don Revie was a smashing fellow to work with. He has been much maligned but he was one of the most decent, kind-hearted people you could hope to meet. Thompson was a bastard – and that's being kind to him,' says Odell who worked with Ramsey from 1966, then Revie, Ron Greenwood and Bobby Robson until 1989. 'You had to get to know Alf Ramsey. It took him a long time to accept people. I worked with him for a whole year before he stopped calling me Mr Odell. But once you got to know him, he was a great person. Thompson, though, was a very rude man who made life very awkward for both Don Revie and Alf Ramsey. He was the prime mover in getting rid of Alf Ramsey who should never have been sacked. It was disgraceful how the FA treated him and Thompson was the man behind it. He would have been the prime mover in getting rid of Don Revie as well, without question.'

The crucial match of the Revie era came a year later when England faced Italy in Rome in their World Cup qualifying group, which also included Finland and Luxembourg. England's campaign had started well enough with two wins over the Finns in June and October 1976, but with just one team qualifying for Argentina from each group, defeat by Italy would have left England needing to beat one of the world's best defensive sides by a greater margin back at Wembley. The match was widely regarded as Revie's make-or-break. Having failed to qualify for the 1976 European Championship finals, further failure would almost certainly result in Revie's removal, or at the very best in a vigorous campaign by the press to have him replaced. The cumulative pressure of England's failure to qualify for a major finals since 1970 was now resting on Revie's shoulders.

England had beaten Italy six months earlier in New York in a triangular tournament to mark the bicentenary of the United States' independence from the United Kingdom. England were losing 2–0 at half time and looked in danger of being swamped by the *azzurri* until a remarkable turnaround in the second half, during which the Italians suffered a collective loss of temper and composure, saw Revie's side fight back for a 3–2 win. The recall of QPR's mercurial forward Stan Bowles, who had supposedly cleaned up his bad boy image since he marched out of a Mercer training camp and down to the nearest bookmaker's, dominated the extensive coverage in the build-up to the Rome qualifier. Later, Revie would be criticised for playing Bowles in what turned out to be, as predicted, a highly physical contest, but in the week before the match every tabloid newspaper campaigned for the player's inclusion. Revie, in the meantime, was trying to downplay the importance of the occasion. 'We are the underdogs, the pressure is on them,' he said. 'Even if we lose, it's not the end of the world. They still have to come here and then play Finland twice.'

Revie's preparations for the match were disrupted by a flu epidemic which claimed Bowles, Emlyn Hughes, Trevor Cherry and Dave Clement, as well as himself. The eleven chosen by Revie to take the field in the intimidating atmosphere of the Stadio Olimpico was consistent only in its inconsistency. Showing six changes from England's last match against Finland at Wembley, the following were selected: Clemence, Clement, McFarland, Hughes, Mills, Cherry, Brooking, Greenhoff, Bowles, Channon and Keegan. On the eve of the match, the *Daily Mirror* claimed the Italians were in a state of disarray following the inclusion of Bowles in the

England line-up, and that they had hastily called up Juventus hardman Claudio Gentile to shadow the QPR playmaker. 'SHOCKED ITALY MAY BRING IN THE HATCHET MAN TO BEAT BOWLES BOMBSHELL' ran the headline; the report began: 'Italian football was thrown into confusion last night by the news that Stan Bowles will play for England in tomorrow's game here.'

If Italy were in a state of disarray that night, it was chilling for England fans to wonder how they might have played had they been organised and confident. Italy played England off the park, and their 2–0 win was a poor reflection of their superiority in every department. The front-page picture on the *Daily Mirror* showed a miserable Revie with furrowed brow staring down at his feet under the headline 'THE FACE OF DEFEAT'. On the back page, the message was equally simple: 'WORLDS APART'. 'The Italians did not need to be ruthless. They were so much better than England,' wrote Frank McGhee. 'It wasn't manager Don Revie's fault that England lost a vital World Cup qualifying match here. It was the failure of English football as a whole.' But Revie seemed to understand the significance of England's defeat as he struggled unconvincingly to declare that there was still hope of qualifying. 'I believe, because I have to believe it, that England can still make it to Argentina by our own efforts,' he said. 'Football has taught me that no competition is ever decided by one match.'

Unfortunately for Revie, England's next match, in February 1977, was against a powerful Holland side at Wembley. Once again the gulf between England and the best sides in the world was laid out painfully bare for all to see as the Dutch, inspired by Johan Cruyff, the greatest footballer in the world at the time, toyed with Revie's side during an embarrassingly easy 2–0 victory. It was after this Dutch defeat that Revie began to roll out his excuses, and though he was probably justified in blaming the structure and nature of English domestic football for the ills of the national side, he was probably as aware as anyone that headlines like 'INFRASTRUCTURE MUST GO!' just did not sell newspapers. 'In the domestic game we give the fans what they want – football played at a hundred miles per hour,' said Revie. 'We have been brought up on that type of all-action football, but at international level I doubt that this is how we can make progress. We need to slow down and develop our skill and technique.'

The defeat by Italy, compounded by the exposure of England's shortcomings against the Dutch, had extinguished the last traces of optimism that followed Revie's appointment and his successful first season in charge. The attacks in the press grew in their frequency and intensity. Revie said later he was convinced it was just a matter of time before he was sacked. The sense that England were being overrun and ridiculed on the international stage was given dramatic expression by the scenes that followed the 2–1 defeat at the hands of Scotland at Wembley in June 1977. At the final whistle, thousands of Scottish fans swarmed on to the hallowed turf at the spiritual home of English football, pulling down the goalposts and digging up the turf as souvenirs of their country's victory. The scenes of chaos rubbed in the sense of England's humiliation. Alan Hoby in the *Sunday Express* wrote: 'Where do ragtail, mediocre England go from here? I shudder to think. Revie – what will he do now? – slumped off, the bitterness of this conclusive defeat in a match which England desperately needed to win stamped on his taut features. The stark truth is that England seldom looked like a team at all. They were bereft of ideas – a shambles.'

Unknown to anyone at the time, Revie was starting to plan his escape. When the England party flew off for their summer tour of South America, Revie was not among them. He told the FA he was going to Finland to watch Italy train ahead of their World Cup qualifier in Helsinki. In fact, he boarded a flight to the Middle East to hold negotiations with officials from the United Arab Emirates who had held out the temptation of a salary six times what he was receiving from the FA. He then covered his tracks by flying to Helsinki for the match itself before joining up with the England squad in Rio de Janeiro. (The tour itself turned out to be a qualified success after the disasters of the previous six months as England achieved creditable draws against Brazil, Argentina and Uruguay.)

While England were in Buenos Aires Revie demanded a

meeting with Dick Wragg, the chairman of the FA International Committee, and dropped his bombshell. Without mentioning his negotiations with the UAE, Revie told Wragg that he believed there was a conspiracy within the FA to have him removed and that he wanted to resign. He demanded £50,000 in compensation, justifying his claims on the improved gates at Wembley. Wragg was flabbergasted. He told the England manager that if there was a conspiracy to remove him then he of all people would have known about it, and that his position would only have come under review were England to fail to qualify for Argentina. (Revie, though, might have been justified in at least suspecting his number was up by reading the newspapers of the previous six months, in which it seemed a case of when rather than if he was going to be sacked. After the South America tour James Mossop wrote in the *Sunday Express*: 'Has the England football team's unbeaten sweep across Latin America been encouraging enough to postpone the sacking of manager Don Revie?') Wragg reported Revie's request to his colleagues, who took a dim view of what they saw as Revie's effort to break his contract and be paid handsomely for it. Revie's first escape bid failed. The FA were not prepared to meet his compensation claims and nor did they want to be subjected to the inevitable criticism that would follow if they released their manager while there was still hope of England qualifying for the World Cup finals.

Following his failure to extract a deal from the FA, Revie turned to Fleet Street in search of money. He sold the story of his resignation, one of the biggest sports 'scoops' of the decade, to Jeff Powell of the *Daily Mail*, from whom he received a large fee – thought to be £20,000 – to add to the £60,000 annual salary and signing-on fee he would receive from his £340,000 contract with the UAE. Revie flew out to Dubai via Switzerland and Athens accompanied by Powell, who left two sealed envelopes at the *Daily Mail*, one with the story of Revie's decision to quit, the other for the following day giving details of his move to the Middle East. Copies were delivered to the FA that evening, 10 July, but they arrived after Lancaster Gate had shut. The following morning, Revie's employers woke up to read a front-page newspaper headline informing them that their most high-profile employee had quit. They were not amused, and went straight to their lawyers before announcing that they had charged their former employee with bringing the game into disrepute. Revie's lawyers declined to attend the subsequent hearing, claiming that the FA had no jurisdiction over their client.

In the story, Revie was quoted as saying: 'I sat down with my wife Elsie one night and we agreed that the job was no longer worth the aggravation. It was bringing too much heartache to those nearest to us. Nearly everyone in the country seems to want me out so I am giving them what they want. I know people will accuse me of running away, and it does sicken me that I cannot finish the job by taking England to the World Cup finals, but the situation has become impossible.' He quickly found himself in the stocks of public opinion as the criticism rained in on him from all directions. Bob Stokoe was one of the first in the queue. 'He should have been castrated,' said Stokoe, whose greatest moment in football had come when his Second Division Sunderland side beat Revie's Leeds in the 1973 FA Cup final. Alan Hardaker was another who could not resist the opportunity to put the boot in on the man with whom he had had so many acrimonious confrontations in the past. 'Don Revie's decision doesn't surprise me in the slightest. Now I can only hope he can quickly learn to call out the bingo numbers in Arabic.' The *Mail*'s rival papers, furious that they had been caught out by Jeff Powell's stunning scoop, quickly tried to make up for lost ground by running as much anti-Revie material as they could fit in their pages. The *Mirror* splashed its allegations of bribery as Fleet Street pilloried Revie as a corrupt traitor and deserter who put cash before country (Revie denied the bribery allegations, but he never started libel actions against his accusers). The man who came to the job with one of the most formidable reputations in world football became an object of hate and ridicule. In the *Daily Express* David Miller called Revie's earlier attempt to extract some compensation while deserting his post 'an outrageous piece of cheek'. He added: 'The attempt to leave the sinking ship and be paid for desertion merely confirms the impressions of those who deplored, for example, his request and acceptance of £200 for speaking for a few minutes at a football publishers lunch . . . Revie has said his resignation came because his family were upset by the pressure, but his daughter's appearance straight from boarding school to sing in a Luton night club was hardly the action of a sensitive, publicity-shy girl.'

Alan Odell says the news of Revie's departure took everyone at the FA by complete surprise. 'We were all astonished when we heard,' he recalls. 'But I suppose the writing was on the wall for him and he knew the FA was going to give him the elbow. I remember I was in a Suffolk hotel on a short holiday after getting back from the South America tour. I got up and turned on the radio and the first thing I heard was that Don had resigned and gone to Dubai. I was flabbergasted. But I think the only thing he did wrong was to sell his story. That was a mistake and he admitted it was later. If he had just told the FA and called a press conference then no one would have blamed him. We had virtually no chance of qualifying for Argentina, everyone knew he was on his way out and he had just been offered a salary five times what he was getting. But once he sold the story the other newspapers were furious and so the criticism of him was vicious. It was stupid of him because he didn't need the extra ten or twenty grand he got from the *Daily Mail*. He lost a lot of goodwill by doing that and I think it tarnished his reputation as a manager. It's a shame because I will personally always remember him as a lovely man.'

The summer of 1977 was a golden period for English sporting scandals. International cricket was plunged into chaos when it was announced, out of the blue a few weeks earlier, that most of the world's leading players had signed up to play for Kerry Packer's World Series in Australia, and ten days before the Revie saga erupted, Tommy Docherty was sacked as Manchester United manager for having an affair with the club physiotherapist's wife ('I have been punished for falling in love,' he told reporters). 'Revie and Docherty have compromised the game off which they have lived so luxuriously and the shame will survive long after their shabby, selfish actions are forgotten,' wrote David Miller. 'Revie has ruthlessly exploited a position which invested in him the aspirations of every schoolboy in the country . . . His vision would seem to be not glory but wall-to-wall bank notes.'

Following his failure to appear before their disciplinary hearing, the FA suspended Revie from all involvement in football. Twelve months later Revie finally agreed to face his former employers at a hearing which was set for 18 December 1978. Revie's QC, Gilbert Gray, claimed the FA could not ban his client from football because they had no jurisdiction over him. Gray also said Revie could not expect a fair hearing with his old adversary Sir Harold Thompson sitting as chairman of the disciplinary committee. The arguments were brushed aside – by Thompson – and Revie was banned from all football activity for ten years. Revie took his case to the High Court where Justice Cantley presided over the case for eighteen days in November and December the following year, during which time some of the most famous names in English football arrived to give evidence on behalf of the FA and Revie, who sought a quashing of the ban on grounds of restraint of trade. During the testimony, the court heard stories of how Revie had developed insomnia while in charge of England, and had suffered the insults of increasingly abusive fans. A sense of Revie's profound insecurity came across as he revealed his pain when he discovered that his famous dossiers had been used by players to keep scores at cards, and that he became so nervous that he lost his voice. Revie also told how he had rejected highly lucrative offers from Barcelona and Saudi Arabia out of loyalty to England. The upshot of his testimony was that he was always fearful of his future and forever worried about the security of his family. Revie was convinced everyone was 'out to get him'.

Sir Harold Thompson was asked in cross-examination if he thought Revie had behaved badly. 'I believe that to be true, so did my colleagues at the FA, and so far as one could tell, so did everyone else in the country.' Revie, though, had his supporters in the case, among them Johnny Giles, Jimmy Hill, Jock Stein and Lawrie McMenemy. Obliged by legal precedent, Justice Cantley, with transparent reluctance, upheld Revie's bid to have the ban lifted and agreed with the claims that Sir Harold Thompson had not been in a position to take an impartial view of Revie's case. But before announcing his decision the judge left no one in any doubt about his feelings for Revie. 'Mr Revie is a very prickly man and I think he has been brooding on imagined wrongs,' he said. 'Mr Revie was the English team manager. He held the highest position of its kind in English professional football and he published and presented to the public a sensational and notorious example of disloyalty, breach of duty, discourtesy and selfishness. His conduct brought English football, at a high level, into disrepute.' Though Revie could claim a victory in having his ban lifted, his claim for damages was rejected and he was made to pay two thirds of his own costs. The FA were left with a massive bill of £150,000. Later, Lord Harewood, the fair-minded former president of the FA, described Justice Cantley as 'an ass' and said: 'If he really thought Sir Harold Thompson had behaved "admirably" and Don hadn't, then he is a very, very poor judge of character.'

Revie returned to his new job in Dubai, where he stayed for three years. He enjoyed the luxury of a sumptuously fitted villa and a swimming pool, but he applied himself to his job with the same enthusiasm and application he had shown throughout his career. Revie did much to improve the quality of football at all levels in the Arab kingdom, but he was abruptly dismissed by his capricious employers on the grounds that the national team needed an Arab speaker. (Revie, incidentally, was said to be disturbed by his players' traditional habit of getting into each other's beds when staying at a hotel before a match.) Shortly after his dismissal, he landed a new job with Al Nasr, one of the leading Emirates club sides, but he soon returned to England where he did some consultancy work for Leeds United. In 1984 he returned to the Middle East to take up a two-year contract to manage Cairo Al-Al FC, but he stayed just a few months because his wife Elsie was tired of living abroad. In 1986 he moved for a final time to Perthshire, near to Elsie's birthplace.

That summer Revie began to complain about aches in his legs, and when on holiday at his villa in Marbella he felt a curious floating sensation and noticed that he had started to trail his left leg. A few weeks later he went to see a London doctor who told him that he was suffering from motor neurone disease, an incurable condition in which the motor neurones in the brain slowly die and cause the muscles to waste away. Revie spent the rest of his life in a wheelchair, and the simplest tasks became major challenges (shaving, he revealed, took up an hour of his day). The last time he was seen in public was when he returned to a hero's reception at Leeds in May 1988 for a match in his benefit, the proceeds of which he gave to research into motor neurone disease and a local children's hospital.

He died on 26 May 1989 in Murrayfield Private Hospital in Edinburgh. Within hours the gates at Elland Road were draped in scarves, messages and flowers as the people of his adopted city swarmed out to mourn the man who had turned their football club into a name known all around the world and whose teams are still today considered to be among the finest ever produced in England. His ashes were buried at Warriston Crematorium in Edinburgh with a bottle of cognac, his favourite drink, placed on the lid of his coffin. Shortly afterwards, Kevin Keegan, who would follow Revie into the job a decade later, paid tribute to the man. 'It saddens me that the public at large still have the wrong impression of him. He was kind, generous and caring. When he left the England job he did the right thing for his family, but did it in the wrong way. He was a big enough man to admit he had gone about it in the wrong way.' The vast majority of his former players at Leeds were at the funeral to pay their final respects. Eddie Gray told reporters he was 'more like a father than a manager'. Referee Jack Taylor, who officiated at more Leeds matches during the Revie reign than any other and was often on the receiving end of some harsh words from him, said: 'Revie was personally charming. I have all the time in the world for him.' No one from the FA turned up for the funeral, prompting 'FA'S FINAL SNUB' headlines the following day. FA secretary Ted Croker, though, never held a grudge against Revie, despite his anger at the manner of his departure. 'He was a strong and very likeable man who, like all of us, had strengths and weaknesses.'

Croker is one of only a handful of leading figures in football to hold a balanced view of Don Revie. Even in the curiously masonic world of English football, where former players and managers are generally loath to speak ill of each other, Revie still provokes strong feelings, both in his defence and in his prosecution. He will be remembered as a man of multiple contradictions whose better qualities were demonstrated during his days at Leeds, where they still will not hear a bad word said about him. At Leeds he preached and practised loyalty, but as England manager he was fickle in his selections, and as Alan Ball's experience bears out, he could be heartless in his treatment of players. He was both pragmatic and rational, yet sentimental and superstitious. As a player he was attack-minded and was never accused of being dirty, but as manager of Leeds he was forever criticised for the brutality and cynicism of the teams he turned out.

It is unfortunate, and perhaps indicative of what the England job can do to a man's enduring reputation, that some still struggle to recall him in a positive light. Revie claimed in his self-pitying interview with Jeff Powell and in the subsequent court case that he left the England post because of the unbearable pressure he found himself under. But, his critics point out, Revie was a bright man, highly sensitive to criticism, who must have realised that the manner of his departure would create ten times the amount of criticism and stress he would have suffered had he seen out his contract. All the anguish could have been avoided if he had waited until England played Italy (a match they won 2–0, only to lose out on qualification for the 1978 World Cup on goal difference) and then resigned, claiming that the whole structure of English football needed a major overhaul.

For Jimmy Armfield, who succeeded Revie as manager of Leeds, his predecessor never came to terms with leaving the club where he thrived on the day-to-day contact with players. 'When I took over at Leeds, the players were in awe of him,' recalls Armfield. 'The problem for Don Revie was leaving Leeds. He couldn't get it out of his system. He was a superb club manager. In the first year after he left we got to the European Cup final, and he followed us right through every game. He was in Barcelona when we won there. He was in Anderlecht. He went to all the games. I wonder whether he ever really put Leeds out of his mind when he was England manager.'

4 The Impossible Job
Ron Greenwood 1977–1982

THE REPUTATION OF England's football team had reached the lowest point in its history at the time when Don Revie took flight to the Middle East. If the currency of the national side had been slowly falling against its foreign competitors since about 1970, it had crashed to critical levels by the summer of 1977. England was in recession in more ways than one: there was anarchy rumbling on the terraces; public confidence was low; industry on the pitch poor; skilled labour was in short supply; and although England could still boast a number of priceless national assets, the final product had about as much appeal on the continent as an Austin Princess. A once great footballing nation, feared and admired in equal measure around the world, had become a laughing stock. Even England's reputation for integrity and fair play had been sullied by the grubby skulduggery of Revie's departure. Not only were England a poor football team, their former manager was apparently more proud of the size of his pay packet than the honour of leading his country. England craved the return of stability and integrity – and quickly. England's first international of the new season, a friendly against Switzerland at Wembley, was fewer than two months away. Shortly after that, England faced Italy at Wembley in a match which would decide which of the two countries would qualify for Argentina.

Aware that the leading candidates to succeed Revie – Brian Clough and Bobby Robson – were under contract with Nottingham Forest and Ipswich Town respectively, the FA turned to one of the most respected and experienced coaches in European football. For years Ron Greenwood had been living in semi-retirement in his home near Brighton having handed over the full-time manager's job at West Ham to John Lyall. He was coach of the England Under-23 side but, deprived of his daily involvement on the training ground, Greenwood had slid into such a depression that he could not even bring himself to join the West Ham players at the celebration party which followed their 1975 FA Cup triumph over Fulham. At the end of July, Sir Harold Thompson invited Greenwood to meet him at the Park Court hotel around the corner from Lancaster Gate and asked him to take over the England job on a caretaker basis until December. Greenwood realised that he was no more than a stop-gap measure as there was virtually no one else available to step in at such short notice. Thompson told Greenwood bluntly that the FA were going to advertise the job and that if he wanted it on a permanent basis he would have to put himself forward for an interview like other prospective candidates.

Having appointed Bill Taylor and Geoff Hurst as his assistants, Greenwood went to Anfield on the opening day of the season to watch a Liverpool side who a few months earlier had been crowned European champions. Greenwood realised there was little time for him to establish a settled side for the crucial match against Italy, so he decided to put his faith in Liverpool's Englishmen: Clemence, Neal, Thompson, Ray Kennedy, Hughes, Case, McDermott and Callaghan, the veteran winger who had last represented England against France in the 1966 World Cup. All but Jimmy Case were chosen for the Switzerland match – a dour contest which finished 0–0 as Trevor Francis, Channon and Keegan, who had just left Liverpool for Hamburg, failed to gel up front. England were equally uninspiring when they ground out a 2–0 win in Luxembourg, and their failure to score more goals that day ultimately cost them their place in the 1978 World Cup finals. If the match had been boring, the same could not be said about what happened in the streets of the tiny duchy as England's hooligans went on the rampage.

Italy flew into London in mid-November with a reputation as one of the meanest defensive sides in world football. England would not have to just beat them, but beat them well to stand any chance of pipping them for a place in Argentina; both teams had eight points, but Italy had one more game against Luxembourg to improve their already superior goal difference. But if qualification was highly unlikely, then the match did at least present England with the chance of restoring some much needed confidence. Inspired by Coppell and Keegan, England produced one of their best performances of the decade in a magnificent 2–0 victory. Greenwood had decided before the match that Keegan held the key to the match and he played him 'in the hole' behind Everton's in-form centre-forward Bob Latchford, with Manchester City's Peter Barnes and United's Steve Coppell providing the width on the flanks. Trevor Brooking and Ray Wilkins were handed the central midfield roles with instructions to keep possession. Greenwood announced his team at the last minute, fooling his old friend Enzo Bearzot into playing two hardmen in the middle on the assumption that England would play three midfielders. The plan worked to perfection as England, playing with a passion not seen for several seasons, outplayed their much-vaunted hosts. Keegan and Brooking each set up a goal for the other, but if the victory was not enough to see England into the finals, it did at least ensure that Italy suffered a nervy final encounter with Luxembourg, whom they overcame 3–0 to qualify by the narrowest margin. After the match, Greenwood sat down with the England players and staff at the dinner table and said, 'Perhaps this isn't the Last Supper after all.'

The result had boosted Greenwood's prospects of landing the job on a permanent basis when he went to be interviewed by the FA the following month; Clough, Robson, Lawrie McMenemy and Allen Wade, the FA's Director of Coaching who wanted the England job to be run by area coaches around the country, were the other candidates in the waiting room. (Incredibly, Greenwood was close to being given the job fifteen years earlier. His coaching mentor Walter Winterbottom had approached the young West Ham manager about succeeding him, but when Winterbottom was overlooked as successor to Sir Stanley Rous in the position of FA secretary, the plan collapsed.) Clough, the people's choice and the bookmakers' favourite, emerged from Lancaster Gate to tell reporters that he had enjoyed 'a magnificent interview'. Greenwood was in the room for half an hour but had no idea that he had landed the post until a few days later when he heard the news on his car radio outside his local restaurant. Greenwood knew what he was in for. Asked by reporters to whom he was accountable as England manager, he replied: 'The whole country.' He knew that years of failure followed by the Revie scandal had increased the pressure on the England manager to unprecedented levels. 'I was fully aware of all the press criticism that would come with the job if things went badly, as well as the high expectations in the country at large,' he recalls. 'For me it was a question of getting a group of good people together, and I was lucky to have Bobby Robson and Don Howe in the set-up. After Don [Revie] had gone overseas, there was even greater interest in the position, but we just got stuck into the job and tried to forget about the pressure. But I enjoyed it from the beginning. It was an enormous challenge and I was happy to get back on the training field again. I'd been with the youth team and the Under-23s, so I just tried to see it as a continuation of that.'

The man they used to call 'Reverend Ron', who was 55 when he took the job, arrived with a reputation as one of the game's great thinkers. His teams were always attractive to watch, but his detractors accused him of being idealistic and his teams of lacking grit. During his time at West Ham, the club won the FA Cup in 1964 and 1975, were runners-up in the League Cup in 1966, and reached the final of the European Cup-Winners' Cup three times, winning the trophy in season 1964/65. Greenwood always disputed that the type of skilful football he encouraged shied away from the more physical aspects of the game, and pointed out that his favourite players – Best, Beckenbauer, Moore and Blanchflower – were all great tacklers as well as ball players. But he believed the frantic pace of British football had restricted the development of technique and movement off the ball. An unashamed enthusiast of continental football, Greenwood believed that speed of foot was no replacement for speed of mind. For Greenwood, football was a battle of wits, a rapidly moving game of physical chess.

One of the big problems facing him when he took over the

England job was the variety of football styles in the English League. Whereas there was a certain uniformity to the continental game in which teams built their attacks from the back, patiently keeping possession until movement off the ball created an opening, English football was a boiling pot of different styles. Some teams played with wingers, some relied on the long ball, some, like Liverpool and Forest, played a passing game at pace – all of which made it difficult for the new manager to establish a pattern of play his players felt comfortable with. Greenwood wanted to employ a continental-style sweeper and toyed with the idea of playing Bryan Robson in that role in the 1982 World Cup campaign before deciding that his eye for goal and effectiveness in the final third of the field made him a more valuable asset in his customary central midfield role. In his early games, Greenwood reverted to the traditional use of two wingers, a sight not seen regularly in England teams for nearly two decades. In Peter Barnes and Steve Coppell he had two fine exponents of the art, and the policy not only brought excitement to watching England, but also success. England qualified for the 1980 European Championship finals in Italy with ease. They failed to win just one of their eight qualifying games – a 1–1 draw in Dublin – against Bulgaria, Denmark, Northern Ireland and the Republic of Ireland. Greenwood stuck with a fairly experienced group of players during the qualifiers, but he also gave youth its chance to impress by handing debuts to Bryan Robson, Glenn Hoddle and Kenny Sansom. The only blots on Greenwood's copybook came in the form of away defeats by the odd goal to West Germany and Austria, and an extraordinary 4–1 thrashing by Wales at Wrexham.

Greenwood, having successfully restored England to the First Division of world football, found himself welcomed by the nation's sports writers who, after years of embarrassments, were happy finally to be reporting some good news. The players, too, were happy with the more relaxed regime off the pitch which allowed them to have a pint or three in the evening rather than don the plastic smiles as the carpet bowls were brought out. 'If players like to relax by having a drink, why stop them? They're grown men,' said the England manager.

According to Trevor Brooking, Greenwood succeeded in quickly restoring the morale of the squad. 'Under Ron, there was a much happier, more relaxed atmosphere in the squad and that was reflected on the pitch. There was less of the tension which had built up under Don Revie. Like Joe Mercer, he simply told the England players to go out and enjoy themselves and the results would come.' Like all his predecessors, though, Greenwood was frustrated by the small amount of time the Football League were prepared to yield to the national side. 'It's completely different from managing a club side because you are only with the players for a short time,' he says. 'It's not like being with them every day. The one thing I tried to establish was some continuity whereby whenever we met we felt as if we had never been apart. I tried to create a club atmosphere with all my staff and players.'

In March 1980, England beat Spain 2–0 in Barcelona with a performance of such virtuosity that one Spanish newspaper described their play as 'out of this world' and suggested that Spanish footballers should go to England to finish their education. After watching Greenwood's side toy with Spain for 90 minutes, Italy's manager Enzo Bearzot said England were now the 'logical favourites' to win the European Championships. But England's preparations for their first finals of a major championship for a decade suffered a major blow when Trevor Francis, Britain's first million-pound footballer, injured his Achilles tendon. England beat world champions Argentina 3–1 at Wembley in May, with two goals from Liverpool's David Johnson, but their form deserted them in the first two matches of the Home Championship. That 4–1 defeat by Wales, a team that had not qualified for the World Cup finals since 1958 and then only because the country's name was the first to be pulled out of a hat after a series of withdrawals, was not the best result to improve a team's self-esteem. A 1–1 draw against Northern Ireland followed, and when England arrived in Scotland for their final match they were presented with a giant wooden spoon. The amusing gift was handed back the next day as Greenwood's side silenced 80,000 demonic Scots at Hampden Park with goals from Brooking and Coppell.

After a cocktail party with Margaret Thatcher at Downing

Street, England, in good spirits, flew out for the European
Championships to their base at Asti near Turin in northern
Italy. They had won twenty and lost just three out of 29 since
Greenwood took over and they were considered to have as
good a chance as anyone of being crowned champions of
Europe three weeks later. In the event, the championships were
as disappointing as any major finals since the advent of
international competition. The football was largely negative,
the crowds were demoralisingly small, England fans battled
with riot police on the terraces, and the final was contested by
West Germany and Belgium – not exactly a fixture to get the
world's pulse racing at the best of times. England drew 1–1
with Belgium in their first game, which was suspended for five
minutes after the tear gas being used by police to beat off the
hordes of England's hooligans had drifted on to the pitch and
incapacitated goalkeeper Ray Clemence. Greenwood was
incensed by the disallowing of what seemed a perfectly
legitimate goal by Tony Woodcock, and was even less
impressed by the behaviour of England's fans. After the match
the England manager appeared before the BBC cameras and
suggested 'the troublemakers should be put on a boat and
someone should pull the plug' – comments which provoked an
angry response from an Open University sociology professor
who criticised Greenwood for not attempting to understand
what social injustices drove men to behave this way. In their
next match England faced the hosts, who had not been beaten
on their own territory for ten years. A tight game was settled
by a Marco Tardelli goal, ending England's hopes of reaching
the final. A 2–1 victory over Spain kept alive hopes of making
the play-off for third place, but a goalless draw between Italy
and Belgium ended their campaign.

The criticism that followed England's exit was relatively
mild, but by the same time the following year the press was
clamouring for Greenwood's head following an astonishing
slump in form. The draw for the qualifying rounds had
provided England with what seemed a straightforward passage
to the 1982 World Cup finals in Spain. In a group of five from
which two teams would go through, England's opponents were
Norway, Romania, Hungary and Switzerland – reasonable

teams all of them but not exactly world-beaters. Defeat in Bucharest in October 1980 and a 0–0 draw in the return match in April 1981 were a setback to England's hopes, but having beaten Switzerland and Norway there was no immediate cause for panic. England, though, were clearly struggling to find their rhythm and confidence as they suffered their worst ever sequence of form at Wembley, losing to Spain, Brazil and Scotland and drawing with Romania and Wales.

Greenwood grew used to the sound of 'What a load of rubbish!' echoing around the ground as he made the long walk back to face a group of journalists who were becoming increasingly hostile with every match. The tabloid newspapers of the period make for uncomfortable reading for those, like Greenwood, of a sensitive nature. Such was the directness and intensity of the attacks that the mild-mannered Greenwood exploded at one press conference, and a few days later made up his mind to resign in the summer. Sub-editors at the *Sun*, the most unforgiving and unrestrained of the tabloids in the 1980s, showed an especially vicious wit in their headlines. After the goalless draw with Wales in May 1981 the back page read 'WALK SMALL' and Frank Clough, the chief footballer writer, warmed up for what would become an all-out assault in the coming weeks. 'The worry lines are back and biting deeply into Ron Greenwood's brow . . . Not to beat about the bush England were pathetic.' Greenwood's discomfort was increased by a comment from Mike England, the Wales manager, that left English fans shuddering with hurt pride. 'Wales are now the best in Britain,' said England as a matter of fact after the match. 'England haven't got it together right now.' Greenwood was starting to experience the massive difference between managing a club and managing the country. 'If West Ham or Preston lose, only the people of West Ham and Preston are upset, but if England lose then it is national disaster,' he says. In his engaging autobiography *Yours Sincerely*, ghostwritten by Bryon Butler, the veteran football reporter of the BBC and the *Daily Telegraph*, Greenwood put the experience more poetically: 'Victory is a slice of heaven and defeat is a step towards the fire below.'

But there was much worse to come. On the day of the Scotland match, 23 May, the *Sun* ran the headline 'FOR

PETE'S SAKE'. In his report Clough claimed that Greenwood had been pressurised by the players to drop Peter Barnes. 'Axed England winger Peter Barnes and hundreds of fans are entitled to ask this morning: What the hell is going on? Barnes yesterday became the first victim of player power in the England camp . . . Greenwood is WRONG in allowing them to sway him and he is WRONG to drop Barnes.' After England's 1–0 defeat a thunder-faced Greenwood marched into the press conference and flew at the massed ranks of raincoats and notepads ranged before him. 'To all of you a big thank you. I have been stabbed in the back. The prefabricated messages that went out today about my speaking to the players was the biggest load of journalistic licence I have ever read.' And with that he turned on his heel and stormed from the room. The papers clearly enjoyed the confrontation. 'RON HITS ROCK BOTTOM' ran the headline in the *Sunday Mirror* (note that it is 'Ron', not 'England') and in his report Ken Montgomery showed his quarry little mercy: 'England's goalless, guileless soccer squad head for Switzerland and Hungary on Thursday – facing the worst results sequence in their 109-year history. Don Revie had a run of six winless games in 1977 – and that signalled his departure. Incredibly, Greenwood still has the backing of the FA.' The *Sun* continued the battering on Monday. The two main headlines in the sports pages – 'THE FINAL RON-DEZVOUS' and 'WRONG AGAIN, RON!' – left little room for doubt about the paper's feelings for the England manager, as Frank Clough cranked up the calls for his removal. 'There is a school of thought in the England camp that the press are never more delighted than when the team is struggling,' he wrote. 'It has been there since Sir Alf Ramsey's days – and it is still flourishing, to judge by Ron Greenwood's astonishing outburst against the media after yet another defeat . . . For Greenwood to claim that the media have put the knife in is too laughable for words.' His final comment that 'Nobody wants to see Greenwood and the England team successful more than I do' can hardly have reassured the manager.

Today, Greenwood claims that he never let the press criticism get to him. 'I just ignored the headlines. You appreciated they had a job to do but what you had to do was try and win them over by getting close to them and letting them know what's going on and not trying to keep anything secret. You wanted to get them on your side, that was the main thing. I found it easy to relax after games because I went home to a strong family, to people not connected with the job, and so I could shut it out of my mind. They insulate you from the pressures and take your mind off the snipings. Of course the English public are unreasonable in their expectations of success, but you can't blame them for that. They expect everything from you and quite rightly so. As England you are a public servant, like a politician. You are answerable to the country. 'Whoever is in charge of England is going to be under pressure and you have to expect that. That's why it's so important to have a team of people around you to absorb the pressure. I was lucky to have Bobby Robson, Dave Sexton and Don Howe who soaked up a lot of it for me. It's an impossible job to do on your own. You need people around you with intelligence and knowledge.'

Greenwood needed every friend he could get as England set off for Basle the following week. 'Defeat by Switzerland, the no-hopers in the qualifying group, will kill off any chances of going to the finals in Spain next year, and will surely end Greenwood's reign as manager,' wrote Clough on the day of the match. He was almost right on both counts. England lost 2–1 and, indeed, their hopes of reaching the finals appeared to be over after picking up just five points from five of their eight qualifying games. The front and back pages of the following day's newspapers reported 'ENGLAND'S DAY OF SHAME'. The news pages carried ugly pictures of English fans battling police and local supporters. One picture showed two fans hurling a Swiss supporter down the steep concrete terracing. On the back pages, Greenwood was told to pack his bags. The *Sunday Mirror* carried the apocalyptic headline 'END OF THE WORLD'. Greenwood's cause was not helped by the comments of his Swiss counterpart Paul Wolfsberg, who said after the match: 'When Hungary win in Budapest, England will be out of the World Cup. I cannot see this England team containing Hungary's forwards. England's play was easy to read – it was simple for us.' Trevor Brooking believes that a major factor in England's defeat was the fact that the Liverpool contingent arrived less than a day before the match, exhausted after their efforts winning the European Cup final. 'It was overlooked at the time but Ron Greenwood only had his full-strength side together on the eve of the match when the Liverpool lads flew in. Twenty-four hours is no time to prepare an international side for a World Cup qualifying match.'

The England manager had decided that enough was enough: he was going to resign, whatever the result in Budapest the following Saturday. So as not to undermine the squad's already low morale, Greenwood decided to keep his thoughts to himself until after the match. England had not won in Hungary for seventy years, but with Robson, Keegan and Brooking in outstanding form in the midfield they produced one of their best performances of the modern era as they swept to a 3–1 win. Brooking scored two of the goals, the second a stunning left-foot drive that flew into the corner of the net and lodged behind the stanchion. 'It was the best shot of my career,' says Brooking.

England, though, were still highly unlikely to qualify, and only an improbable sequence of results elsewhere would deliver them to their first World Cup finals since 1970. On the plane back to England, Greenwood drew the curtain separating the squad from the press and, close to tears, announced to his players that he was leaving the job. When he sat back down, Keegan, Brooking, Clemence and other senior players huddled together before descending on the manager to urge him to change his mind. Greenwood, though, was not for turning and had already telephoned Dick Wragg to meet him at Luton airport so that they could announce the news at a press conference. As the squad disembarked from the plane Greenwood was still holding his ground, but the players continued to badger him as they waited for their luggage to appear. Greenwood finally cracked, and just minutes before the press conference he told Wragg that the support of his players had prompted him to reconsider. Greenwood remembers the occasion well. 'I was very moved by their support. I had begun to feel very downhearted, but it was touching that they still believed in what we were doing. We had built up that kind of spirit in the squad despite the run of bad results.'

Bryon Butler, who knew Greenwood as well as any of his contemporaries, believes the relationship between the England set-up and the press changed beyond all recognition at the start of the 1980s. 'The thicker the skin an England manager can get hold of these days the better,' says Butler. 'Now the media coverage has become an absolute circus. When I started covering England on the radio for the BBC I never had to say at a press conference "Hello, Bryon Butler BBC Radio" because everyone knew who you were. I was the radio man, the only one. Even at the beginning of Greenwood's time in charge there was still a manageable amount of media. There was a chap from each of the main papers and that was that.

'On the day after the match about half a dozen of us would go and have breakfast with Ron and discuss the game – but there were no photographers allowed because they would wait until he bit into his sandwich to try and get a picture of him with egg on his face. We would all be there for up to a couple of hours just chatting about the match. It was all very friendly but after a while other TV companies and radio stations started to say "Why can't we come along?" So the FA started to hire a room in the hotel and there would be about 12 or 15 reporters there. But it was still nothing compared to recent years. Now radio people queue, TV people queue and then there are all the papers who want it carved up for themselves. The evening papers want something, the morning papers want something, the foreign papers want something, there are requests for one-to-ones – if the England manager today did everything asked of him he wouldn't have any time left to do any football at all. The amount of media attention on the England set-up is monumental now.

'For the last 20 years or so the manager has become part of a circulation war or the victim of an editor or journalist trying to establish his reputation. There is a competition to see who can produce the spikiest headline. They're trying to outdo each other at the England manager's expense. It's a policy at some newspapers. They decide whether they are pro or anti the man in charge and stick to that line. The broadsheets generally take a more balanced, fairer view of events, but in the other papers the England manager is just a pawn in a wider, nastier game. There was always aggro in Revie's time but it got really nasty in the Greenwood/Robson era. The problem is the increasing number of media organisations, which has brought more competition and a hardening of attitudes. I think most of the sports reporters are England fans – but they're journalists first.'

In England's five previous encounters with Norway they had scored no fewer than four goals on each occasion, and they travelled to Oslo knowing that anything less than a victory would, barring miracles, finally put them out of their World Cup misery. But Norway, then still largely an irrelevance in international football, pulled off the greatest result in their history as England slumped to a 2–1 defeat amid the deafening roar of the tiny Ulleval Stadium. In a broadcast that has become part of football folklore in both countries, Norwegian TV commentator Borge Lillelien exploded in a frenzy of nationalistic pride at the final whistle. Screaming into his microphone, he said: 'We are the best in the world! We have beaten England! Lord Nelson ... Lord Beaverbrook ... Sir Winston Churchill ... Sir Anthony Eden ... Clement Attlee ... Henry Cooper ... Lady Diana. We have beaten them all! Maggie Thatcher, can you hear me? Maggie Thatcher, your boys took a hell of a beating! Norway have beaten England at football!'

Predictably, the criticism of Greenwood and his team rained in from all directions back home; the matter of England's evident decline as a footballing power even provoked a debate in the House of Commons. Romania and Hungary were now almost certain to go through – until Switzerland, the no-hopers in the group, came to England's rescue by beating Romania at home and holding them to a goalless draw in Bucharest. England now needed only a draw at home to Hungary in a match which prompted discomforting parallels with the contest against the Poles eight years earlier. On the day of the match, 18 November, stories appeared on the front pages of the tabloids reporting that Glenn Hoddle and others had been on a drinking binge the night before, but England, though never convincing, won the match 1–0 thanks to a goal from Paul Mariner. As Greenwood strolled, head up, back to the tunnel 92,000 voices boomed out a rendition of 'You'll Never Walk Alone'. England and Greenwood had pulled off what one paper called 'The Great Escape'. For the whole week after the match the England manager wore the tie he had bought in Switzerland.

England's struggle to qualify for Spain seems all the more extraordinary when you consider the array of talent at Greenwood's disposal. In Shilton, Clemence, Sansom, Thompson, Robson, Mariner, Woodcock, Rix, Keegan, Brooking, Francis, Hoddle, Wilkins, Coppell, Butcher and Mills – all of whom made the final tour party – England could boast some of the most illustrious names in world football, and at least six of them could retire in the knowledge that they had proved themselves to be among the finest players ever to have represented the country. The draw was good to England, pitching them in a relatively easy-looking group with France, Czechoslovakia and Kuwait, and basing them in the northern coastal town of Bilbao. The San Mames Stadium, known locally as 'The Cathedral', was similar to English grounds in its design with the crowd pressed right up against the pitch. There were understandable fears among Bilbao's 600,000-strong population in the industrial port that England's notorious hooligans would cause mayhem, but a few months before the finals Greenwood struck a diplomatic blow for the country when he took over an England XI to play Atlético Bilbao in a testimonial match that drew a crowd of 40,000 and finished in a 1–1 draw.

Greenwood spared no detail in his preparations for England's first appearance in a World Cup since 1970. Accompanied by the FA's administration officer, Alan Odell, Greenwood went on a reconnaissance mission to test everything from the firmness of mattresses in hotels to the security and cooking arrangements. He opted for a hotel called Los Tamarises a few miles outside town, owned by a jolly, hospitable figure called Jesus who gave each of the England players a bottle of wine from the year of their birth from his extensively stocked cellar. Shortly after the name of England's hotel was announced, a photographer took a picture of a dead dog on the beach outside and the image appeared in most newspapers with articles suggesting England had chosen a godforsaken dump as their base camp. The hotel, in fact, was of the very highest quality, boasting one of the best restaurants in the area as well as a large games room where the players could relax playing pool and table tennis. Just to be on the safe side, England brought with them industrial quantities of brown sauce and cornflakes. The hotel was built into the cliff face behind, making it safe from unwanted intrusions, but amid fears that the Basque terrorists might exploit the publicity potential of the tournament, England were given round-the-clock armed protection, and when the players first arrived at the hotel they found a tank sitting in the car park.

'Greenwood felt that one of his achievements in Spain was that there were no stories unearthed by the news hounds,' says Bryon Butler. 'The hotel was up against a cliff side and so it was impossible for anyone to get in. The press were only allowed in every now and then. There was one occasion when the press officer Glen Kirton, informed him that the London Ballet were in town and were wondering if they could pop in and say hello to the England players, but when they came in with virtually nothing on and their legs up to their armpits it was quickly realised that this was a hoax by one of the papers trying to get amusing shots of the England team in compromising positions. But there were no scandals at the 1982 World Cup and the management were very careful about making sure the news hounds were not able to manipulate situations.'

England's first match was against France, a team they had not played since 1969 but who had improved considerably since Hidalgo took over as manager in 1975. In Platini, Giresse, Soler and Tresor they could boast one of the best midfields in the competition. With Brooking and Keegan battling to overcome injuries, Greenwood opted for Shilton in goal; Mick Mills, the captain, and Kenny Sansom; Thompson and Butcher in central defence; Coppell on the right of midfield with Wilkins and Robson in the centre and Rix on the left, but with a brief to roam; and Francis and Mariner were handed the strikers' roles. England had not appeared in the World Cup for twelve years, but they took just 27 seconds to let everyone know they were back. Wilkins passed to the right from kick-off, the ball was forced into touch, Coppell took the throw-in, Butcher flicked on and Robson volleyed into the net. Robson earned a gold watch from the organisers as well as a place in the record books for the fastest ever goal in the World Cup finals. The French hit back with an equaliser by Soler before half time, when the players staggered out of the 100-degree heat into the cool of the dressing-rooms. Some players complained of feeling dizzy as the coaching staff draped them in cold towels and plied them with salt tablets and hot tea. England, though, looked the stronger team in the second half as Robson scored a second with a header and Mariner added a third to give England the perfect start. All the players lost weight in the debilitating heat, the worst affected being Mariner, who lost nearly a stone, while Rix and Coppell were so badly dehydrated that it took them nearly three hours to produce urine samples for the dope testers.

England's next matches were entirely forgettable affairs; 2–0 and 1–0 wins over Czechoslovakia and Kuwait respectively as England made sure of their progress into the second group stage. (It was unfortunate for Kuwait's players that the World Cup coincided with the holy month of Ramadan. They took to the field on empty stomachs and refused even to drink water at half time.)

The complicated format of the finals meant that the twelve teams who had qualified for the next stage would be split into four groups of three, the winners of which would go on to the semi-finals. England, who moved to a new base camp at Nava Cerrada in the mountains above Madrid, found themselves in the same group as European champions West Germany and the hosts Spain, but the group stages had exposed the mediocrity of both teams. The Germans had not been beaten by another European nation since Jupp Derwall took over from Helmut Schoen after the 1978 World Cup, but Derwall's emphasis led Pele to describe them as 'Rummenigge and ten robots'. In one of the biggest upsets in the history of the World Cup West Germany had lost 1–0 to Algeria before scraping into the next stage with a 1–0 win over their central European brothers

Austria, a match the cynics dubbed 'the Anschluss agreement' after Austria gave little or no suggestion of wanting to win. Derwall left out three of his most exciting players in Pierre Littbarski, Horst Hrubesch and Klaus Fischer in a team clearly designed to contain England. Greenwood stuck with the team that had so far won three games. It was Madrid's first experience of the World Cup, and 80,000 fans turned out at the Bernabeu Stadium in the hope of seeing two of the biggest names in world football lay on a spectacle. They were deeply disappointed. England had the better of a tight match, but knowing that defeat would spell the end of their chances of reaching the last four, neither side was prepared to take risks. West Germany mustered just two chances on goal all game, the second of which five minutes from time almost won them the match when Rummenigge crashed a 25-yard drive against Shilton's crossbar. Boos and whistles greeted the final whistle.

England had a whole week before their game against Spain, allowing Keegan and Brooking to return to near full fitness. In the meantime, West Germany beat Spain 2–1, which meant that England would have to beat the Spaniards by two goals to go through. A controversial rule based on classification in the group stages meant that England and West Germany would draw lots if England beat Spain 2–1. Spain, who had already been beaten by ten-man Northern Ireland in Valencia, were already out, but they wanted to end their disappointing campaign on a high note and had nothing to lose. It turned out to be a frustrating night for England, who produced their best football of the tournament but failed to convert a string of chances. With half an hour to go Greenwood sent on Brooking and Keegan. Both of them, however, showed they were still some way from match sharpness and missed chances they would normally have buried. For both players, those 30 minutes were to be the only experience of World Cup football in their careers.

England were unbeaten, but bowed out of the tournament as they were made to pay for their lack of a truly world-class striker. The Germans went on to win a controversial semi-final against France in which their goalkeeper Schumacher somehow survived being sent off after a horrifying challenge on

Battiston, who was rushed unconscious to hospital, leaving behind a shaken team fearing for his very survival. Many felt that a victory for West Germany in the final would have been a defeat for football, but Italy made sure it was not to be.

England could consider themselves unfortunate, but at least Greenwood could now retire from football knowing that his reputation as one of English football's best coaches had been restored following the ferocious battering he had suffered in the press twelve months earlier. 'I honestly thought we could have won the World Cup in 1982,' said Greenwood. 'We were strong in almost every department, and if we had been a little sharper in front of goal, who knows?'

Shortly afterwards, Greenwood published his autobiography in which he called for the radical overhaul of English football to aid the national team. 'The earth will be flat and the moon made of cheese before England's manager is given all he needs to do his job properly. We are talking about the impossible.' Greenwood proposed that all foreigners, including players from Scotland, Wales and Ireland, should be banned from playing in English football. 'Ninety-two clubs employ 1,800 players, but only about 50 of them are of any interest to the England manager.'

For Jimmy Armfield, Ron Greenwood was one of the best English coaches of the post-war era. 'Ron was the first one who really got me interested in coaching,' he says. 'I was captain of the Under-23s when he was coach, and I used to hang on every word he said. He was a big disciple of Walter Winterbottom – another extremely nice man – and, like him, he was one of the first real thinkers in the game. He imposed his views on us but he also wanted us to have freedom to play.' Armfield rejects the most common criticism of Greenwood that he was too nice. 'People respond to different types of people, but he certainly stimulated me. Anyone who rants and raves at me would get nothing out of me. I respond to someone who knows what they're talking about. Winterbottom, Ramsey and Greenwood were like that for me. I learnt something from all of them.'

5 Total Rancour . . . and Other Headlines

Bobby Robson 1982–1990

T SAYS SOMETHING ABOUT the perverse fickleness of the English mentality that Bobby Robson found himself being hailed as a national hero on the day he left the job. For the eight years before that, he had been an object of ridicule and contempt. He had been spat at in the street, lampooned in satirical TV shows, his private life had been splashed all over the nation's newspapers in gory detail, he was called 'stupid' and 'bungling' and 'useless' and 'a plonker' by the critics, and one paper even suggested on its front page that his brother's heart attack had been brought on by Robson's decision to take a job with PSV Eindhoven after being told by the FA his services would not be required after the 1990 World Cup. Murderers and child molesters have suffered less abuse. Even allowing for the peculiarly English relish for seeing public figures humiliated for no better reason than the sheer fun of it, there is something especially illogical about the treatment Robson received.

According even to his fiercest critics, he was (and is) an immensely likeable, kind, loyal, dignified and enthusiastic man. As the most public face of English football, Robson's personal charm made a small contribution to the improvement of the Englishman's image abroad at a time when the country's hooligans had generated in their compatriots not just the customary sense of embarrassment at their behaviour but, following the Heysel Stadium disaster, also a profound sense of shame and revulsion. But the main point about his likeability is that it failed to gain him not even so much as a reduction in sentence, let alone a reprieve, from those who felt they had the right to judge and execute him. Others, like Terry Venables, have found that affability and good humour can be handy weapons in fending off the critics, but with Robson . . . well, he might just as well have told them to stick their typewriters in a dark place for all it was worth. They could not have been more abusive if they tried.

But what about his record as England manager, the only truly relevant test of his achievements? Under Robson, England reached the World Cup quarter-finals in 1986 and the semi-finals in Italy four years later. He lost just one qualifying match out of 28 in four major competitions over eight years. The only England manager whose record in competitive matches compares favourably to Robson's is that of Sir Alf Ramsey – and he enjoyed home advantage for his greatest moment in 1966. Aside from that, England's record under Ramsey lies somewhere between mediocre and poor. Reaching the quarter-finals of Mexico 1970 from a group which included Romania and Czechoslovakia was no more than expected, while the failure even to qualify four years later – regardless of how many chances England had in their final match against Poland – is not easy to applaud. Under Winterbottom, England won just three out of fourteen matches in the World Cup finals; under Revie and Taylor England failed to reach the finals at all; under Greenwood they reached the last twelve of the strange grouping system in 1982; Venables was shown the door before he had the chance to lead England in a World Cup campaign; and Hoddle took England only as far as the last sixteen in 1998.

In short, Robson's record is as good as that of anyone who has ever managed England. So why the vitriolic abuse, and why did the FA dump him? Nearly ten years later, Robson says that time has not diminished his astonishment at the treatment he received both from his employers and from the press. 'It was a hell of a shock coming up from Ipswich where you were well loved and a bit of a local hero,' he recalls. 'I had fourteen years of tranquillity and happiness working with lovely people and then . . . well, then the England job. I was a successful club player. I represented my country twenty times. I had played in a World Cup. I had won trophies as a manager for Ipswich. I had worked for England in a coaching capacity at other levels. I had had about as much experience of top-grade football as it was possible to have. But nothing, nothing, can prepare you for the England job. It was a severe test of character.

'But despite it all, at the end I didn't want to leave. I had got to know the job and I got better and better at it and I was handling it very well by the time I left. I knew more about what the job entailed than anyone. It's daft: you get on top of the job and then you have to leave. Before the World Cup I had a meeting with Bert Millichip [FA chairman] and the International Committee and they told me that they felt it was time for a change. Had they waited until after the World Cup I don't think they would have made that decision. I definitely would have stayed for another World Cup. I wasn't ready to leave. They bring in Graham Taylor in my place – they had to bring in someone – but he had no experience. I had been there for eight years and then they decide to get rid of me and bring in someone to start all over again from scratch. He had a wee bit of success at club level, and no disrespect to him but he was suddenly being asked to take on one of the most difficult jobs in world football. They threw away my experience overnight. It's quite ridiculous! I mean, can you imagine that happening at a major corporation? It would be madness. There was no one better qualified to do the England job than me. If only they had waited until after the World Cup and not been so hasty, things might have turned out very different.'

Robson barely had time to arrange his family photos on his new desk at Lancaster Gate when he found himself knee-deep in controversy. The new England manager took the bold decision to leave out Kevin Keegan from his first squad for the vital European Championship qualifier against Denmark in Copenhagen on 22 September 1982. Keegan, the best English footballer of his generation and captain of the national side under Greenwood, had recently joined Newcastle in the Second Division. Robson, who found himself being spat at on his next visit to St James's Park, justified dropping the former European Footballer of the Year on the grounds that he needed to look ahead to the 1986 World Cup. Keegan himself made no attempt to hide his fury and promised that he would never play for England again. 'I was upset because he didn't tell me before he announced it to the press,' Keegan said at the time. 'After 63 caps and ten years' experience I thought I was worth a ten-pence phone call.' In his 1986 World Cup diary Robson said that he feared that Keegan would stir up unrest in the England squad. 'I spoke to a great many people involved and learned that, because of his back injury, he was being a little difficult and had lost some of his huge popularity with his team-mates,' he wrote. 'As he sought a solution to his personal troubles he became something of a disruptive influence.'

Robson had no time to experiment in a friendly before facing a Denmark side who, under German coach Sepp Piontek and with the talents of Michael Laudrup, Preben Elkjaer and Jesper Olsen, were fast emerging as one of the most exciting forces in European football. In the event, a Keegan-less England were extremely fortunate to come away with a point. The match finished 2–2, but it was the very least the Danes deserved for they outplayed England for most of the match and were only denied their first ever victory over England in eight attempts by an outstanding performance from goalkeeper Peter Shilton. Robson made no attempt to claim England had played well and admitted he made mistakes in choosing Aston Villa winger Tony Morley in attack as well as defenders Phil Neal and Russell Osman, both of whom struggled against the speed and guile of Denmark's strikers. 'It was a travesty of a result,' he said. 'They overran us and it was one of football's mysteries that they had to wait until the last minute to score their second goal.'

With Hungary, Greece and Luxembourg never in the running, the qualifying group quickly became a two-horse race that reached its most critical point when the Danes visited Wembley the following autumn. Robson was left in no doubt about the importance of the occasion. 'Bobby Robson wrestles with the problems that could secure his international reputation or expose him to the merciless criticism that bit deep into Ron Greenwood and Don Revie before him,' wrote Terry McNeill in the *News of the World*. 'Robson, perhaps more sensitive than either, knows his credibility will be on the line ... So much is at stake that defeat would be a calamity and, while such instant damnation would be dreadfully unfair, that's all part of the job he accepted a year ago this week.' Robson, showing a firm grasp of economics at the height of the Thatcherite revolution, said on the eve of the match: 'Beating the Danes means everything. We must get to France for the European Championship finals next year to sustain public interest in a product that is being hit by the recession.'

As it turned out, the match prompted more public inquiry than public interest as England were toyed with by the Danes, who virtually guaranteed their passage to France at the expense of their hosts with a 1–0 win. The history books show that only a penalty – awarded against Neal for handball – separated the two sides, but no one who left Wembley that night was in any doubt that the gulf in class was considerably wider. While England were being booed off the pitch there were wild celebrations beginning in Denmark; such was the excitement at the biggest result in the country's history that the best-selling newspaper with an average circulation of 250,000 sold an extra 85,000 copies the following day. 'England's performance created the biggest stink since the sewermen went on strike,' wrote Terry McNeill in next Sunday's *News of the World*. 'I sat until the lights went out, feeling first anger then shame that millions throughout Europe were laughing themselves silly.' Brian Glanville in the *Sunday Times* admitted that the dearth of world-class talent and the absence through injury of Bryan Robson was a problem for the manager, but lambasted him for ignoring Glenn Hoddle who was not even given a place on the bench. Glanville, perhaps Robson's most trenchant critic throughout his eight years in charge, declared that 'the true charge against Robson is that he did so pathetically little with pathetically little ... He simply sticks to bad players, leaves out good ones and seems to listen to some dubious advice, of which in the coaching establishment at Lancaster Gate, there is no shortage.'

Robson admits he made a psychological blunder by ramming home the talents of the Danes to his players in the build-up to the match. 'I think it made them freeze up a bit on the night,' he recalls. 'I should have given our lads more confidence by talking *them* up rather than hammering on about the threat the Danes posed.' Robson, though, was not the only one to come in for criticism. Many correspondents believed they could see the influence of Arsenal coach Don Howe, Robson's assistant, behind England's dour, over-cautious display. Howe, though, rejected the suggestions that he had influenced Robson or the players. 'In the few hours we have together there is no time to fill the players' heads with my ideas, even if I had the power, which I haven't,' he told reporters. 'I've never changed Bobby's mind over selection or even tried for that matter.'

The criticism which followed England's defeat by Denmark and the consequent failure to qualify for France was as nothing compared to what followed in the second half of the 1983/84 season when England lost 2–0 to France in Paris, 2–0 to the USSR at Wembley and 1–0 to Wales in Wrexham. The *Sun* and the *Daily Mirror*, battling each other more furiously than ever in the eternal circulation war in Fleet Street, both launched campaigns to have Robson removed forthwith. The *Sun* handed out badges declaring ROBSON OUT – CLOUGH IN, and TV pundit Jimmy Hill declared there was little point in England going to South America for their scheduled summer tour. 'Unfortunately for Bobby the 1980s was a time when the circulation war between the tabloids stepped up a gear,' says the *Daily Telegraph*'s Bryon Butler. 'By the end of his time the relationship between the press and the England camp reached melt-down point. The press has always been split down the middle about the qualities of an England manager, but the anti-Robson faction were particularly harsh. I remember when he first started and Robert Maxwell, the owner of the *Daily Mirror*, was apparently watching an England game and saw Robson appearing to be indecisive over whether to make a substitution and said, "Right, this man must not manage England." '

Brian Glanville's criticism of Robson may have been more sophisticated and constructive than that of his colleagues in the popular press, but it was no less damning. Yet Glanville says he grew to like Robson as a man, but claims that his success owed more to luck than anything else. 'Bobby Robson is the original man who fell down the lavatory and came up smelling of *eau de Cologne*. I was violently critical of Robson. His problem was that he was not very intelligent. When I was at the *Sunday Times* it was arranged that I would go to Lancaster Gate for a one-to-one debate with him. We spoke for about two hours and we thrashed the whole thing out. I actually like Bobby Robson – I like most of the football people I come into contact with – but I regard journalism as an adversarial activity. If you go on criticising people for the right reasons and you do it honestly, you end up making many more friends than enemies.'

Shortly before England left for South America, and with calls for his head being bellowed from the rooftops of Fleet Street, Robson was presented with a gilt-edged chance to escape: 'Barcelona, the biggest club side in the world, contacted me, for the second time in my career, and offered me a fantastic package to take over. But I told them I still had three years to run on my contract and that I was not prepared to break it, so I recommended Terry Venables instead.'

Robson appeared to be on a hiding to nothing when he set off for South America with a young and inexperienced squad. But in the first match against Brazil in the intimidating atmosphere of the massive Maracana Stadium, he witnessed perhaps the most extraordinary result of his England career – as well as one of the great goals. John Barnes, a young winger with Watford, dribbled through half the Brazilian team from the halfway line to score a goal that was to be repeated over and over again on Brazilian TV for months to come. Mark Hateley, an old-fashioned centre-forward with Second Division Portsmouth, scored a second with a powerful header as England inflicted a rare defeat on the mighty Brazilians in their own back yard. A 2–0 defeat at the hands of Uruguay and a 0–0 draw with Chile followed, but the victory over Brazil had provided Robson with an unlikely, if short-lived, stay of execution.

England's World Cup qualifying campaign got off to a flying start in 1984/85 with victories over Finland (5–0), Turkey (8–0) and Northern Ireland (1–0), but the press began to sharpen the guillotine again at the end of the season when away draws with Finland and Romania were followed in May

1985 by a 1–0 defeat by Scotland at Hampden Park – a result which prompted Maxwell to insist on a front-page story in the *Daily Mirror* calling for Robson's dismissal. A triangular tournament in Mexico City in June, designed as a taster for the following year's World Cup, saw England beaten by Italy and Mexico before a 3–0 victory over West Germany helped the national side avoid a record fourth straight defeat.

The world of football, though, had bigger things to worry about than the performances of the England football team at this time. Shortly before England's summer tour 39 Juventus fans were killed during a riot before the European Cup final with Liverpool at the Heysel Stadium in Brussels. The images of the tragedy, beamed live to hundreds of millions of viewers around the globe, left football in a state of numbed shock. The apocalyptic sensationalism of the tabloids' coverage of the England scene now seemed grotesquely absurd. 'The club sides were immediately pulled out of European competition, and for a while I honestly thought the same would happen to the national side,' says Robson. 'Heysel was a horrible, horrible shock. You felt ashamed. It made you get your own worries into perspective.'

The following season, though, Robson had less to worry about than at any time since he took over. England finished top of their qualifying group and, although the failures to beat Northern Ireland and Romania at Wembley inevitably drew unfavourable reviews in the national press, Robson and his squad arrived in Mexico in buoyant mood on the back of an eleven-match unbeaten run. First stop, however, was a training camp in Colorado Springs in the Rocky Mountains, where it was felt the players could get used to the type of intense heat and high altitude they would experience in their group matches in Monterrey. After a send-off party laid on by Minister of Sport Dick Tracey at Government House, the England party flew off (with no fewer than 176 items of luggage) only to find a blizzard swirling around their base camp, the Broadmoor Hotel. For the first few days the hotel's saunas provided the only means of acclimatisation.

For Robson, though, the weather was just a minor irritation compared to the chilly buffeting he was receiving in the press from Sir Alf Ramsey, his predecessor at Ipswich and England. Robson had never got on particularly well with Ramsey and admitted that he always felt uncomfortable in his company. Shortly before the 1986 World Cup finals, they ran in to each other at a function and Robson, eager to pick the great man's mind on his experiences of Mexico in 1970, offered to give him a lift home. Ramsey replied coldly: 'I came by train and I shall return by train.' Robson admits that he was mystified by Ramsey's coldness towards him and positively astonished by his outspoken assaults on him in the newspapers, not least because Sir Alf was now accepting large sums of money from the people he used to treat with such contempt. Robson had plenty of other critics, the most ferocious of them former England players Keegan, Ball and Malcolm Macdonald, but he found it easier to come to terms with their snipings because Keegan had never even managed a football team while the other two had tried and failed. Ramsey's comments, though, hurt him as he felt that of all people, the last person to be undermining him should be a man who had experienced the pressures of the job himself. 'I don't really want to get into the Ramsey business, but it did hurt at the time,' recalls Robson. 'It's not what we needed before heading into a World Cup.'

The two and a half weeks hidden away deep in El Paso country proved to be a happy and relaxing period for the England players, who were joined by their wives and girlfriends for the second half of their stay. Between training sessions and conditioning, the squad lounged by the swimming pool and went on sight-seeing expeditions into Indian territory and stamina-building treks organised by officers at the local US Air Force Academy. While they were in the States, England played two competitive matches, beating World Cup hosts Mexico 3–0 on 17 May in front of 70,000 mostly Mexican immigrants at The Coliseum in Los Angeles, and then Canada a week later by a single goal in Vancouver. The Canadians played with all the physical subtlety you would expect from a country that gave the world the lumberjack in a match that almost proved disastrous for England's World Cup hopes. After crashing to the ground under a heavy challenge, Gary Lineker was led from the pitch clutching his left arm in obvious agony. Physiotherapist Fred Street and doctor Vernon Edwards feared a fracture, and the young Everton striker was rushed to a local hospital where, to Robson's relief, the doctors reported that he had suffered only a bad strain. England's only other injury, predictably, was Bryan Robson, who had dislocated his shoulder against Mexico and then picked up a hamstring injury.

Two days later, with Lineker's fragile arm now in a protective cast, the squad flew into Monterrey where they were escorted to their hotel, the Camino Real, by a police entourage of presidential proportions. Four police cars, six outriders and a helicopter, all manned by officers armed to the teeth with machine guns, pistols and stun grenades, sped the England party high into their luxurious mountain retreat. With Robson and Lineker recovering well from their injuries, the only setback to England's preparations came when team doctor Vernon Edwards collapsed having suffered a major heart attack.

England were widely expected to overcome the relatively lightweight challenges of Portugal, Morocco and Poland and win their qualifying group. Their first match in Monterrey's Technológico Stadium was against Portugal, a team who had beaten them just once – 3–1 in Oporto in 1955 – in fourteen meetings since 1947. Lineker's wrist had recovered enough for him to play wearing only a light padded bandage, while Robson had convinced his namesake manager that his battered body was in good enough condition for him to lead out his country. The final eleven on the teamsheet read: Shilton, Gary Stevens (of Everton, not the Tottenham player also in the squad), Butcher, Fenwick, Sansom, Wilkins, Hoddle, Robson, Lineker, Hateley, Waddle. It had rained so heavily in the days immediately before the match that Robson feared the game might be called off. With hindsight he probably wishes it had as England slumped to a 1–0 defeat when some Sunday park football defending allowed Carlos Manuel to pounce from close range. It was a shattering blow for Robson and England, who were lucky not to concede more against a lively and skilful Portuguese side. After four years of waiting, an unbeaten qualifying campaign and a month's intensive training, Robson's first-choice XI had fallen flat on their faces at the first hurdle against an opposition they were supposed to sail past.

The press were not coy about their feelings. 'DISASTER!' screamed the back page of the *Sun*, while 'WORLD CUP WALLIES' was the *Daily Mirror*'s message. The day after, the press attack switched to Robson himself. Under the headline 'FOOL ON THE HILL', John Sadler in the *Sun* gave it to him straight: 'Bobby Robson has returned to his hideaway up the road from Monterrey – but he's no longer being called the Maestro of the Mountains. To be honest he's in distinct danger of being renamed the Fool on the Hill.' Butcher and Sansom were the players to come in for the heaviest criticism, not least for their errors which led to Portugal's goal, but the wisdom of playing the dubiously fit Bryan Robson was also called into question.

Robson, though, refused to be swayed by the advice that came his way and named an unchanged line-up for England's second match against Morocco, an unknown quantity who were considered in English circles to be nothing more than an irrelevance thrown up by the statutory quota of African countries insisted upon by FIFA. The match was being seen as the make-or-break of England's World Cup and Robson's international career. 'Who would have thought England's hopes and, perhaps, Bobby's job would depend on 90 minutes against the unrated makeweights of Group F – Morocco?,' wrote John Sadler in the *Sun*. The match was a disaster for England, mitigated only by the fact that it finished goalless and thus left England with a chance of reaching the last sixteen. Apart from England's failure to see off the North Africans, Bryan Robson, 'Captain Marvel', was ruled out for the remainder of the tournament after dislocating his shoulder for the third (recorded) time in his career shortly before half time. The captain's arm band was tossed to Ray Wilkins, but minutes later he too was leaving the field – not in pain, but in disgrace. Wilkins, normally the most self-disciplined of players, in a rare fit of pique reacted to an offside decision by hurling the ball in the direction of the Paraguayan referee, who responded with a far more hurtful weapon: a red card. With hindsight, it can be seen that the next 45 minutes were the most crucial of Robson's time in charge. One lapse at the back and both England and Robson would have been packing their bags. England, though, survived the second half, and might even have won it as they produced their best football of the tournament to date.

Back home, the newspapers were in uproar. The front page of the *Sun* called it England's 'NIGHT OF SHAME', but the story was squeezed into a side column to make way for the news that Canadian snooker star Kirk Stevens was in a cocaine coma. There was, however, plenty of room at the back of the paper for the sub-editors to enjoy themselves: 'YOU MUGS!' ... 'DON'T LET 'EM LAUGH AT US' ... 'THEY WOULDN'T BEAT THE SALLY ARMY'. In his report, Alex Montgomery said the result was a humiliation 'against a team with no pedigree and no tradition from the Third World'. Nor was the criticism confined to the newspapers as England's fumbling displays sparked a stampede of former players eager to trample on Robson's reputation. Foremost among them were TV panellists Mick Channon and Emlyn Hughes, who called the England manager 'a stupid man'. Speculation about Robson's future dominated the newspaper columns as well as television and radio airtime in the five days before England's last group match against Poland. Robson, though, insisted he would not resign if England failed to beat the Poles. 'I am not going to pack it in. I have done the best I can but I suppose at the end of the day you are in the hands of players.' When the FA were called upon to say that they were sticking by the manager, Robson must have realised that his days were numbered – probably at about five. 'I want Bobby to stay on and I think the whole of the International Committee would agree,' said Dick Wragg. But what else could he say? 'I want Bobby to go if we lose'?

Two days after the Morocco match Robson unwittingly provided a photographer with an image that was worth more than a million words of negative comment. He was captured with his hands over his ears and his elbows on the railing of his hotel balcony staring downwards as if in miserable contemplation. He was the very picture of despair and the image was splashed all over the nation's papers. What the photograph didn't reveal, though, was that Robson was actually listening to Whitney Houston on his Walkman and was simply pressing the headphones into his ears. But what the heck.

'BOBBY'S LAST STAND – THE VULTURES ARE READY TO SWOOP' declared the *Sun* on the eve of the Poland game. Robson says now that it was during those five days that he began to understand the behavioural pattern of 'the vultures' in the press. 'The difficulty of the job is the press,' he says. 'If you strip away the pressure of the press it's a marvellous job. You work with great players, you work for mainly good people at the FA, you are also working for the country who are basically behind you, you travel to some wonderful places around the world and you get paid a reasonable amount of money for doing it. But the press will condition and brainwash the public [at this point Robson lets out a howl of pain] – if you say something over and over again, then eventually the public will believe it. It's often dressed up as public opinion, but it's just what the editors want their journalists to say. But it's *not* public opinion. When we were in Mexico I realised that many of the reporters were under pressure to write particular types of story. After one press meeting before the Poland match the reporters were all filing their stories around the hotel. I went out to sit by the swimming pool where I heard one reporter, Steve Curry, who I liked because his criticism was always constructive, making a telephone call just around the corner. I wasn't paying much attention but my ears pricked up when I heard him say, "But Bobby didn't say that and I don't want to write that. That's not how it is here." I realised he was obviously speaking to his editor or someone back at base in London, and it brought home to me that he was under pressure to twist a story about me and England so that it was negative.'

Journalists and editors will argue that they are only as fickle as England's performances, that a story is only relevant for the day on which it is printed and that today's newspapers are tomorrow's fish and chips paper (at least until the European Commission decided that newspaper ink posed a risk to the health of the English people). Indeed, twenty-four hours after the whole of Fleet Street had been predicting the end of the world as England knew it, the headlines were trumpeting the country's glory to the heavens. England thrashed Poland, their most dangerous rivals in Group F, as Gary Lineker, inspired by the wizardry of Liverpool's Peter Beardsley, suddenly hit form and bagged a stunning hat-trick. The *Sun* beamed 'ROBSON LIONHEARTS ARE ON THE MARCH' and said of England's battered manager: 'He started with his head on the block and ended with it high in the clouds.' Robson had been reminded that ninety minutes is a long time in football, and the following day he admitted he would have quit if England had lost. 'If I was at a press conference or in front of the TV cameras then I would have said, "I've done my best, and if that's what you want then bye-bye." '

The England party headed off for Mexico City where they would face the little-known and even less fancied Paraguayans at the start of the knockout stage of the tournament. England had never played Paraguay, a country with a population of just under four million sandwiched at the heart of the South American continent between Argentina, Brazil, Uruguay and Bolivia. Howard Wilkinson and Dave Sexton, Robson's 'eyes' when his own were focused on other matters, had reported back that England had little to fear from a team that was fitfully dangerous in attack and consistently poor in defence.

Unable to unearth any scandals within the England camp itself during this time, the news hounds had to settle for knocking the team hotel, the Valle de Mexico, which, situated in the ugly surroundings of an industrial estate, was described as a 'dump'. It was not Robson's first-choice hotel but the players had insisted on being as near to the training ground as possible. After three days of noise from the local traffic and complaints from the players about non-flushing toilets and cold showers, Robson and his squad moved out to the quieter and more luxurious Holiday Inn. The only other 'extra-curricular' story to arise during the week before the match was a front-page splash in the *Sun* headlined 'DOLE'. An England fan is pictured wearing a T-shirt saying DHSS WORLD TOUR 86 and holding a sultry local girl in one hand and a cocktail in the other. The story claimed that dozens of unemployed England fans were enjoying a month of sun, sea, lager and football at the taxpayers' expense.

Paraguay, as predicted, were no match for an England team whose confidence had surged after their dramatic discovery of form in the Poland match. In front of a crowd of 100,000 at the Aztec Stadium Lineker scored twice to take his goal tally to five, while Beardsley grabbed the other, England's second, just moments after Lineker had been carried from the field for treatment after being punched in the throat by Delgado. The Paraguayans had started brightly but they grew more fractious by the minute and began to badger the Syrian referee and roll around on the ground in apparent agony as if auditioning for a part in a local pantomime. It was a highly professional performance from Robson's side with Lineker and Beardsley establishing their reputation as the most effective strike pairing in the competition.

Victory set up a quarter-final clash with Argentina, a fixture that the organisers, the security forces and the respective governments of the two countries least wanted to see. It was to be the first time the two teams had met since the end of the Falklands War, and within minutes of the final whistle at the Paraguay game Robson had found himself playing the role of Foreign Secretary as reporters fired questions at him about the political significance of the encounter. He insisted that he was 'a football manager not a politician', but there was no escaping the fact that this match carried a significance that extended well beyond the touchlines of the Aztec Stadium. Predictably, the *Sun*, the most bellicose and nationalistic of the British papers during the conflict, led the battle cry. 'BRING ON THE ARGIES, ENGLAND VICTORY SETS UP BATTLE' bellowed its front page after the victory over Paraguay, and two days later the paper declared 'IT'S WAR SEÑOR'. There were reports that thousands of Argentinian veterans from the war were on their way to exact revenge for 'Las Malvinas', while some of England's 'crack' hooligans were also said to have answered the unspoken call to arms and were boarding flights in their scores. The forces of law and order were taking no chances and thousands of troops were placed on alert while helicopter gunships and armoured cars were called in to keep the peace between 5,000 England and 10,000 Argentinian fans. The England party were also given four armed guards to escort them on the coach to and from the ground, while a decoy coach would be waiting at the stadium so that the squad could escape unnoticed in the event of a riot.

Over 115,000 fans were packed into the giant concrete bowl of the Aztec Stadium while a record British TV audience for a football match tuned in for the game, the main events of which are well known even to those with only a passing interest in the affairs of the national football side. For entirely different reasons, Argentina's two goals remain two of the most talked about in the history of the World Cup. The first, Maradona's infamous 'Hand of God' goal, broke the deadlock five minutes after the break; his second, four minutes later, broke English hearts. The BBC commentator Barry Davies screamed in near orgasmic excitement at the time: 'You have to say that was magnificent!' The Argentinian underlined why he was widely considered the best player of his generation in the world by dribbling from the halfway mark through half the England team, leaving Peter Reid, Terry Fenwick and Terry Butcher puffing like tired old pit ponies in his wake, before sliding the ball under Shilton. England, to their credit, were galvanised into a stirring comeback, and Robson's introduction of John Barnes almost brought off a remarkable recovery. Barnes crossed for Lineker to head England back into the game, and then repeated the action just before the end only for Lineker to miss his header by an inch.

By very fair means and very foul, England were out of the World Cup. In the changing-room many of England's players were in tears, but there was also anger that the Tunisian referee had allowed Maradona's first goal. Television pictures and 'stills' clearly showed the little Argentinian dunking the ball basketball-style into the net as Shilton rose to gather Hodge's fluffed overhead clearance. England's players had chased the referee all over the pitch after the goal was awarded, and Robson stood anxiously on the touchline hoping the linesman would confirm Maradona's sleight of hand to the referee. It never happened, and afterwards Robson could only rue what might have been had England gone on to play Belgium in the semi-finals.

The *Sun*, predictably, were not impressed, but the paper's indignation was directed not at Robson and the England players but at the Argentinian villain of the piece and the South American nation as a whole. In an ironic reference to the famous headline 'GOTCHA!' which followed the sinking of the *Belgrano* battleship, the front page of the paper howled: 'OUTCHA! ARGIES GET THEIR OWN BACK ON US'. 'Brave England last night failed to prevent the Revenge of the Argies,' ran the report. 'The South Americans knocked us out of the World Cup to get their own back for the hammering they took in the Falklands War four years ago.' The back-page headline left little room for doubt about the paper's interpretation of Maradona's idea of fair play, reading simply: 'DIEGO THE CHEAT'.

Robson, though, emboldened by England's improved form in their final three matches and with Maradona's handball diverting criticism away from the England camp, could face the press with confidence. 'You shouldn't get decisions like that in the World Cup. That decision cost us the result. The match was so close it ruined everything for us.' The England manager, who almost certainly had come within one result of losing his job before the Poland match, confirmed he would be staying in charge for England's European Championship campaign. 'It's a unique position and it takes two years to get to know it. We reached the last eight and went out to one of the best sides in the world in very unfortunate circumstances. It has been a great experience and I believe I am a better international manager now than I was two months ago.'

When England arrived in West Germany for the 1988 European Championship finals, they were being widely touted, mainly outside of Britain, as one of the favourites. They had sailed through their qualifying group against Yugoslavia, Turkey and Northern Ireland with five victories and a draw from six matches, scoring nineteen goals in the process. The Turks were thrashed 8–0 at Wembley but England saved their most impressive performance until last when they swept aside a much-vaunted Yugoslavia side 4–1 in Belgrade in November 1987. England's breathtaking attacking football in the first half of that match did much to silence the increasingly vociferous band of critics who had pilloried Robson earlier in the year during a four-match winless sequence which saw them lose to West Germany and draw with Scotland, Brazil and Turkey. But the sharpening of knives could be heard again in the first few months of 1988 when England drew 0–0 with Israel in Tel Aviv, 2–2 with Holland at Wembley, 0–0 with Hungary in Budapest and 1–1 against Colombia in their last match at Wembley before setting off to Germany. Robson was forced to remind his insatiable critics that England had lost just two games in the two years since Mexico.

England were drawn in the same group as Holland, the Republic of Ireland and the USSR, and Robson was eager for success and confident it could be achieved, despite fears that the ban on English clubs following Heysel had left English players short of experience at the highest level, simply treading water in a sea of technical mediocrity. 'I had been in the job for nearly six years and I thought we had a very good, balanced team when we went to Germany. I wanted to go down in the history books and I wanted it very badly,' he recalls. 'That's why you take the job. I wanted to push myself and England to the very limit. As it turned out I now think of those few weeks as the lowest point of my time in charge. Everything about it was just very, very depressing.'

England's first match was against the Republic of Ireland who had reached the finals of a major competition under the bullish, no-nonsense Englishman Jack Charlton. England were outright favourites to beat the Irish, who were derided in many circles as nothing more than a group of second-rate English journeymen who had qualified to play for the country by virtue of having a grandmother who had once been to Ireland on a holiday. England played all the football and created a host of chances, but Lineker was unusually sluggish (he was later diagnosed as suffering from jaundice) and Ireland made them pay as Ray Houghton converted one of Ireland's three chances in the match. England could still qualify, but the *Sun* urged Robson to cut his losses and run. 'ON YER BIKE, ROBSON' was the unequivocal message on the following day's back page. Inside, John Sadler predicted: 'If Robson fails and England do not even qualify from group matches then it is impossible for him to survive. Public opinion would be of such intensity that the FA would have no option but to make a change.' In his match report Alex Montgomery said England were stuffed like 'fourth division nobodies . . . It was a defeat – it was a disaster – and a national disaster at that.'

If England's footballers had arrived as something of an unknown quantity, the same could not be said of their supporters. The violence involving England fans was the worst that had ever been seen at a major championship, prompting the *Sun* to run the front-page headline 'WORLD WAR THREE', which carried more than a discomforting whiff of patriotic pride. The ugly images of running battles with police and rival fans that were beamed around the world served only to dramatise the sense of shame and humiliation of England's performances on the field.

Hopes of qualifying from their group ended in England's next match with a 3–1 defeat at the hands of the eventual champions, Holland, for whom Marco Van Basten scored a stunning hat-trick. If England had performed creditably against a highly talented Dutch side boasting the talents of Ruud Gullit and Frank Rijkaard as well as Van Basten, their performance in the 3–1 defeat against the Russians was inexcusably dire. For once the *Sun*'s headline 'A GUTLESS SPINELESS SHOWER' seemed just about spot on after a display curiously lacking any sign of pride and fight. Inside, the paper produced a picture of Robson with a cone-shaped dunce's cap superimposed on his head next to a story detailing 'The ramblings of the bungling boss who brought shame to England'.

Robson found himself under attack from virtually every direction at the end of a traumatic week in which England's reputation abroad plumbed new lows. The *Observer*, though, went out of its way to praise the dignity of the national manager. 'It's hard to have a decent wake when so many people are confused about the identity of the corpse,' wrote Hugh McIlvanney, who feared that a ban on the international team would have disastrous consequences for English football. 'But Bobby Robson has handled the cruel demands implicit in a stunning loss to the Republic of Ireland and a more predictable beating inflicted by Holland with admirable dignity. Keeping control of his emotions, even injecting a little humour into press conferences reflected immense credit on the manager.' What a shame, Robson must have thought, that more people didn't read the *Observer*. Jack Charlton, the original mastermind of Robson's misery, also came out in his fellow Geordie's defence. 'I just wouldn't take all the aggravation that Bobby is suffering,' he said. 'If I was returning home to be hounded and booed the way he is going to be, I'd be off.'

'The 1988 European Championships were the worst period of my time in charge,' recalls Robson. 'Apart from all the nonsense going on off the pitch, from a football point of view it was heart-breaking because we lost all three matches having played very well in the first two. We were very unlucky to lose against Ireland and Holland, but that can happen in international football. In the Irish game, we had seventeen strikes at goal, they had three, and we lost 1–0. It was one of those matches in which you can play very well and still not win, and you got that feeling that the harder you try to score the less likely it is to happen. But that's a commonplace of international football. If you fail to take your chances or you make a mistake you'll be punished for it. If you make a little error, like you play for offside and you're half a yard out or you underhit a backpass, then you'll almost certainly get punished – the ball will finish in the back of the net. If you make a mistake at League level there's less chance of it resulting in a goal and then you have 41 games to make up for it; at international level, you often only get one chance. For me, the European Championships highlighted how much you are at the mercy of forces beyond your own control.

'It was also a painful reminder that with England you're representing the whole population, not just a small area of it. At Ipswich, it was Ipswich and Suffolk people you affected, but with England it's the young lad in Stockport, the old lady in Plymouth and the bloke selling petrol in Carlisle. You are aware of this the whole time, especially when you walk out on to the pitch at Wembley and you see the crowd and all the flags. The pressure obviously is intense and if you don't win then I'm afraid it's just the way it is, but you will be in for some very heavy criticism indeed. When I was there I think the criticism was OTT. It got very personal, vindictive and vitriolic. But I tried to deal with it by saying to myself: "I'm not going to behave like them. I'm going to be above that." It got under my skin, of course. I am a human being with blood and veins. I had a family and I know they were hurt and my boys would say to me, "Is it worth it, Dad?" It was dreadful when you lose like we did in 1988, but when you win ... it's the greatest feeling in the world, better than anything you will experience at club level. What better feeling can you have as a football person than to know that you and the players have made the whole country feel good about itself? And what worse when you lose?'

Between the disastrous European Championships and the 1990 World Cup finals in Italy, Robson experienced that losing feeling just once: a 2–1 defeat by Uruguay in England's last match at Wembley before setting off for the Mediterranean. The statistics of the period back up Robson's subsequent contention that he was getting better at his job – played nineteen, won ten, drew eight – yet England, despite being unbeaten in their qualifying matches, made it to Italia 90 literally by about an inch. In their final qualifier, a nerve-jangling 0–0 draw with Poland in Katowice in October 1989, an eighty-ninth-minute shot shuddered Peter Shilton's cross bar. Had it gone in, Sweden would have gone through in their place. And far from finally being treated with a bit of respect, Robson found himself subjected to ever more intense and personal attacks, and by the start of Italia 90 the relationship between the press and the England camp had completely broken down. Suspicion on both sides had given way to open hostility and the vicious circle of mutual antipathy which had been slowly rotating throughout Robson's time in charge span out of control. The press criticised the England camp, the England camp grew less helpful towards the press, the press were annoyed and increased their attacks, and the England camp – apart from Robson, the most vilified of them all – refused to co-operate with the press.

'At 1990 there was no real relationship between the press and players at all,' recalls Brian Glanville. 'It became ludicrous.

They simply refused to speak to us. But relations between the press and footballers have generally been getting worse and worse down the years. This is partly down to the enormous pressure placed by tabloids on general news reporters to uncover scandals about the players, but I think all reporters for the tabloids are under great pressure to write much more vilifying and critical pieces. I remember Ted Croker, the former FA secretary, complaining to us about the press, saying: "We're not talking about you sports people, we're talking about the rotters." So we nicknamed these people, the news reporters, "the rotters".

'David Beckham was recently quoted as saying that he just never speaks to journalists. In the past this was just unthinkable. For many years as football correspondent for the *Sunday Times* covering England, you had your friends among the players. People talk about Alf Ramsey being anti-press, but in retrospect when you consider the people who followed him, he was actually very benign. During Ramsey's time on these long tours of Latin America press and players used to mix quite freely. I often used to sit next to Francis Lee on these trips and I was very friendly with many of them: George Cohen, Jimmy Greaves, Bobby Moore and plenty of others. Then, the idea that players didn't speak to journalists was out of the question. Now, the problem is that footballers have become so rich. They think they're above it all. Things have deteriorated, there is no doubt about it. There is a paranoia floating around football. Players and managers don't differentiate between people who are going to turn them over and those who are not.

'I think things reached a climax in 1990 when there was a terrible tension between the press and the players. This was largely because Bobby and Bryan Robson, the manager and the captain, had both been turned over by the news reporters. The tabloids were running all sorts of squalid stories about Bobby Robson's private life. All this was being done by the news reporters, not by us – over the years there has been an entire conspiracy of silence among football reporters to hush up these stories. They made our lives considerably more difficult. There was never much confrontation with the news reporters, but we made it perfectly clear what we thought of them.'

And there are a number of examples of reporters setting out to stitch up the England manager. Robson is famous among players he has coached and the press for forgetting people's names – even those of people he has worked alongside for years. Bryan Robson, his captain throughout his eight years in charge, recalled how once the manager had greeted him at breakfast with a 'Good morning, Bobby!' The *Telegraph*'s Bryon Butler recalls how one journalist set a trap for Robson before England's 1–1 draw with Saudi Arabia in Riyadh in November 1988. It was England's third match after the disastrous European Championships and the campaign to have Robson removed was still in full swing. 'One tabloid sports reporter who was very much in the anti-Robson camp asked him at a news conference what he thought of the Saudi manager and mentioned a specific name. Robson replied with the usual stuff: "I'm sure he'll keep it tight at the back and then try and hit us on the break", and so on. When he finished, the journalist said: "Well, actually, so and so was sacked a few months ago and the manager now is so and so." Next day the headlines, predictably, were 'WHAT A PLONKER' and 'IN THE NAME OF ALLAH, GO!' The idea was that if Robson didn't even know who his opposing manager was then he had obviously lost the plot.'

Robson says that the only newspaper he and his wife Elsie read during his time in charge was the *Guardian*. Looking at the front page of the *News of the World* on 27 May 1990 it is easy to understand why. The paper had decided that Robson's private life was a subject of legitimate moral interest to the nation. Under the headline 'ROBSON'S OTHER WOMEN' the newspaper alleged that there were three 'love secrets' in addition to two others that had already been exposed. Referring to him throughout the piece as 'Romeo Robson', the paper revealed 'No.3 Blonde Bosom Buddy – No.4 Dishy Dutch Treat – No.5 Soccer Star's Missus', all of whom apparently had fallen to the charms of 'the silver-tongued Robson'. 'That was unfair,' says Rob Shepherd, football correspondent for the *Express* but then working for the now defunct *Today*. 'Robson never spoke publicly about morality. He wasn't a fair target. If a manager starts to expound his moral views on subjects then he is putting those opinions on the line and inviting a reaction to them. But Robson never did that. He never preached to anyone about anything not relating to football. The problem is that top football people now enjoy superstar celebrity status and the front ends of newspapers have inevitably started taking an interest in them. It's bad news for the sports reporters because all journalists get categorised as one group, but what can you do about it? You can't go up to the general news desk and say, "I don't think you should be running that story." They would tell you to fuck off.'

Apart from the fact that Robson was a football manager and not the Archbishop of Canterbury or a Cabinet minister whose personal morality could be regarded as falling within the public interest, the allegations are all the more extraordinary as Robson had just announced that he was leaving the England job after the World Cup and would be taking a job with PSV Eindhoven in Holland. Those who wanted him out of his job had got what they wanted. In the sports pages of that *News of the World* edition Robson was also described as 'the most vilified Englishman since Lord Haw Haw – and they hanged him as a wartime traitor'. It was not his decision to leave the job, but the FA's, yet the insinuation was that he was betraying his country for securing his future by taking a job with PSV. It is not difficult to understand why Robson had reached the point where he thought he could not win no matter what he did. With hindsight it becomes all the more incredible that throughout Italia 90 he cheerfully continued to co-operate with the press at all, and all the easier to understand why the England squad felt that their country's press appeared to be bent on breaking their morale. It was a typically messy English affair which, regardless of which camp you were in – the England squad or the press corps – reeked of hypocrisy and gratuitous malevolence. At around the same time, Franz Beckenbauer had told the West German FA that he would be resigning after the World Cup to take a job with Bayern Munich. There was not a word of criticism, but back in Little England Robson was being slaughtered for the crime of being forced out of his job against his will.

But football was not the only area of sporting life invaded

by the news journalists during the 1980s. Mike Collett, a veteran of Fleet Street for 22 years and currently the global football editor for Reuters, the world's biggest international news agency, recalls the 'rotters' invasion of the Wimbledon tennis championships. 'The news guys would go to John McEnroe's press conferences with the sole purpose of goading and winding him up, hoping that he would explode,' he says. 'I remember a fight breaking out on one occasion between two rival tabloid journalists, one from the news and the other from sports. The news guy asked McEnroe a provocative question about his private life, hoping to get a rise out of him, and immediately the sports guy jumped to his feet and told him to shut up. A few moments later they were trading blows. McEnroe just sat there smiling while it was going on, and then said, "You two seem good enough at making your own trouble." Then he just walked out.

'Football players and other sportsmen often think that all journalists are on the same side, but that is not the case. Within the press corps there are lots of running battles between the various factions. I remember at the Mexico World Cup in 1986 I was working for one of the international news agencies and we all found ourselves being frozen out by the English newspaper boys. They don't like the agencies because they know that shortly after the press conference the stories will be on the wires where they picked up Teletext, the radio, TV and the evening newspapers. It is a problem for them because there is a long delay between them getting their stories and them appearing in the papers the following day, during which time the news will come out some other way. You can understand their anxiety, but it often leads to a very confrontational and unpleasant atmosphere. In Mexico, we were so frustrated about being denied access to the players that we went to see Glen Kirton, the FA's press officer of the time, so he set up separate interview sessions for us. In the end, it worked to our advantage because every day the likes of Bryan Robson, Glenn Hoddle, Ray Wilkins and Peter Shilton would come and talk to us for up to an hour safe in the knowledge that we were going to talk about football and not turn them over. The same thing happened in France 98 where on two occasions I had a toe-to-toe shouting match with guys from the tabloids who didn't want me to file my story because they would have had no original story for the next day.'

One man who found himself at the epicentre of the media storm during Italia 90 was David Bloomfield, the FA's press officer, who had the unenviable job of trying to placate both camps. Bloomfield recalls his amazement at Robson's relentless cheerfulness in the face of the most personalised attacks to which a football figure in Britain had ever been subjected. 'There are a number of reasons,' says Bloomfield. 'He loved talking – full stop. He particularly loved talking about football. He didn't hold any grudges, he wanted to get his point across rather than let silence lead to misunderstandings, but above all he was an incredibly patriotic man and I think he felt a great sense of duty to the English public. He was the first manager who made it on to the front pages of the newspaper on a regular basis, and it was unfortunate for him that the conflict between the *Sun* and the *Mirror* was at its height. There was a rough parity of circulation between the two papers at the time which made the battle to be Britain's best-selling paper all the more intense. At one match I got talking to two journalists who didn't know who I was, and they said, "We are here to fry Bobby Robson."

'Much of the problem in Italy was caused by the news reporters. They had to come back from their overseas adventure having justified their salary and expenses with the most salacious and dramatic stories possible. These guys were there for one big hit, they weren't there for the long haul, and thus they felt no obligation to build up any relationship with the England camp because a couple of days later they would be assigned to another story. When their stories appeared in the papers, the players didn't stop to differentiate between the news and sports reporters. As far as the players were concerned the reporters are all on the same team, so they decided to withdraw their co-operation *en masse*. It was a strange situation for me because I had a foot in both camps, although my allegiance lay with the players. One night I would have dinner with the players and they would all be analysing and moaning about the press. The next night I would be having dinner with the press and they would all be analysing and moaning about the England team, discussing team line-ups and tactics and so on. You would have thought it would be the other way round: the journalists would be talking about journalism and the football people talking about football.'

Ten days before their opening group match against the Republic of Ireland, England flew out of their base camp in Sardinia for a final warm-up match against Tunisia. A late goal by Steve Bull brought a 1–1 draw, but it did not spare England a lashing in the press. According to the *News of the World*, after the match 'the continent of Africa will reverberate with mocking laughter at England's obvious unease'. It transpired after the match that Terry Butcher had headbutted an opponent, leading to calls for him to be sent home in disgrace – calls which Robson rejected. England's failure to beat the North Africans and the subsequent refusal to punish Butcher provoked a furious response from the *Sun*. 'PATHETIC! ARROGANT! SMUG!' screamed the headline as the paper set up a phone line on the 'big England crisis!' inviting its readers to air their views on the Butcher incident. Robson, meanwhile, pointed out that there were no calls for Ronald Koeman to be sent home after he had rugby tackled an Austrian player a few days earlier.

On 8 June, three days before England's opening match, the *Sun* stepped up their campaign against Robson by running a front-page story reporting that his brother Keith had had a heart attack while at work in Middlesbrough and had been rushed to hospital. At the end of a short story, the paper implied that the attack had been brought on by the recent behaviour of his famous brother. It said: 'Brother Bobby caused uproar shortly before the team left for the World Cup when he revealed he was quitting to join top Dutch club PSV Eindhoven.' A few days later, the news reporters whipped up another controversy when it was claimed that a local girl, 'olive-skinned' Isabella Ciaravolo, who was working at England's hotel, the Is Molas, had enjoyed some fun under the duvet with three unnamed members of the England squad. The story was run shortly after the players' wives and girlfriends had returned to England, and for several days afterwards the telephone lines between Sardinia and England buzzed with reassurances from the squad members that the story was no more than spiteful fabrication. The story was never substantiated, and a friend of the girl accused told the press that there were a number reasons why Isabella would not have gone to bed with any of the players, chief among them being that 'England are the ugliest team in the World Cup'. Bryon Butler of the *Daily Telegraph* recalls being bemused by the scandal: 'I was staying at the England hotel during the World Cup and we all knew the girl. It was absolutely ridiculous. She was just a normal Roman Catholic family girl. It was total nonsense.'

Robson stuck up for his players and was lambasted by an editorial in the *Daily Mirror* – the paper that ran the original story – for his troubles. The three-in-a-bed scandal served only to force the England squad deeper into their self-imposed isolation, and the relationship with reporters got so bad that players began to call their team-mates 'scab' if they were seen talking to the press. Jeff Powell in the *Daily Mail* accused the 'sullen' England players of 'retreating into fortress paranoia' and 'polluting the atmosphere in a cloud of arrogance and suspicion'. He added: 'Small minds never won great trophies. World Cups are conquered by gifted adults, not spoiled boys.' Powell, though, made a point of singling out Robson for his decency in the face of animosity. 'Amazingly, the most vilified individual of all is retaining his integrity to the bitter end ... Bobby Robson accommodates even the most sadistic of his persecutors with great dignity.'

If victimisation by the press was one thing Robson could have predicted, another was that his captain and namesake Bryan would either be carrying an injury or would pick one up that would rule him out of the competition at some stage. The inspirational Manchester United midfielder was the first name his manager wrote on the England team-sheet throughout his time in charge; unfortunately, though, his name was more often than not the first to go down on the casualty list at the hospital or the physiotherapist's. The list of serious injuries he has sustained during his career is so long it is remarkable that he still managed to become the fifth most capped England player in history with 90 appearances. (For the record, Robson suffered three broken legs, two dislocated shoulders, two broken noses, concussion twice, a broken finger, severely torn ankle ligaments, torn hamstrings twice, rib damage, a hairline fracture of the leg, a hernia, a torn Achilles' tendon, damaged toes, bruised heels and a severely bruised foot twice.)

Despite carrying an assortment of knocks, Robson made England's first game against Jack Charlton's Ireland. England's full line-up makes for impressive reading: Shilton, Stevens, Butcher, Walker, Pearce, Waddle, Gascoigne, Robson, Barnes, Beardsley, Lineker. England had four of the most exciting ball players in European football in Gascoigne, Waddle, Barnes and Beardsley, but in a howling gale and against an Irish side whose first object was to disrupt the opposition, there was precious little football played in what was universally described as the worst game of football anyone could remember. It finished 1–1, Kevin Sheedy having equalised Lineker's early goal sixteen minutes from time. Earlier in a woeful day for British football Scotland were beaten by Costa Rica (the joke doing the rounds in offices the next day was that now the Scots can't even beat a brand of coffee), and one Italian newspaper ran the headline 'NO FOOTBALL PLEASE, WE'RE BRITISH' while another described the match as 'PEASANT FOOTBALL'. The *Daily Mail*'s Ian Wooldridge, the sports writer of the year, said of the England match: 'Have you ever witnessed a more embarrassing exhibition of wasted energy and spilled adrenalin? It was like watching Aldershot play Aldershot reserves.' The *Sun* was so appalled by the performance it suggested in a front-page editorial piece that England should pull out of the World Cup. In the sports pages, there was a picture of Robson walking towards a bicycle – and straight into the perfect tabloid photo opportunity under the headline 'ON YER BIKE'. The press inquisition the following morning was, according to Robson, 'the most intense' he had ever experienced. 'I was taken aback by the hostility and the pessimism,' he recalls. 'We had drawn a match in very difficult conditions against a team who were the third most successful in world football the year before, and everyone was talking as if our World Cup was over. I pointed out that Argentina,

Scotland and the Russians had all lost to supposedly inferior opposition and that we were still in a good position to go through. But it was a tough session. They really went for me.'

Despite the criticism, Robson took the biggest tactical gamble of his managerial career for England's next match against European champions Holland when he decided to play Mark Wright as a sweeper alongside Paul Parker, Stuart Pearce, Des Walker and Terry Butcher. Robson, like Greenwood before him, was accused of succumbing to player pressure and criticised for experimenting with an alien system in a vital World Cup campaign. Don Howe, Robson's right-hand man, denied that a players' revolt had forced Robson into the switch. 'The suggestion that Bobby is indecisive is bloody nonsense, put about by people who don't know him or just want to knock him,' said Howe. 'It seems to stem from the fact that he is prepared to listen to the opinions of others.' In the end, Robson's bold decision was rewarded by an excellent team performance in a highly entertaining contest. England dominated the game and had 'goals' by Lineker and Pearce disallowed. The Holland players, riven by in-fighting throughout their World Cup campaign, admitted they were lucky to escape with a point. The group was yet to produce a win and had come to be dubbed 'The Group of Sleep' because of the lack of goals, but England were in pole position to go through to the last sixteen as they faced Egypt, supposedly the weakest team, in their final match. 'We knew that if we didn't come through against Egypt then we didn't deserve to go any further,' says Robson.

The day after the Holland match Bryan Robson informed the manager that he had sent for a faith healer, Olga Stringfellow, in a desperate final bid to sort out his Achilles' tendon problem, which was getting worse each time he took the field. Robson, convinced that they would be unable to keep Stringfellow's presence a secret, told his captain that he was worried by the inevitable uproar in the press. The FA said that they were happy for her to come so long as they were not associated with her. Robson's fears proved well-founded. On the day of her arrival FA chief executive Graham Kelly called him to say that the story was on the front page of the *Sun* and that the paper had had a reporter on the plane with her. The tabloid news stories about the England squad were now coming thick and fast: Gascoigne was spotted larking about in a hotel on the wrong end of a few pints of lager, while Barnes was upset by a story in the *Daily Mirror* which claimed he had had a difficult childhood growing up in Jamaica.

Robson abandoned the sweeper system for the Egypt match, reverting to a flat back four and dropping Butcher for the first time since his old boss at Ipswich had taken charge of the national side. It was a highly disappointing game, with Barnes and Waddle again curiously ineffective on the flanks. It was settled midway through the second half by a towering header by Wright from Gascoigne's free-kick. At the final whistle, the Egyptians were so upset that many of them rolled around on the pitch in tears. The goalkeeper, Shoubeir, went into hysterics and had to be treated by medical staff. England, meanwhile, returned to the hotel to celebrate with a champagne dinner as they looked ahead to a last sixteen clash with the highly rated Belgians in Bologna on 26 June.

Relations with the media reached a new low on the eve of the Belgium match when the local press officer, Signore Machiavelli, switched venues for the press conference at the last minute. When the reporters finally found their way to the training ground for the rearranged meeting, Machiavelli allowed only the Italian press inside. The English press corps were understandably furious, and matters got worse when the England players were boarding the coach to return to the hotel. When Paul Parker got off the coach to speak to a reporter from the *Evening Standard*, Gascoigne sparked a scene when he threw a paper cup full of water at the pair before Parker was dragged back inside by his team-mates, who took exception to him talking to the press.

Meanwhile, Bryan Robson was coming to terms with having kicked his last ball in a World Cup after the spiritual powers of Olga Stringfellow failed to heal his injured Achilles' tendon. England's only other injury was to the manager himself, who cracked his ribs when he slipped getting out of the hotel swimming pool. The captain's place went to Liverpool's Steve McMahon, whose blunder against Ireland after he had come on as a substitute had led to Sheedy's equaliser. He would play alongside Gascoigne in the heart of the midfield with Lineker the lone striker and Barnes and Waddle on the flanks, while Robson reverted to playing Wright at sweeper and brought back Butcher in a five-man defence. Belgium, though, were sure to present stiff opposition with players of the calibre of Preud'homme, Gerets, Scifo, Ceulemans and De Gryse in their ranks.

In the event, the match proved to be one of the most entertaining of the finals as both sides, freed from the shackles of ensuring they qualified from the group stages, attacked each other with the cut and thrust of medieval duellists. Scifo and Ceulemans both cracked an upright, Barnes missed an open goal and then had a perfectly good goal disallowed for offside, and Waddle was a constant threat as he took on defenders and bombarded the Belgian box with a string of crosses. It was anybody's game. Midway through the second half Robson sent on Platt for McMahon in what later proved to be the crucial decision of the game, and three minutes later he pulled off Barnes and sent on Bull. Extra time saw no let-up in the tension, but it seemed the match would have to be settled on penalties before some quick thinking by a shattered-looking Gascoigne and a flash of genius from Platt saw England snatch victory with just seconds left on the clock. Gascoigne was dumped by Gerets wide on the left, and from the ensuing free-kick he floated a perfect curling ball into the box. Platt had timed his run to perfection, and as the ball dropped over his right shoulder he swivelled and struck a stunning volley past Preud'homme. England, perhaps a shade luckily, had reached the quarter-finals of the World Cup for the second successive time.

Next stop was Naples, to face Cameroon, who became the first African side to reach the last eight of the World Cup and had guaranteed themselves the status of tournament darlings by beating reigning champions Argentina in the opening game despite being reduced to nine men. The Africans played their football with a potent mix of exuberant skill and clumsy brutality, and in Roger Milla (officially 38, but some reports said he was as old as 44) they had a striker as deadly and in-form as any in the tournament. Robson made just one change from the Belgian game, retaining substitute Platt for McMahon, and he also decided to stick with the sweeper system. It was another emotion-convulsing classic, even more open and incident-filled than the memorable game against Belgium. After riding an early onslaught from 'The Lions', England took the lead with a bullet header from Platt to set them on course for a semi-final showdown with West Germany, who had beaten Czechoslovakia earlier in the day. Cameroon, though, were playing the better football as they sliced up England's defence with an ease and frequency that had Robson throwing the tea cups around at the interval.

In the second half, the Africans' greater adventure was rewarded when they took the lead with two goals in four minutes. Gascoigne, who had barely put a foot right all night, tripped Milla in the area. Kunde converted the penalty, and moments later the jubilant Africans were lying in another green, red and yellow heap by the corner flag when Ekeke put them in front. Biyik came close to killing the game when he narrowly missed adding a third with a cocky back-heel. ('There would have been no way back from there,' admits Robson.) The manager immediately rung the changes, sending on Trevor Steven for Butcher and abandoning the sweeper system. Perhaps mindful of his error in felling Milla, the hyperactive Gascoigne suddenly sprung to life and began to boss the match from midfield. With eight minutes remaining he split the Cameroon defence with a slide-rule pass to Lineker, who was brought crashing to earth by Kunde just inside the area. Lineker converted from the spot and the match went into extra time. England had been awarded just two penalties during Robson's eight years in charge, but they were awarded their second of the match in the 105th minute. Again it stemmed from another laser-accurate pass from Gascoigne, and again it was Lineker who converted the penalty after being chopped to the ground. 3–2. England, thanks largely to Gascoigne's vision and Lineker's composure, had escaped. Leeds manager Howard Wilkinson had 'spied' on Cameroon in their group matches and had reported back to Robson that England had as good as a bye into the last four. As Waddle left the pitch, he said to the manager, 'Some fucking bye that!'

England had reached the last four of the World Cup for the first time on foreign soil in forty years of trying. The team had undergone a rapid and radical transformation in the nation's press: 'Bobby's Bunglers' had become 'Bobby's Beauties'. They now faced a West German side who had started with a rush in their group matches, crushing Yugoslavia 4–1 and the UAE 5–1, but had begun to show signs of fatigue beating an unsettled Dutch side and a relatively weak Czech side, both by a single goal. England, by contrast, had improved considerably since the horror show against the Irish, although they had looked strangely dishevelled and directionless for long periods of the Cameroon contest. Robson admitted that were England to show the same laxity and lack of organisation against the Germans, then Franz Beckenbauer's side would stroll into their third successive World Cup final without having to break sweat. Another worry for Robson was the condition of his players who had been pushed to their mental and physical limits in their last two matches, both of which had gone to extra time. At the end of each encounter the players were virtually walking, and now they had just two full days to recuperate before facing the super-fit and powerful Germans in Turin.

England had already featured in what were widely regarded as three of the four most entertaining matches of the World Cup – albeit ones that would not go down in the memory as some of the best in the tournament's sixty-year history. The games against Holland, Belgium and Cameroon were all fabulous spectacles for the neutral, but the semi-final against West Germany was without question not just the best match of Italia 90 but one of the great international football contests of all time. The prize of a place in the final against a relatively unimpressive Argentinian side combined with the traditional rivalry between the two heavyweight nations of north European football brought an unbearable tension to the match before even a ball had been kicked. What followed over the next nerve-shredding 150 minutes or so exceeded the most fanciful expectations of the billions who tuned in worldwide to watch it. There have been plenty of more technically accomplished and skilful sides than the two who took the field on 4 July 1990 in the magnificent Stadio delle Alpi, but few can have generated more raw excitement than England and West Germany did on that night. 'It was probably the best England performance since the day we won the World Cup 24 years earlier,' says Robson.

England once again started with a sweeper in a line-up that read: Shilton, Parker, Walker, Butcher, Wright, Pearce, Platt, Gascoigne, Waddle, Beardsley, Lineker. For West Germany, Beckenbauer chose: Illgner, Berthold, Brehme, Kohler, Augenthaler, Buchwald, Hassler, Voller, Thon, Matthaus, Klinsmann. Both teams attacked from the first whistle, and in a breathless, breathtaking first half Gascoigne and Pearce for England and Thon (twice) and Augenthaler for West Germany all had good chances. Barely a single foul had been committed despite the frenetic action, and as the players walked off to booming applause at the interval, England had good reason to believe that they had shaded a pulsating first 45 minutes. The Germans, though, were first out of the blocks in the second half and took the lead on the hour mark thanks to an enormous slice of luck after Pearce was penalised for a questionable foul on Hassler outside the area. Brehme's free-kick took a huge deflection off Parker, who had rushed out of the defensive wall to block, and looped agonisingly over the stranded Shilton, under the cross bar and into the net. 'The world just seemed to grind to a halt for me,' says Robson. 'I could barely hear the German fans celebrating. It was like I was in shock, feeling numb. But I knew I had to do something to retrieve it.' Robson waited ten minutes and then, just as he had done against Cameroon, he abandoned the sweeper system and sent on Trevor Steven for Butcher and pushed Waddle further out to the right. With eight minutes remaining England pulled level when Parker fired over a cross from the right, causing mayhem in the last line of German defence. Lineker seized on the hesitation and squirmed into position before firing a left-foot shot across goal into the bottom left corner of Illgner's net. 'I wanted to explode I was so happy,' says Robson. 'It was nothing more than we deserved, and I began to think, Well, maybe our luck *is* in.'

For the third match in a row, England found themselves

having to muster all their reserves of energy for an extra half an hour. And what a half an hour. Far from being an exercise in caution with both exhausted sides holding out for the lottery of penalties, England and West Germany both went all out for what would almost certainly be the winning goal. Waddle, who Robson had considered leaving out altogether, came within an inch of delivering England into the final with a rasping low drive that cannoned back off the upright. At the other end, Buchwald also hit a post, while Shilton needed to be at his sharpest to deny Matthaus and Klinsmann.

Halfway through the first period of extra time came a moment that gave rise to one of the most enduring memories of Italia 90. Gascoigne brought down Berthold with a challenge that was more tired and clumsy than malicious and was shown the yellow card by referee José Ramiz Wright. It was his second booking for the tournament and, realising that he would now miss the final if England went through, Gascoigne burst into tears. 'It wasn't *that* bad a challenge, but the whole German bench jumped to their feet right under the nose of the referee,' says Robson. 'If it had happened somewhere else on the pitch, I am sure Gazza would never have been booked.' Lineker, Gascoigne's team-mate at Spurs, immediately ran over to the bench and told Robson to watch the young midfielder. But his warnings proved needless as Gascoigne quickly recovered his sense of purpose, if not his energy. With fatigue oozing out of every limb of the 22 exhausted players, extra time finally ground to a halt, and after 120 minutes of gut-twisting tension there was nothing to separate the two great rivals of northern hemisphere football.

'We did not have two of our best penalty-takers in Robson and Barnes, but I was still confident we would go through,' says Robson. 'I wanted Lineker to go first so that the pressure would always be on the Germans.' Lineker did go first and did score, but if the Germans were feeling any pressure they sure weren't showing it. Beardsley and Platt were successful with the second and third kicks, but each time, first Brehme, then Matthaus and then Riedle kept the Germans on terms. (For the record, each time Shilton guessed which way they would shoot, but each time their efforts narrowly avoided his grasp.) Pearce,

England's second-choice penalty-taker after Lineker according to Robson, fired England's fourth into the legs of Illgner. 'I knew that was it,' says Robson. Thon stepped up to make it 4–3 and leave England's hopes resting on the sloping shoulders of Waddle, who ran up to the ball and smashed it wildly over the cross bar. England were out of the World Cup. 'It was an appalling way to go out,' recalls Robson. 'As we shook hands afterwards Franz Beckenbauer said to me, "Neither side deserved to lose." I thought whoever won our semi would win the World Cup as Argentina were one of the weaker finalists in the history of the tournament. It was an awful sight in the dressing room. Everyone was tearful. You just didn't want to say anything. There was nothing to say that would have sounded meaningful. I wanted to cry myself but I knew I had to hold it together and face the world's press.'

At least Robson could now look the press straight in the eye with the confidence of knowing that he had taken England to within a penalty kick of the biggest stage in world football, and within one match of its biggest prize against opponents England would have been fancied to beat. The England players were deflated by their agonisingly narrow defeat and exhausted by their efforts over the previous three weeks, but they had to pick themselves up for Robson's last match in charge: the third-place play-off against Italy in Bari. The players responded with a performance as good as any they had produced in the tournament, but an entertaining if meaningless match was settled in Italy's favour five minutes from time when Toto Schillaci secured the Golden Boot award with his sixth goal of the tournament from the penalty spot after Parker was dubiously adjudged to have fouled the shaven-headed striker. Five minutes earlier Platt had equalised Baggio's 71st-minute goal with a towering header from Dorigo's cross. The match had been played in a carnival-style atmosphere with both sets of fans mingling happily, and there was no evidence of the trouble which had marred England's group matches in Sardinia.

Fifteen minutes after the match, Robson was taken back out into the arena where thousands of England fans stood on the terraces chanting his name. Back at the hotel Robson was presented with a Wedgwood dinner service (he must have wondered what he had done wrong) as well as a painting and a watch before Terry Butcher, Robson's protégé at both Ipswich and England, stood and made an emotional farewell speech on behalf of the players. Moments later, the England manager found himself being lifted into the air and hurled into the swimming pool, fully suited and clutching his cracked rib. Robson missed the diving board by about an inch but, in true Charlie Chaplin style, still managed to cut his foot getting out of the pool. The following day England flew back to a tumultuous reception at Luton, where 100,000 fans packed the streets to hail Robson and his players.

After eight years and 95 matches (won 45, drew 29, lost nineteen), Robson's rollercoaster ride of a reign had ended, if not in triumph then at least in celebration. 'Robson walked out with his head held high,' says Bryon Butler. 'For a long time it looked as if that would never happen, especially after the first two games in Mexico when he was absolutely slated. In the end he was given a right royal send-off.'

One of the most peculiar aspects of Robson's relationship with the press is that all the reporters loved him. Many of them on the tabloids may have spent eight years calling for his head, but to a man they will not hear a bad word about him. 'We were just doing our job, reporting what we saw and how we saw it,' they say. 'He was a very likeable man, incorrigibly enthusiastic,' says Butler, who as an employee of the BBC and the *Daily Telegraph* was able to report the Robson era from a less sensational angle than his colleagues in the tabloids. 'Even when the press were having a go at him, about his private life or about an England performance, he was always there the next morning talking away with great enthusiasm. You couldn't help but love the fellow. No matter how much of a battering he took, he'd still be there making himself available for interview.' Brian Woolnough of the *Sun*, a paper which hammered Robson relentlessly, both front page and back, is equally fulsome in his affection for the man. 'He was absolutely brilliant for us. He was a very passionate and loveable person. Yes, he made mistakes on the pitch and in what he said. But he always made great copy. He said some wonderful things, made a big effort for us and always gave us plenty of material. He was someone you always wanted to put an arm round because he was such a lovely bloke.'

Robson warned Graham Taylor, his ever cheerful-looking successor, that he would be in for a shock. 'In a perfect world, the new manager should have worked with me for a couple of years to find out what it's all about,' he recalls now. 'The first two years can be a lonely, terrifying nightmare. I thought I was prepared, but the first time I led England out at Wembley and heard *God Save the Queen* the realisation of my responsibility to the nation came as a shock. The hairs actually stood up on the back of my neck, like they do in a cartoon.'

6 From Top Man to Turnip

Graham Taylor 1990–1993

I N THE 44 YEARS between 1946 and 1990 just six men had managed the England team. Nine years later that figure was eleven. The pressure on the national manager to succeed had reached the stage where mediocrity of performance or errors in judgement, whether on or off the pitch, would no longer be tolerated. There were no second chances for fools or losers. The experiences of Graham Taylor, Terry Venables and Glenn Hoddle make for unhappy reading, a catalogue of frustrated ambition and merciless criticism in the press. Each of them started with a beaming smile (perhaps more of a furrowed brow and an awkward grin in Hoddle's case) and each left the job with a grimace, nursing a sense of injured pride, bitter at their treatment either at the hands of the press, their employers or the public – or all three.

Graham Taylor arrived in the job on a wave of national optimism following England's vibrant showing at Italia 90, only to be swept out on the low tide of public opinion towards oblivion via Wolverhampton and Watford. He had sat down on the hottest seat in English football and got up with a burning backside, smoke trailing behind him all the way up the A1 to his native Midlands. It is difficult to discuss Graham Taylor's time in charge with people still involved in English football without making them feel uncomfortable. There is a near universal reluctance to advance any form of criticism of him, almost instead a sense of polite embarrassment. Bring up his name with anyone apart from journalists and members of the public and almost without exception you will hear a sharp intake of breath, followed by a long pause, a loud exhale, a bit of umming and ahhing and some shuffling of feet, and then the words, 'Well, he's a bloody good bloke and he did an incredible job at Watford.' We all know that, but was he any good as England manager? 'I think he was very unlucky . . . We almost qualified . . . He gave it absolutely everything . . . You had to feel a bit sorry for him . . . He was a square peg in a round hole . . . He didn't deserve to be slated like he was, no one deserves that' – just a selection of the responses elicited by the above question. Taylor himself is perhaps the most reluctant person of all to discuss his experiences in those three and a half increasingly unhappy years during which England flopped at the European Championship finals of 1992 and then failed to reach the World Cup finals in the United States two years later. (No amount of faxes and telephone calls could bring him to the interview table for this book, although, according to his agent, this was partly out of fear that his chances of securing his own book deal in the future might be jeopardised, an anxiety expressed by a number of potential interviewees still involved in the game in the 1990s.)

When it was revealed that Taylor, then manager of Aston Villa, would take over as England's national manager, John Sadler in the *Sun* interviewed his old friend – the man, according to the sub-heading, 'who's gonna be the king'. Sadler was confident that the qualities Taylor had shown in transforming Watford from a backwater irrelevance into a significant power in English football and then in restoring the fortunes of fallen giants Aston Villa would take England to new heights on the international stage. 'The appointment of Graham Taylor will be the best thing to happen to our national game in twenty years,' he wrote. His optimism was shared by many in the game as well as in the press and public – but not everybody was as convinced. Jeff Powell in the *Daily Mail* predicted difficult times ahead for both England and the new manager. 'Graham Taylor is poised to become the least prepared and most pressurised England manager of all time,' he wrote shortly before the start of Italia 90. 'The giant leap into the unknown which Taylor is about to make from Villa Park to Lancaster Gate will be more hazardous and unsighted than any attempted by his predecessors . . . It has to be hoped that he is at least as thick-skinned as Ramsey when it comes to shrugging off the vitriol, abuse, insult and accusation which has reached a crescendo in Robson's reign.' Brian Glanville was more blunt, describing Taylor's appointment as 'an abysmal decision', and he raised fears that together with Charles Hughes, the FA's much maligned director of coaching at the time, the pair would seek to promote the virtues of 'Route One' football.

Taylor arrived in the England job with a reputation for making the most of limited resources, and not even his harshest critics could deny him praise for his remarkable achievements at Watford. Recruited by Elton John on the advice of Don Revie, Taylor took the sleepy Hertfordshire club into the bright cosmopolitan lights of the First Division in just five seasons. In their first season in the top flight, 1982/83, Watford finished second to Liverpool in the League championship, and in 1984 they reached the FA Cup final, which they lost 2–0 to Everton. In 1988 he took over at Aston Villa who, six years after being crowned European Cup winners, had spiralled into the Second Division. Taylor's reputation as a trouble-shooter was enhanced further when he took the Midlands club straight back up to the top division and turned them into title contenders by 1990 when, for the second time in his career, his team was denied the championship crown by Liverpool. Taylor proved that he was a manager who could turn a demoralised squad of players into a highly effective force in a very short space of time and with a minimal amount of funds. If he could achieve such success with the group of players at his disposal at Watford, his supporters would say, just imagine what he could do with the best talent in the land.

But there were a number of nagging doubts about Taylor. The sceptics pointed out that for all his success, Taylor had never actually won a trophy. To that his supporters would say that his miraculous transformation of Watford was as impressive as any manager's achievement in the modern era. They would also claim that he was on the verge of great things after just two years at Aston Villa before the meteoric rise of his reputation catapulted him into contention for the England job. And there were two other causes of worry expressed at the time of his appointment to the England job. Firstly, some observers felt that his lack of experience as a player at the highest level was a handicap. The pinnacle of an undistinguished career as a full-back came with Lincoln City in the Third and Fourth Divisions, and there were concerns that a star-studded England squad would struggle to respect someone who had not played at the highest level himself. 'I think it's very difficult for someone who has no international experience whatsoever to take over the England team,' Lineker said of Taylor at the end of his career. 'He was never an international player himself and I think it was difficult for him to appreciate the game and the differences that there are.' Secondly, it was pointed out that Taylor's success as a club manager was achieved by playing a tactically simplistic long-ball game, and that in the more sophisticated world of international football his methods would be found wanting.

Taylor, the son of a sports journalist, was mindful of the havoc wreaked by the press on his predecessor and was determined to take a positive approach. 'He had all sorts of plans for the media,' recalls the *Telegraph*'s Bryon Butler. 'He always tried to be on the front foot, making himself available as much as possible. You quickly got the impression that he had given a lot of thought to how he was going to try and handle the reporters.' Brian Woolnough of the *Sun* thought Taylor was too preoccupied by the press and was unmoved, even mildly irritated, by the manager's contrived efforts to endear himself to his critics. 'He tried too hard to be what the media wanted. Some of the PR gimmicks they came up with were slightly embarrassing. We criticised him once for only speaking to the press for a brief time and the next time he came in with an alarm clock. It was meant to be funny. On another occasion, after England had drawn 2–2 with Holland at Wembley making us a bit wobbly for qualification [for the 1994 World Cup], he walked into the press conference the following morning singing Buddy Holly's "O misery! what is to become of me?" We just sat there staring at him aghast. But it was a dream to work with him because the copy was magnificent every time.'

England were unbeaten in Taylor's first year in charge and

lost just one of his first 23 games – a 1–0 home defeat at the hands of Germany in a friendly. Qualifying for the 1992 European Championship finals was a struggle, though, and it was there, in Sweden, that his troubles began. In their group matches England were twice held to a draw by the Republic of Ireland, Turkey were beaten by just the single goal on both occasions, and it took a hard-fought draw in Poland for them to scrape into the finals. But if the jury had been out during Taylor's moderately successful if unspectacular first two seasons in charge, they came running back in screaming 'guilty' when England crashed out of the European Championship finals. After goalless draws in Malmö against eventual champions Denmark and a modest French side, England were beaten 2–1 by the host nation in the capital city, Stockholm. Not only had England lost, but Taylor had invoked the wrath of the country by taking off Gary Lineker – the Queen Mother of English football, who had become something of a national treasure after scoring 48 goals in 80 games – and replacing him with the worthy if workmanlike Alan Smith of Arsenal. Taylor's supporters pointed out that Lineker, who was just one short of matching Bobby Charlton's record number of goals for England, had not scored in six matches, but the manager's subsequent explanation that he had wanted to send on someone who could 'hold the ball up' prompted snorts of derision from his critics. Another of Graham Taylor's problems was Paul Gascoigne – or rather the lack of him. The rising star of English football, even European football, played in just 11 of Taylor's 38 games after almost wrecking his career with a maniacal challenge on Gary Charles at the start of the 1991 FA Cup final between Tottenham and Nottingham Forest. England, who were also without the injured John Barnes, were painfully short of creativity in Sweden, but many felt that Taylor did not help his own cause by ignoring Chris Waddle and Peter Beardsley, two of the most talented forwards of their generation with enough left in the tank to drive England to the next World Cup. After retiring from international football, Lineker complained that the England strikers barely had a chance to speak of at the European Championships. 'If he had his time back I'm sure Graham Taylor might rethink his decision to have left Waddle and Beardsley at home,' he said.

The defeat inspired the *Sun*'s sub-editor Dave Clement to produce one of the most memorable headlines in the history of the tabloids: 'SWEDES 2 TURNIPS 1'. Taylor himself has admitted that even he saw the humour in the headline, but the following day he was less amused when he saw his face superimposed on a picture of a turnip. 'It was a magnificent headline but it was aimed not at Taylor but at the players,' says Patrick Barclay of the *Sunday Telegraph*. 'The next day when Taylor himself was caricatured as a turnip, the players were effectively let off the hook and the responsibility of defeat was seen to rest entirely with the manager.' Brian Woolnough of the *Sun* feels that the subsequent competition among rival sub-editors to match the brilliance of the turnip headline led to the treatment of the England manager getting out of hand. 'The turnip headline was just a brilliant piece of tabloid journalism,' he says. 'But I do think it was taken too far when things went increasingly wrong for Taylor. You felt a bit sorry for him.'

The European Championship finals in 1992 marked the turning point in Taylor's relationship with the press which, though tense, had been what the Downing Street press office might call 'cordial'. David Bloomfield, the FA's press officer throughout Taylor's time in charge, believes that his former employers made a major mistake in not injecting significantly more resources into the media side of the England set-up. He believes that in-fighting at the FA and their ignorance of the growing influence of the media in football, and especially in the England team, might have helped their own image as well as that of the manager. 'I was the only press officer for the whole of the FA,' he says. 'I wasn't just dealing with the press interest in the England team but for every aspect of English football. I remember David Davies, who was then a reporter for the BBC, asking me if he should take the job with the FA and I told him that he would be unwise unless they could guarantee that he would be given a team of people to work alongside him. While I was there, it was ludicrous. At an average press conference with England I would have a hundred journalists, fifty photographers, ten to twenty TV crews and any number of radio people, who all had different demands and needs. I was constantly trying to deal with umpteen requests for interviews and God knows what else. The TV crews wanted their interviews and shots and they didn't give a monkey's about the written press, who didn't give a monkey's about them or the radio, and then there were the photographers who don't give a monkey's about anyone. They are all naturally selfish groupings who created a highly combustible atmosphere.

'It was very, very difficult. I thought I was pretty good at my job, but I used to say to the FA, "Look, Maradona is a good player but the Argentinian FA give him another ten players when he goes out to play." I was constantly urging them to switch more resources to the media side, but no one listened. There were a lot of people fighting their own corners in the FA who didn't want to see their little empires threatened by greater influence being given to other areas. Graham and I were both aware that it was totally unsatisfactory, and in the end he told them that he himself was bringing in someone else and if they didn't pay for him, then he would. In the end I think they paid.'

Bloomfield, who now runs his own consultancy company in London, believes that in the end Taylor's openness – he even gave out his telephone number for journalists to contact him in an 'emergency' – as well as his willingness to debate with reporters and a laudable determination not to show preferential treatment to any of them, worked to his disadvantage. 'He wanted to be fair to all the journalists, give them all equal time and show no favourites,' says Bloomfield. 'But I think it backfired because what his fair-mindedness meant was that he didn't have anyone to rely on who could put a more positive slant on stories when he hit choppy waters. I think the journalists felt he was fair game because none of them had any special investment in him doing well. He was the first England manager to realise the importance of the media, but perhaps you could say that the more you acknowledge their importance the more you can be affected by them.'

Bloomfield also believes that the criticism that came Taylor's way in the second half of his tenure was even harsher than that suffered by Robson. 'It was much more virulent,' he says. 'The journalists and sub-editors had a lot of practice at ridiculing and cartooning the England manager under Bobby, and there was a climate and an appetite for it when Graham Taylor took over. They had sharpened their knives so well in the Robson years that by the time his successor arrived they were experts at making incisive and scathing cuts.'

After wrestling all summer with the disturbing idea that he was a turnip, Taylor discovered that he had become an onion following England's first match of the new season. It was something of an improvement, perhaps, on being a tasteless root vegetable – at least, in vegetable terms, he was considered to be sharp and popular – although it is unlikely that he saw anything positive in his latest manifestation in the tabloids. England had lost 1–0 to Spain in Santander on 9 September 1992, and the following morning the headline in the *Sun* read 'SPANISH 1 ONIONS 0'. What the joke may have lacked in surprise, it made up for in bite. Taylor realised that unless his teams began to improve on their increasingly rustic displays, the only trophy he was likely to win would be for the biggest pumpkin at the National Agricultural Show.

The draw for the World Cup qualifying stages had thrown England into the same group as Holland, Poland, Norway, Turkey and San Marino, from which two would be making their way to the finals in the United States. England's campaign started poorly on 14 October with a 1–1 draw against Norway at Wembley, and while they could consider themselves unlucky that their greater share of possession and chances did not bring them victory, the dropped point put them on the back foot from the outset and set the tone for an ultimately disappointing attempt to join the world's élite in the finals two years later. Comfortable victories over Turkey (4–0 and 2–0) and San Marino (6–0) were no more than the country had been expecting before England faced the Dutch at Wembley at the end of April 1993 in one of the key games of the group. It looked as if it was going to be England's night when Barnes and Platt fired England into a 2–0 lead, but two future heroes of North London ensured that Holland left the English capital with a vital point. Dennis Bergkamp reduced England's lead with a goal of exquisite skill before the pace of Marc Overmars forced Des Walker to bring him down in the area for Van

Vossen to convert from the ensuing penalty. England's failure to kill off the game, or at least close it down, was to prove crucial not just to England's hopes of qualification, but also to Taylor's reputation. Football is full of 'ifs', but it is worth considering that had England won that match and gone on to reach USA 94, our impressions of Graham Taylor might have been entirely different. The experiences of Bobby Robson in Mexico where failure to beat Poland would almost certainly have ended in the termination of his contract bear out the point that an England manager's job and his reputation often depend on just one 90-minute period of his years in charge.

A month later England flew out for games in Poland and Norway knowing that a victory in at least one of the games was essential if they were to have any realistic chance of qualification. Having emerged with a creditable point against Poland from the atmospheric inferno of Katowice, England took the field in Oslo with a team that had most observers shaking their heads in disbelief. Worried by the threat of the tall striker Jostein Flo wide on the right, Taylor deployed centre-back Gary Pallister at left-back, with disastrous consequences. They lost 2–0 in one of England's worst performances of the modern era, and not for a minute did they look like a team with any shape or tactical purpose.

A year earlier, the FA, at Taylor's insistence, had brought in media specialist David Teasdale, a kind of Red Adair figure who would try to help dowse the flames of recrimination that raged around Taylor after Sweden. But there was little he could do to prevent the eruption of violent criticism that followed England's humiliation in Oslo. 'NORSE MANURE!' and 'OSLO RANS!' were the pick of the following morning's headlines as the nation woke up to the fact that England were now highly unlikely to reach USA 94. Teasdale, a senior civil servant at the Ministry of Sport in Whitehall, saw his role as two-fold: to relieve some of the enormous burden on Bloomfield and to offer advice to Taylor before addressing the media. 'The "NORSE MANURE" headline was the nadir of my involvement with the England set-up,' says Teasdale. 'I was "on duty" that day and that's not what you want to see the next day if you are a media specialist like I am. But sometimes you are powerless, and with England you were always at the mercy of events on the field. I had no control over what happened there.

'I was brought in after the turnip business in the European championships. The FA were very bad about the media at the time. David Bloomfield had to deal with every aspect of the FA's press relations. It was incredible. He was dealing with the disciplinary hearings, referee issues, the birth of the Premier League, the hooligan issues, any number of interview requests, and then when he had a bit of spare time left he would look after the England manager, who was arguably the single most exposed media personality in the country. Just dealing with the England side of the job was much, much more than one man's job. Football had become big business and the media interest was enormous and growing by the month. To expect him to deal just with the England set-up by himself was bad enough, but to ask him to be the PR man for every aspect of the FA was totally crazy.

'One of the things I tried to do was make contacts among the media, to try and get a feel of what they were after, find out what stories they were working on. The press hunt in packs. Every now and then you'll get a wild card, but generally all the tabloid boys get together and decide what the story is. So I saw my job was to keep my finger on whatever was brewing. At the last possible moment I would grab Graham before a press conference and quickly brief him about what they were after and what the mood was like. We would generally only have two or three minutes and I would tell him to be cool and calm and not talk too much.

'When I joined the England set-up I knew I had to be able to improve the present situation, which was ludicrous. One of the first things I did was write a report saying the FA needed a lot more people employed on the media side. My objectives were to persuade the press to take a realistic, balanced view of Graham and to take some pressure off his back by doing some of the thinking for him to give him more time.'

Teasdale, who worked for Margaret Thatcher in the 1980s, believes that the England manager is one of the most sought-after figures in British public life, but the media structure to protect and support him has always been wholly inadequate. 'Whatever is happening in the country the England manager is getting as much media attention as the Prime Minister or the very top pop star. You go to an England press conference and there will be hundreds of journalists from TV, radio and the papers from all around the world – and there is one poor manager whose main job is to coach his players.

'What often happened was that by the time Graham got to a press conference he was already mentally and physically tired from a gruelling day in the field. In an average day he goes to see the doctor and physio for bulletins on the fitness of players first thing in the morning, then he takes a training session, holds talks with the players collectively and individually, and then, barely before he's had time to gather his thoughts about his team selection or tactics or think about the opposition, he has to go and face the press who, let's face it, are not on his side and have had plenty of time to prepare their inquisition. Alistair Campbell, the Prime Minister's press secretary, would never let Tony Blair face the press when he was so tired and unprepared. He would be much more careful than that. But in the England set-up most press conferences take place straight after training or a match when his head is swimming with a million different worries and when the adrenalin and the emotions are still swirling. These are not good times for a man to face the world's media. In an ideal world you would want him to shower and change and relax, but it doesn't work like that.

'Imagine what it is like: you come off the training field sweating with a hundred worries, you're not sure who's fit and who's going to play where, and then you walk into a room with the dozens of bright lights from the TV crews in your face and there is a forest of microphones and a sea of faces before you, and then the questions start coming at you from every angle. And he has to put on a masterful performance. If he slips up, he'll be jumped on. This is not what football managers are trained to do. Prime ministers are, but not football managers. No wonder they trip up.

'In the end the England manager is a very lonely, exposed figure – no matter how many people he's got around him. He's the only one who is going to be shot at. Kevin Keegan, the darling of the media, had the statutory honeymoon period, but even then you can guarantee that out of about a hundred journalists you are going to have about ten minimum who are bent on knocking him.'

Shortly after the Oslo débâcle, England flew out to the United States for a mini tournament involving Brazil, Germany and the host nation which was designed to whet the American appetite for the World Cup the following year. The American public certainly liked what they saw in Boston, where painful memories of the 1950 World Cup were evoked as the States sent Taylor's demoralised team spinning to a 2–0 defeat. Some credibility was clawed back with a 1–1 draw against Brazil in Washington, but a 2–1 defeat by Germany in Detroit pushed Taylor a step closer to the revolving door at Lancaster Gate. Everything now hinged on England's last three qualifiers at the start of the 1993/94 season, which began well when Poland were dispatched 3–0 at Wembley in September in what was one of England's best performances under Taylor, keeping alive faint hopes of pipping the Dutch for the second qualifying place behind runaway leaders Norway.

While in the United States, reports had emerged in the English papers that some of the squad had lost faith in Taylor. 'The press were running stories that the players were not behind Graham,' recalls Teasdale. 'I think what happened there was this. There were 22 players and only eleven get picked. The other eleven are not going to be that happy and journalists know that, so if they want to get a negative comment they can go to one of the eleven not in the team, and even though the player might stick up for the manager, the journalist will take the couple of lines in which he says "I think I'm good enough to be in the team" and then they would blow it up into an issue. The journalists are looking for a manager who will blame the players and players who will blame the manager – then they can create a nice stink.

'But we never tried to keep the players away from the press. In my experience of the media, the more you try to deflect attention from something, the more you draw attention to it. If journalists can't get information or they meet evasion or stonewalls they'll write more negative stories. You have to remember that when England travel they are on the same plane as the press. David Bloomfield and I did not get paranoid about it. We worked on the basis that if a journalist tried to grab Graham on his own, then unless Graham expressly said to me he didn't want to talk to that guy we would let him deal with it as he wanted. It's the same when I've worked with politicians. Everyone is aware that every now and then they're going to have to cross the street and they're going to meet somebody. You can't protect someone from the media all the time, and nor do I think to do so is a good idea. Graham can't say, "Excuse me, I only talk when my press officer is present." '

And Taylor loved to talk, much to the delight of the press, but many felt that by trying to be helpful and honest he unwittingly and naively contributed to his own downfall. 'He was very honest and very sincere, possibly even too earnest,' says Colin Malam, a veteran reporter of the England scene since 1973, first with the *Sun* and then with the *Sunday Telegraph*. 'My own feeling was that he talked too much and in the end talked himself into trouble. I have been chastised by some of my colleagues for saying that because they say journalists want people to talk as much as possible. From our point of view it was marvellous, but from his I think it was self-destructive.' Like Malam, Teasdale believes that such openness leaves an England manager exposed to attack. 'One thing Graham had which nobody could take away from him was his honesty,' he says. 'I realised after a while there was no point advising him, in the language of politics, to be slightly "economical with the truth" or to "dissemble". That was never Graham Taylor's way. He was an engagingly honest man. He didn't want to duck any questions, and after games he would always hold his hand up and be honest.'

Rob Shepherd says he was amazed by Taylor's naivety on occasions. 'He tried very hard to deal with the press as best as he could, but it would often rebound on him. I remember when we played Turkey in Izmir in 1991. Before the match he was talking about playing Alan Smith and was joking about how he would be criticised for going back to "Route One" football. "I suppose there will be some people out there who will be ready to put a noose around my neck," he said. And surprise, surprise, the next day in the *Daily Mirror* there was a picture of him with a noose superimposed around his neck. It was a good example of him being good-natured and self-effacing but a bit naive, perhaps.

'After the turnips headline, which everyone thought was funny, I think it got a bit out of hand and a bit personal. I never fell out with him, though, and I based my criticism on what I saw as his professional misjudgements. I think what really upset him was when he got turned over by a couple of journalists he had tried to befriend earlier in his reign. He took one or two out to dinner and a couple of others to the theatre, but when the shit hit the fan they turned on him as well and I think he felt let down by that.'

Tensions were running high before England's match against the Dutch in Rotterdam on 13 October 1993. At stake was a place in the World Cup finals. Taylor had one last chance to save his job. On the eve of the match, Taylor clashed with Rob Shepherd at an extraordinary press conference which was captured by a TV crew filming a Channel Four documentary on the England manager. 'I remember going out on the Monday and getting a tip-off from one of the players about the team,' recalls Shepherd. 'I found out that Carlton Palmer and Paul Merson were going to be in, which was pretty controversial. We ran the story on the Tuesday, so when I turned up for that press conference I was a bit nervous because *Today* was the only paper to run it, and if I had got it wrong I would have looked like a right twit. I also thought it was a bad team and I felt depressed about our chances of winning and qualifying for the finals.'

David Bloomfield saw the confrontation unfold from behind the advertising screen. 'Graham Taylor was trying to motivate the players before the match. I think what happened was that he was trying to create a really positive atmosphere for the match, and he walked into the press conference having just been trying to gee up the players and fill them with confidence on the training ground. Rob Shepherd was looking glum and asked him a question with a downbeat tone, and I think Graham Taylor was put out by the air of pessimism in the room.' Shepherd had asked Taylor if he thought he was making the same mistake as he had before the disastrous game in Oslo, when he had made some extraordinary team changes. 'That was fine, but when he started answering a similar question from Joe Lovejoy, who was working for the *Independent*, I started shaking my head in disagreement,' says Shepherd. 'Taylor spotted me doing that and that's what triggered him, I think. He was pumped up and trying to be positive, but also I think there was an element of him knowing he was being filmed for that documentary. I always felt that he agreed to do that programme because he felt it would be a eulogy to his time in charge. If we had won the Holland game and gone to the World Cup it would have been a different programme altogether. But as we lost it ended up being an epitaph to the bad side of his management. Anyway, we argued for a bit and it was getting a bit silly, and I could sense the whole meeting was going to disintegrate if I turned it into a proper argument. He was up for it, but after making a couple of points I backed down because I didn't want to destroy the press conference.'

Brian Glanville, who has seen dozens of club and international managers come and go during fifty years of reporting football from around the would, believes Taylor was preoccupied with the press to the point of paranoia (although even the most level-headed and self-confident person is perhaps entitled to the odd surge of neuroses when he opens his newspaper and sees himself depicted as a grinning turnip with a silly hairstyle). Long before Taylor became England manager, Glanville was given an insight into the man's sensitivity to criticism. After a match between Watford and QPR at Loftus Road, Taylor walked into the press conference and refused to shake hands with the reporter. Glanville recalls: 'I had been knocking him for a while over his use of the long ball, and he confronted and called me a liar. "You write lies, lies," he said. It turned out he was referring to something I had written three and a half years earlier about him substituting a player who disagreed with him in a youth game in Israel.' Glanville also recalls an amusing run-in with Lawrie McMenemy, Taylor's assistant coach. 'When Taylor appointed McMenemy as his right-hand man he said that Lawrie had a big shoulder for him to cry on. I wrote a piece in which I said "When Lawrie McMenemy gets over his rheumatism . . ." A few days later I received a letter from McMenemy saying, "I've never had rheumatism in my life. If this charge is not withdrawn then I'll be taking legal advice." I said, "But Lawrie, it's just a joke," but he was having none of it. Retract, or face the consequences.'

Taylor was not the only man in Rotterdam feeling the tension before the decisive clash against Holland. The Dutch security forces also had cause to feel that there were more rewarding jobs to be had as they battled with hordes of rival hooligans from both countries for two days leading up to the match. The match itself provoked a riot of emotion. Both sides had good chances in a first half of furious action. Platt, Adams and Dorigo all went close for England, while Rijkaard had a perfectly good goal disallowed shortly before the interval. Perhaps the most significant moment of Taylor's time in charge occurred fifteen minutes into the second half when Ronald Koeman, a man who had rugby-tackled players to the ground in the past, crudely brought down Platt on the edge of the area as the England captain raced in on goal. Koeman should have been sent off for a professional foul, but he survived, and two minutes later took advantage of his good fortune to give Holland the lead amid more controversy. Ince fouled Wouters just outside the penalty box, and though Koeman fluffed the ensuing free-kick, he was given a second chance as Ince was booked for encroaching. This time, with goalkeeper Seaman scurrying to and fro on his line like a squirrel with haemorrhoids, the giant Dutchman made no mistake as he chipped the ball over the wall and into the net.

On the touchline, Taylor looked like a man who had just been told he was going to be peeled and boiled vigorously for twenty minutes before being mashed into a nice squash and served up with a healthy portion of humble pie. You could almost see the steam coming out of his ears, and the lid blew off completely as he launched himself at the FIFA official outside the dugout, stabbing his finger at him and bleating that the referee had just cost him his job. The blank expression of the official gave the impression that he did not even know who the jabbering man in the glasses was as he ushered him away from the pitch. Merson hit the woodwork moments later, but Bergkamp soon buried England's chances of reaching the World Cup, as well as any hopes Taylor had of staying in the job.

When the Dutch beat Poland in their final match, England's 7–1 success against San Marino was rendered meaningless. The match in Bologna, however, threw up one final humiliation when the eleven representatives of the tiny republic (with a population of 23,000 and where the largest share of government revenue comes from the sale of postage stamps) took the lead after just nine seconds. England had won just five of Taylor's last fifteen games, and the following day the *Daily Mirror* printed a mock letter of resignation from Taylor to the FA, inviting him to sign the blank space at the bottom. Taylor got the message.

Jimmy Armfield, the FA's technical director charged with the responsibility of finding a successor, believes Taylor was unfortunate. 'I thought he was very unlucky. I don't think anyone will forget the penalty incident involving Kocman and Platt. That was just damned bad luck. Some people are just unlucky and it's not their fault, and I think Graham Taylor was unlucky. He worked his socks off and gave the job everything he had. I don't think it made too much difference that he didn't play international football. The players would have listened to him anyway. If he selected them, they would have responded to his faith in them. Not everything is the manager's fault.'

Glanville, who had little respect for Taylor as a manager, like many journalists felt he got it wrong with the media. He believes that only Terry Venables, Taylor's successor, was genuinely impressive when dealing with the press, and he claims that Ramsey was better than many of the people who followed him. 'Alf Ramsey could be quite playful at times. I remember him after a match going around the train carriage to each journalist in turn, saying, "I don't know why you keep telephoning me. I never telephone you, so why do you keep telephoning me?" Greenwood was fairly sour, Robson a bit paranoid, Winterbottom a bit so-so, not all that good, Revie was a miserable old devil who used to go to bed terrified he'd wake up poor in the morning, Hoddle was very bad, Terry was very good, a bit of a jack the lad, very good at communicating and always produced a smile. You couldn't help but like him. Taylor was quite hopeless and also a bit paranoid.' The *Sun*'s Brian Woolnough also believes Taylor simply wasn't good enough. 'There was never the great respect for Taylor as an England coach,' he says. 'He was someone you liked as a person and felt sorry for because he was out of his depth.'

David Bloomfield saw close up how Taylor, universally acknowledged as a sensitive and decent man, struggled under the avalanche of criticism that crashed down on him in the second part of his time in charge. 'I can't imagine how the criticism could not have affected him,' he says. 'A lot of the journalists will tell you that they really liked Graham Taylor and that if they were in a bar having a drink then they would get on fine. But when it comes to doing their job, they are journalists first and foremost and they have to get a good story. They say that they tell it as they see it. That is what they get paid for and it is just a fact of life that a bloody story is better to read.'

7 The England Job Writ Large

Terry Venables 1994–1996

TERENCE FREDERICK VENABLES is a unique figure in the history of England managers. He is the only man who can claim that managing the national side rescued his career; the only one not to be given a shot at the World Cup; the only one who can claim that he enjoyed the support of the majority of the press during his brief period in charge between 1994 and 1996; the only one to be disqualified as a company director; and the only who has had to pulp his own autobiography.

Venables' impulse to amuse and his ability to dissect football matters with a sharpness that had made him one of the most respected coaches in world football quickly expelled the awkward, confrontational atmosphere that had come to pollute press conferences in the latter part of Taylor's reign. He had served the game with great distinction as a player with England (two caps), Chelsea, Tottenham, QPR and Crystal Palace before managing the latter two with enough success – relative to their respective size, history and resources – for Barcelona, the biggest club in the world, to recruit him in 1984, having failed to lure Bobby Robson away from the England job. He endeared himself to the Barcelona fans by learning Spanish and Catalan (he even released a version of Frank Sinatra's 'My Way' in the ancient local language). In his first season he steered the club to their first League title in eleven years and then guided them into the 1986 European Cup final, where they lost to Steaua Bucharest on penalties. That, though, was not enough for the Catalan giants, who released him – or, as Venables himself would later put it, 'he negotiated a withdrawal from his contract'.

He returned to his native London in 1987, taking over the manager's job at Tottenham and guiding them to an FA Cup triumph in 1991 before helping to save the club from extinction. New chairman Alan Sugar, the man who founded Amstrad computers, put up the majority of the funds to rescue and restructure the famous North London club, and not content to serve in a purely football capacity, Venables also bought a stake in the club and was appointed chief executive. The new partnership between Sugar and Venables was hailed as 'the dream ticket' at the time, but it ended in bitter recrimination two years later. There followed an ugly legal battle which would eventually lead to the degradation of Venables' reputation as a businessman and to his acrimonious departure from the England job before he had the chance to prove that he had the qualities to lead the country to World Cup glory in France.

Alerted by the eruption of his troubles with Sugar, BBC's *Panorama* launched an investigation into Venables' business affairs. Sugar, like all successful, self-made businessmen, has a ruthless streak and he saw no profit in the club's sentimental attachment to someone he considered was no longer an asset but a liability. For all the scorn he attracted from Venables' friends and legion of well-wishers, and for all his confessed ignorance of football, Sugar was the first figure in the modern English game to make people realise that the success of clubs in the future would depend on how well they were run as businesses. The unsentimental manner in which he cast Venables adrift from Tottenham came as a discomforting shock to those who had grown up with the idea that football clubs should be run by football people. Contempt for directors of football clubs was nothing new – in his autobiography Len Shackleton had famously included an empty page under the heading 'What directors know about football' – but Sugar was different. Whereas businessmen in the past might have invested in their local club for a bit of 'kudos' in their dotage and would have seen only relatively small returns on their investments, Sugar saw the way football was going, and he saw dollar signs.

By the end of 1993 the future looked bleak for both Venables and England; Venables had been dumped out of

Tottenham, England out of the World Cup. They were brought together in adversity and they would part in acrimony, but in between the reputation and fortunes of both parties would be restored. Venables needed England as much as England needed Venables. Some commentators said at the time that Venables got the job four years too late, with negative consequences for both him and England. It was argued that had he rather than Taylor been appointed to succeed Robson then England, more likely than not, would have qualified for the 1994 World Cup finals; and had he been there and not at Tottenham, he might never have suffered the seven-year disqualification period as a company director that followed a damning report into his business affairs by the Department of Trade and Industry.

While general news journalists have taken a more critical line of Terry Venables in the 1990s, the majority of the sports press, more interested in the boot room than the boardroom, have treated him with the respect his unquestionable expertise in football matters deserves, as well as with a warmth generated by his boyish and self-effacing sense of humour. However, the handful of reporters who damned him and drew attention to his murky business dealings more than compensated for those who were happy to be seduced by his apparent openness and cheerful banter. Reading the *Daily Mirror* during Venables' time in charge you began to wonder whether there was any other news in Britain or around the world at the time, such was the sheer volume of the stories in the paper that sought to expose his alleged wrongdoings. There was also Mihir Bose, a sports and financial journalist and broadcaster, who has written a 500-page book exposing the details of Venables' commercial activities and his bitter dispute with Sugar. The two *Panorama* documentaries, meanwhile, made similar accusations to those appearing in some sections of the written press. Venables is convinced there was a co-ordinated conspiracy hatched by his enemies to blacken his reputation as a businessman for ever. He says the attacks in the *Mirror* got so bad that he took 155 'major articles' from the paper to the Press Complaints Commission, but he did not take legal action against the paper because he felt it was 'too expensive', even though the general procedure in civil actions is that the successful party will have the greater part, if not all, of his legal costs paid by the loser. Venables instituted a police investigation alleging a criminal conspiracy against him, but no evidence was found to support his claims.

There was certainly no conspiracy in the sports world to condemn him. 'Venables, without any question, was the best of all the England managers at dealing with the press,' says Brian Woolnough of the *Sun*. 'He knew exactly what they needed. I have a lot of respect for the way he handled the media because he was the master at talking a lot and telling you nothing. Also, with Terry you could have an off-the-record conversation so long as he knew you weren't going to let him down. He might say "I don't know what to do about this guy who has been misbehaving" or whatever, and although you didn't use the information in a story, he had brought you into his trust rather than alienated you. He allowed you information to form a picture in your own mind. With Venables you knew most of what was happening behind the scenes, and therefore you were in a position to make a more balanced judgement of events.'

It is a view echoed among the reporters for the broadsheets. 'I started covering England in earnest at the start of Venables' time in charge, and I was amazed by how media-friendly he was,' says Henry Winter, the *Daily Telegraph*'s chief football reporter. 'He was very clubbable and got on with the majority of journalists, apart from a couple like Harry Harris and the *Mirror* boys and a couple at the *Telegraph*. What I found so impressive about Terry Venables was that he sounded genuinely interested in what you did and what you thought, although you were probably of no relevance to him. You could sit down and have a meal with him and just chat away. I would much rather go out for dinner with Terry Venables than most people in football. He was terrific company. You could have a vigorous debate with him and he would never patronise you like a lot of other managers might. I think he is a genuinely curious, boy-like person, which is a very attractive trait. He is very enthusiastic and simply loves to talk with other people. There was certainly nothing contrived about his enthusiasm.'

At the time of Taylor's resignation, there was probably not

a better qualified person in England to take the national manager's job than Terry Venables, although at the outset Kevin Keegan was the people's and the bookmakers' favourite, despite having just a handful of years' experience in club management. When the first odds for the successor were laid, Venables was a 25–1 long shot. Jimmy Armfield, the FA technical director responsible for helping to secure the appointment of both Venables and Hoddle, says finding someone prepared to take the top job in English football is not as easy as one might think. He believes that the heavy, often personal, criticism suffered by Robson and Taylor has put off many prospective candidates to the ultimate detriment of the national side, just as high-calibre individuals are deterred from embarking on a public life in politics out of the same fear of having their private lives exposed. 'Many of the candidates I spoke to were extremely apprehensive about considering the post after seeing what happened to Graham Taylor and Bobby Robson in the press,' says Armfield. 'They told me that they were not prepared to put their families through that. Another worry was that they would miss the day-to-day involvement with players, but the main concern was the press intrusion into their lives.'

It was only when Arsenal manager George Graham began to champion Venables' cause that the former Tottenham boss emerged as a serious contender. Graham, the most successful English club manager of the day, was then still in good odour with the football authorities before the stink of the 'bung' scandal that broke shortly afterwards. The FA, while convinced of Venables' skills as a coach, were worried about the allegations emerging about his commercial enterprises. The accusations related to his conduct as director of three business concerns: his West London nightclub Scribes, a company called Edennote, and Tottenham. Central to the allegations was Venables' relationship with Eddie Ashby, a friend and business associate who had been declared bankrupt. England managers' contracts have generally been in four-year cycles, starting with the European Championships and going on to the World Cup. It was a measure of the FA's unease that originally they only offered him a one year-contract, which Venables refused. The offer of a two-year contract was then accepted, but the FA insisted that the title of the post was changed from 'manager' to 'coach' for fear that the term 'manager' might carry the suggestion that Venables was involved in 'management' in a wider sense. The FA also had a get-out clause written into the contract which would allow them to release him in the event of his legal difficulties becoming an embarrassment.

In his first season in charge Venables justified the FA's faith in him as he set about restructuring the squad and restoring the confidence that had evaporated over the previous two years. In his first match, on 9 March 1994, England beat Denmark 1–0, and then hammered World Cup finalists Greece 5–0 at Wembley, prompting mixed emotions among fans who were left sighing about what might have been had England reached USA 94. He gradually rebuilt a directionless team and constantly reminded the press that putting together an unbeaten run was the best way of restoring morale, and such a run did materialise: by the end of 1995, England under Venables had played thirteen, won six, drawn six and lost just one, 3–1 in June 1995 to the new world champions, Brazil, England's only defeat in open play in the two and a half years Venables was at the helm (not counting the February 1995 match against the Republic of Ireland which was abandoned at 0–1 after 23 minutes when a group of right-wing hooligans sparked a riot at Lansdowne Road). However, among the opponents in those six wins and six draws – with one exception, all home games – not one could be considered to be a major footballing power; Denmark, Greece, the United States, Nigeria, Uruguay, Japan, Sweden, Colombia, Norway, Switzerland and Portugal are nations England would expect to beat under normal circumstances. (It would have been interesting to see the reaction of the press had it been Taylor overseeing goalless draws at Wembley with the likes of Norway, Uruguay and Colombia.)

But the focus, and Venables' priority, was always on assembling a squad capable of putting on a good show on home soil at the 1996 European Championships, when England would be tested for the first and only time in meaningful competition under Venables' stewardship, and, thanks largely to Venables' motivational powers and tactical skills, the English public had certainly started to feel good about the national side again by the end of 1995. The coach had good reason to feel he was in a strong bargaining position when he went to see the FA about an extension to his contract that would see him through to the World Cup finals in France in 1998. Shortly before starting negotiations with his employers, Venables pulled the time-honoured managers' ploy of publicly declaring that his services were in demand elsewhere by announcing that he had recently turned down a job off from Inter Milan.

'He went to see them when the draw for the European Championships was made in December 1995,' recalls Colin Malam, the *Sunday Telegraph* correspondent and a close confidant of Venables. 'He asked them reasonably enough whether they were going to keep him on or not so that he could make alternative plans if they didn't want him. Noel White, the chairman of the committee, told him that they would not consider giving him a new contract until they saw how England got on at Euro 96. Terry said to Noel White: "You don't want to place your bet until the horse has crossed the line", and pointed out that most other coaches in world football know where they stand in respect of their future. He wanted to stay on to take England to the World Cup, but he was effectively forced out. I remember being stunned when Terry told me, confidentially, that he was going to leave. I tried to talk him out of it because as far as I am concerned he is without doubt the best coach and tactician England has ever had and is likely to have. He is also one great motivator of players, as good as Kevin Keegan, but in a different way. Where Keegan gees up players with his enthusiasm, Terry does it with his knowledge as much as anything else. But the line from the International Committee was that Terry's business connections had become an embarrassment. They were uneasy from the start because he was involved in a lot of legal battles, mainly with Sugar, but there were also a couple of related libel actions. Part of the problem for Terry arose out of his loyalty to his old friends, like Eddie Ashby, with whom he fell out in the end. He was bitter about the way he was treated by the FA from the outset and he decided he had enough after they refused to renew his contract.'

Mihir Bose has a different understanding of Venables and his negotiations with the FA. Bose believes that if there was any conspiracy involving Venables, it is to be found among the vast majority of sports journalists who, he insists, turned a blind eye to his alleged misdemeanours. 'The whole story of Terry Venables is a classic case of media misreporting by people who do not understand or even want to understand the basic facts,' he says. 'It's a very, very sad commentary on the England football press. Most of the people who write about Terry Venables are friends of Terry Venables. He is a very charismatic man – very engaging, very funny, very good company. Given the choice of having dinner with Terry Venables or Alan Sugar, I would choose Terry Venables every time – not that he would want to have dinner with me.

'After Terry Venables got the sack from Tottenham, I started investigating the reasons behind his dismissal. The conventional line was that Sugar, a relatively unknown businessman who knew very little about football, had gone mad and sacked one of the great managers of the modern era. Once I started investigating, a lot of stories started coming out which shed a different light on Venables. Venables lost Spurs to Sugar and Sugar made him pulp his autobiography. If a man has to pulp his own autobiography it raises the question: does the man know his own life?

'The problem with Terry Venables is that he had always been told he was wonderful. Sporting stars get surrounded by acolytes who make them believe they are wonderful. Defeat with Sugar was the first time he was beaten. He came across a hard-nosed businessman who made him realise that he was out of his league. For Terry Venables that was awful, he could not accept it. That was his biggest misjudgement. He could have walked out and come to a compromise and got most of the money he claimed.

'Sugar may not be the most friendly man in the world, but it is interesting that apart from Venables, you do not hear of any legal problems that he has had. If Sugar had mistreated other people, it surely would have come out at the time or since. But it hasn't. It would have made a great story at the time of the legal battle between the two and Terry Venables has a lot of friends in the media, but still no stories about Sugar ever emerged. Sugar, like any businessman, cuts his losses, and he made an offer to Terry Venables, but Venables could not accept it.

'With the England business he presents it as if there was a vendetta against him and, yes, there were people in the FA who felt uneasy about the potentially negative headlines thrown up by his court cases. But once the England manager is involved in matters outside of football, it becomes difficult for the FA.

'What saddens me is that anyone who writes a critical article about him is accused of being an enemy of his. It shouldn't be a case of being pro- or anti-Venables. It should be about proper journalism. Only a few people seemed interested in investigating Venables' affairs, which is sad because football in England, or any game in fact, is meant to have great moral values.'

Rob Shepherd, now of the *Express*, believes there is some substance to Venables' claims that there was a conspiracy among the media at large, and beyond, to besmirch the England coach's reputation. 'Venables was a master at dealing with the media. It was one of his great strengths as an England manager, but, ironically, if any England manager was brought down by the press it was him because of the constant investigation into aspects of his business which made the FA go wobbly on him. When Hoddle talks about a conspiracy against him I think that he is talking nonsense, but in Terry's case I think his claims are more justified. There were one or two people in the media as a whole, not just the papers, who were out to get him and damage his reputation. I'm sure he did have some business problems but a lot of the allegations were never substantiated and came to nothing. But the allegations just went on and on and on, and in the end the drip-drip effect began to destabilise his position within the FA. It was unfortunate for England because he was one of the best coaches the country has ever produced.'

Put out by the FA's failure to back him, Venables announced in January 1996 that he would be leaving the job at the end of the European Championships. The impression which came across to the public via the media was that dark forces within the FA had forced him out – an entirely false impression, according to Bose. 'In answer to the question who or what cost Terry Venables his job as England manager, I would say Terry Venables cost Terry Venables his job,' he says. 'If he had stayed and had had the confidence in himself and England then he would almost certainly have been offered an extension to his contract. It would have been an embarrassment for the FA because in January 1998 he was banned by the DTI for seven years as a company director. The report is one of the most damning documents the DTI has ever produced. 'But I don't see how anyone at the FA could have denied Venables a new contract after the euphoria of Euro 96. It was purely Venables' decision to go. People say Terry Venables resigned. He did not resign. His contract expired at the end of Euro 96. It's a myth that he was sacked, or resigned or was forced out. Venables is the original spin doctor. He's better than Tony Blair's press secretary, Alistair Campbell. He was the first manager to realise that you could go into a press conference and shape the next day's reporting. He realised that you could deflect attention away from a poor performance by starting a row about the referee or a bad foul or a penalty decision. He knew that would then take over as the main story the next day. And he is convincing.'

The players and public, along with the majority of the press, were sad that Venables' reign as England manager would be coming to an end after just two and a half years. There was a mood of confidence in the England camp not experienced since Robson had guided the country to within a penalty or two of the World Cup finals nearly six years earlier. If he had not quite found the winning formula, Venables at least had established one which seemed resistant to defeat, and all the signs suggested that a good showing at Euro 96 would provide the England squad with the foundations and confidence to mount a serious challenge for the World Cup two years later. In addition to senior stars like Adams, Ince, Seaman, Gascoigne, Sheringham and Shearer, there were a number of talented youngsters starting to press their claims: Anderton, McManaman, Gary and Phil Neville, Beckham, Cole, Scholes, Redknapp and Fowler. The national side's rediscovered sense of purpose and tactical shape was demonstrated in their solid build-up to Euro 96, the biggest sporting event to be staged in Britain since the 1966 World Cup. In successive months they beat Bulgaria 1–0, Hungary 3–0 and drew 0–0 with Croatia, a richly talented team and a new face on the international scene following the disintegration of the former Yugoslavia.

As a final warm-up, in May Venables took the squad on a controversial tour of the Far East where, in their only official international, they beat China 3–0. It was on their return from Hong Kong that the biggest player-related scandal of Venables' time with England broke, one which would dominate press coverage on their return in the week before their opening match against Switzerland on 8 June. Allegations were made that damage had been done to the team's Cathay Pacific jumbo jet during a rowdy flight home. Shortly afterwards lurid pictures appeared in the papers of the players enjoying a boozy night out in a Hong Kong bar. The images of players lying prostrate in 'the dentist's chair' while team-mates soaked them in spirits led to a furore of indignation and claims that the squad were just a bunch of lager louts, unfit, physically and morally, to represent their country. The hunt for scapegoats, though, foundered when Venables announced that he would not be taking action against individuals and that the entire squad accepted 'collective responsibility' for what happened. Many felt that Venables' refusal to single out players for blame was a clever piece of 'psychology' as it created a sense of solidarity among the squad.

The incident gave rise to thousands of column inches on the front, back and inside pages of the newspapers as the press went into one of its occasional fits of frenzied soul-searching. It was claimed that foreigners would be amazed by the irresponsible antics of the England players, but when the teams began to arrive for Euro 96 most of the players who were immediately quizzed for their views on the subject professed astonishment at the fuss that had been generated. Many, in England too, felt that too much was made of the incident and that Venables was right to allow his players to let off some steam at the end of the tour and a long season, pointing out that one night off two weeks before the start of the European

Championships was hardly likely to ruin their chances of success. 'If it wasn't for the pictures that were taken, the story would probably never have come out,' says Colin Malam. 'But that is another problem for players – members of the public taking pictures of them knowing full well they can sell them to the tabloids for a few thousand pounds. The players are at risk whatever they do in public now.'

Venables was hoping for a brilliant victory over the Swiss in the opening match of the finals to put an end to the controversy, but England played poorly and in the end they were lucky to escape with a 1–1 draw against a side rated as rank outsiders. The most heartening aspect of the match from England's perspective was that Shearer finally ended his extraordinary twenty-month goal drought with a thumping first-half strike.

The crucial moments in Robson's reign had been the 35 minutes in which Lineker snatched a hat-trick in the group match against Poland in Mexico in 1986; the critical passage of play which would determine Taylor's fate came in those few minutes in Rotterdam when Platt was hauled down by Koeman, who, having survived unpunished, scored from a free-kick at the other end moments later; Venables' moment of truth came against Scotland in the second half of a match that was threatening to run away from England. Venables' side were leading 1–0 thanks to Shearer's first-half header, but they found themselves under increasing pressure from the well-organised visitors who were growing in confidence with every move they put together. Moments after a stunning save from Seaman had kept out a certain goal for Gordon Durie, Adams brought down the Scottish striker and the referee pointed to the penalty spot. As Wembley erupted in delight at McAllister's miss and Scottish heads fell in despair, England raced upfield. Redknapp released Gascoigne who appeared to offer little threat to the goal as he advanced into the left of the area, but in one flash of inspiration he effectively killed the match when he flicked the ball over Colin Hendry and crashed a low volley beyond Andy Goram. It is perhaps pointless and interesting at the same time to speculate about what might have happened to England and Venables' reputation had Gary

McAllister fired his spot-kick one foot either side of Seaman. Victory over the Scots seemed to release a surge of confidence that would sweep England to the brink of the final itself. Would England, so timid and unconvincing until Gascoigne's thrilling intervention, have had the confidence to play with the style they showed against Holland in the next match if they had been pegged back to a 1–1 draw or even lost to a mediocre Scotland team that afternoon? If nothing else, the events of that brief and dramatic passage of play highlighted how the fate and enduring reputation of an international manager can be forged in a matter of minutes rather than years.

England's match against the Dutch on 18 June was beyond question the high point of Venables' reign, and one of England's most majestic performances in their entire history. Shearer and Sheringham each grabbed a brace of goals as the Dutch were routed 4–1 with a swagger and a ruthlessness that had even England's most optimistic fans rubbing their eyes, like cartoon drunks, in disbelief. England were into the quarter-finals, and Venables knew that assuming his team were not humiliated by Spain he could now walk away from the England job with his reputation enhanced. 'Terry has said to me on a couple of occasions: "Well, whatever else happens in my life in football at least I will always be able to sit down in the evening and put the video of that on," ' says Colin Malam.

A wave of patriotic pride swept over the country in the wake of England's astonishing demolition of the Dutch, and in the build-up to the quarter-final against Spain. Some papers were criticised for being xenophobic and jingoistic. 'What have Spain ever given the world apart from syphilis and the Inquisition?' asked one daily. The match itself finished 0–0 and Spain, the great under-achievers of international football, could consider themselves unlucky not to have won the match in the 120 minutes of open play after edging England in terms of possession and chances. It was settled by the lottery of a penalty shoot-out in which the Spanish saw one effort saved by David Seaman and another hit the post. The English headlines and pictures the next day focused on Stuart Pearce, who buried the ghost of Turin 1990 when he strutted into the penalty area and smashed his spot-kick into the back of the net, the veins and muscles bursting out of his magnificently deranged face as he celebrated.

Standing in the way of England and their first ever appearance in a European Championship final was Germany. Bloody Germany. England had not beaten their old north European rivals in a major finals match since the 1966 World Cup final. The build-up to the match sparked a surge of national interest in the fortunes of the England team not witnessed since England had played the Germans (then West Germany) in Turin in 1990. The tabloids, especially the *Daily Mirror*, were heavily criticised, in the House of Commons and by members of the public from both countries, for what was considered to be the nationalistic and aggressively anti-German nature of their commentary. (The *Mirror* ran a front-page piece on the day of the match showing Stuart Pearce wearing a World War One tin hat next to the headline 'ACHTUNG! SURRENDER!')

The match itself was as exciting as any seen at Wembley since the 1966 World Cup. The teams emerged from the tunnel to a riot of colour and noise considerably better-natured than the one that followed in Trafalgar Square after the match. The Germans were clearly still trying to gather their wits in the extraordinary atmosphere when Shearer headed England into the lead after just two minutes. Stefan Kuntz equalised a quarter of an hour later, and the match remained deadlocked at 1–1, despite a flurry of chances at both ends, until the end of the 'golden goal' extra time two hours later. Once again the lottery of a penalty shoot-out would decide which of the two countries would advance to the final of a major championship, and once again it was the Germans who emerged victorious. With the match all square after the first five penalties, Gareth Southgate – whose only other penalty in competitive football, for Crystal Palace, had hit a post – took England's first sudden-death penalty, and saw his effort blocked by Andreas Kopke. Andreas Moller kept his head to deliver the *coup de grâce* and deliver the Germans into the final against the unfancied Czechs.

England had not just lost a match, they had lost one of the

best coaches of his generation. With a mixture of pride and regret, Venables, who had been staring so grimly into an uncertain future fewer than three years earlier, walked away to the applause of virtually everyone outside of the Inland Revenue, the DTI and the odd corner of Fleet Street to spend some quality time with his lawyers.

8 Take Me to Your Leader Page

Glenn Hoddle 1996–1999

'BLAIR GIVES HODDLE THE RED CARD' ran the *Daily Telegraph* headline above the main story on its front page. A visitor from outer space with a passing knowledge of human civilisation and modern British politics could be forgiven for wondering what on earth was going on. Is Mr Hoddle a senior Cabinet minister? Or one of the country's spiritual leaders? And what in heaven's name, he might wonder on being told that Mr Hoddle was a 'football coach', was the leader of one of the most powerful countries in the world doing sitting on the pastel-coloured sofa of an anodyne daytime chat show explaining why he felt that the man who trained a group of the country's football representatives should leave his job forthwith? Should he not be concentrating on more important tasks like trying to advance peace and prosperity among the people he rules over? Has the country that gave the world Shakespeare, Newton, Darwin, Keats, Churchill and Stan Bowles completely taken leave of its senses? Has the world gone mad? What next? Cats living with dogs? Cliff Richard to marry Edward Heath?

By anyone's standards, of this world or not, of this life or any other, the events which led to the dismissal of Glenn Hoddle as the coach of the England football team were nothing if they were not surreal. The *prima facie* case against Hoddle was that he had said disabled people were paying for their sins in a former life. He had made exactly the same comments nine months earlier and they were ignored. So what happened in the meantime to spark this astonishing deluge of indignation and condemnation which had Fleet Street working around the clock for a week and provoked the country's political leader to intervene? Had the country suddenly discovered a passionate sense of responsibility and sensitivity towards those born with physical and mental deficiencies? And why should anyone care about the spiritual views of a football coach any more than they should care if the Archbishop of Canterbury, off the record, told a reporter that he believes Shearer should play in a more withdrawn role with Rio Ferdinand as a sweeper at the back? Stranger things have happened, but not in the history of England's football managers. Hoddle himself was lampooned as an alien and a freak with crackpot views on the meaning of life, but the bizarre manner of his dismissal raises the question: Is he the only one among us living in the twilight zone? If nothing else, the Hoddle fiasco confirmed a handful of interesting aspects of modern life in England: that football has assumed an importance in society way beyond what those oily-moustached Victorians can have imagined when they first started haring around outdoors in pursuit of an inflated leather-bound bladder; that, at the drop of a quote, the British media has the power to whip up the country into a frenzy of moral outrage if it should so choose; and that Glenn Hoddle is not particularly clever.

Despite the general sadness at the departure of Terry Venables, the arrival of Hoddle was greeted with guarded optimism. He was young, supposedly full of bright new ideas, he was one of the most gifted English footballers of his generation, he had no financial and moral skeletons rattling in his locker, and he was the beneficiary of a generous legacy left by his predecessor. Although he had never won a trophy during his brief managerial career with Swindon and Chelsea, Hoddle had gained a reputation as a thorough and thoughtful coach with a promising future. 'I personally got on quite well with Glenn,' says the *Daily Telegraph*'s Henry Winter. 'I liked the freshness he brought with him to the job. He was full of good ideas and intentions and it seemed very promising at the outset. Terry had left him a good squad with a nice balance of youth and experience and there was confidence that Glenn was going to build on that. The straitjacket was off English football after Terry, and you had the feeling that Glenn was about to give young talent its chance.'

Hoddle enjoyed what has frequently been described as the longest honeymoon period ever accorded to an England manager. It lasted about eighteen months, during which time England won Le Tournoi in France in the summer of 1997 with victories over the hosts and eventual world champions and Italy. England won nine of their first eleven matches under Hoddle, losing only by a single goal to Brazil in their final match at Le Tournoi and by the same margin to Italy in the World Cup qualifier in February earlier in the year. That defeat, which left England facing a hard battle to qualify for France 98, was the only black spot in the early part of Hoddle's reign. England barely created a chance all night, and Hoddle was roundly criticised for his tactics. His not-so-secret decision to play wildcard Matt Le Tissier was considered especially foolish. The extravagantly talented if unpredictable Southampton ace spent most of the evening straining to head in crosses – not his strongest suit, and one much better suited to Les Ferdinand, who spent most of the match sitting on the bench fiddling with his jockstrap.

The general consensus after the match was that, with away matches to Poland and Italy still to come, England had blown their chances of automatic qualification for France 98 and the best they could hope for would be for a place in the play-offs as one of the best runners-up. But to the immense credit of both Hoddle and England, they reached the finals at the first time of asking with two of the national side's best performances in the 1990s. First, at the end of May 1997 in the intimidating cauldron of Katowice, they beat the Poles 2–0 and then flew to Rome in October knowing that a draw was all they needed to qualify as the Italians had slipped up against Poland and Georgia. The goalless draw turned out to be one of the great nights in English football, although the Italian security forces and a handful of Roman shopkeepers and street cleaners are unlikely to agree. 'I think Rome was one of the great results of English football history because we were away from home somewhere we had never picked up a point before in a very intimidating atmosphere,' says Henry Winter. 'It was a very un-English performance in many ways. The players weren't just professional, they were cynical in the way that very successful Italian teams have been. Fair play was thrown to the wind. They stayed down and wasted a bit of time when they were tackled and they made sure the opposition got booked, just as the Italians had done down the years. It wasn't the most wonderful sight, but they got the point England needed. I think immediately after that Hoddle could do no wrong. It was a case of "Arise, Sir Glenn." '

It was in Rome, however, that the seeds of Fleet Street's annoyance with Hoddle were first sown. At the press conference on the eve of the match, Hoddle brushed off a question about the fitness of Gareth Southgate. Roy Hodgson, then the Blackburn Rovers manager, was helping out by translating into Italian and, quite innocently it seemed, revealed that the Aston Villa defender was suffering from an injury and was doubtful for the match. At France 98 nine months later, Hoddle blatantly lied about an injury to the same player – he boasts about it in his World Cup diaries – and even forced the player to face the press and go along with the deception. The rest of the squad were also instructed to toe the line that Southgate wasn't injured.

Rob Shepherd of the *Daily Express* says Hoddle's economy with the truth infuriated the press and was a major factor behind Fleet Street's subsequent campaign to oust him. 'I understand there are times when the manager cannot say exactly what is going on, but it's better not to say something at all than to make an outright lie like Hoddle did on a few occasions,' he says. 'I was annoyed by that because the way I have always seen my role as a reporter is as a bridge, or a medium if you like, between the England squad and the public. He obviously just thought he was only lying to a handful of press guys who he might not have that much respect for, but essentially what he was doing was lying to millions of supporters.'

Henry Winter feels that far from benefiting from his numerous deceptions, Hoddle was unwittingly digging the grave in which the press would eventually bury him. 'I can understand that there has to be an element of smokescreen, but Glenn seemed to glory in misinformation and journalists felt patronised. There was straightforward lying about his players, most memorably about Beckham and Southgate, and I know for a fact that Southgate was very, very unhappy to be involved in the deception. It wasn't very clever of him because journalists have instant right of reply in the following day's papers. I think he short-changed the public by not being more open, honest and civil with the press. I didn't want to go out clubbing with Glenn Hoddle, I just wanted some basic and reliable information from him. If I am trying to predict the team on the eve of a big match, I want to have the relevant information to pass on to the readers. Hoddle's lies made reporters look stupid when the truth was revealed the following day. It got to the point with Hoddle that if I was unsure about the truth of what he said then I would quote him verbatim and put in a couple of riders saying Hoddle has been known to give out dubious information in the past.'

By the end of France 98, sports reporters were incensed by Hoddle's deliberate campaign to deceive. 'I have never seen Fleet Street journalists as angry as they were at the World Cup,' says Mike Collett of Reuters, who covered England's campaign. 'Their noses were completely put out of joint because he was constantly feeding them misinformation, so their stories were all wrong and they looked like jerks.'

The comic episode of Hodgson's mistranslation in Rome was soon forgotten amid the jubilation which followed England's heroic performance the next day. The England coach had every reason to feel that 1998 was going to be his 'annus mirabilis'. Rome, though, proved to be the pinnacle of his time in charge. From the peaks of public adulation that followed his miraculous resuscitation of England's ailing World Cup hopes, Hoddle found himself sliding uncontrollably towards an abyss of recrimination and contempt.

The first signs that not all was well on the pitch began to emerge in the new year when England were beaten 2–0 at Wembley by Chile, and were then held to a dour 1–1 draw by the Swiss in Berne and a goalless draw by Saudi Arabia at Wembley. Before the game in Switzerland Hoddle provoked incredulity in the press and in the country at large when he claimed that Michael Owen, the teenage Liverpool prodigy who had smashed goal records at all age groups, was not, in fact, a natural goalscorer. Hoddle later tried to explain himself by saying that what he meant was there was much more to Owen's game than 'mere' goalscoring. Hoddle had either been wrong or he had failed to state what he meant in plain English. His inability to put his strong opinions into unambiguous words, especially when discussing complicated issues of religion and spirituality, was a running problem in his relationship with the press. Added to his inclination for 'smokescreen' misinformation, the sum result was often a fog of misunderstanding. 'His biggest problem was that he couldn't articulate the views that got him the sack,' says Mike Collett of Reuters. 'If he had been able to explain himself, rather than leave everyone walking away scratching their heads, then it might have turned out differently.'

Rob Shepherd believes Hoddle made the fatal mistake of thinking he could outfox the press. 'He was not that articulate,' says Shepherd. 'He fell into that trap of thinking he was more erudite than he was. When he started getting involved in debates you got the impression he had forgotten or was overlooking the fact that many of the guys he was arguing with were reasonably intelligent people themselves. It is a reporter's business not just to write but to have reasoned debates with their subjects and form reasoned opinions on the basis of what they hear. Most reporters are very good at that – that's why they are in that job. You got the impression sometimes that he couldn't really compete on their level. He should have realised that and not tried to outsmart people because he often ended up contradicting himself or simply just not making sense.'

Henry Winter recalls an incident which led to a confrontation with Hoddle, highlighting the England manager's propensity for opening his mouth and putting his foot in it. 'I had a run-in with Glenn after Michael Owen's only Under-21 game against Greece at Carrow Road. I had an agreement that I would speak to him after the match and then I would pass on what he said to my colleagues on other papers. During this Hoddle said to me, "Owen has got to watch his off-field activities." I thought that was absurd and burst out laughing. I said to him, "But Michael Owen is whiter than white. What do you mean?" He said that he didn't want to go into it, but that Michael just needed to be careful. I assumed this was Hoddle's indirect way of saying Owen had to keep his feet on the ground rather than that the young lad had some dark secret. But I passed on what he had said to the other reporters and the next day the tabloids went potty with stories about Baby Spice and that Owen was going to self-destruct and so on. Hoddle then went ballistic, but I had recorded the conversation and ran off transcripts of the tape so that Hoddle would shut up.'

The immediate build-up to the 1998 World Cup finals was a busy and happy time for reporters of the England scene, who found themselves with the best of two entirely different worlds, both of them right here on earth. On the one hand, they would be covering an England team with as good a chance as any in their recent history of succeeding at the World Cup. (Whatever England managers in the past may have said about the press preferring to see the national team fail, most England reporters are ardent England fans.) At the same time, they found themselves dealing with a manager who had begun to expand on his 'crackpot' views of the world with alarming candour. Hoddle's willingness to advance his views on spirituality and existentialism might have alarmed his PR advisers, but it brought a whoop of delight from the country's newspaper editors as they headed towards 'the silly season' when Parliament's long summer recess would empty their in-trays of hard news stories.

When Hoddle first revealed his belief in the virtues of faith-healing as practised by his friend, spiritual guru and former Essex pub landlady Eileen Drewery, there were a few predictable jokes about aliens and Hod the God. Most commentators, though, seemed prepared to accept that as a last resort, after conventional treatment had failed, there could be no harm in an injured player trying alternative methods. Hoddle's image was not helped by the claims of 'TV spoon bender' Uri Geller that the England coach had performed a bizarre mystical ritual on him. 'I've been to witch doctors and tribal rituals, but nothing like this,' Geller told reporters. Hoddle angrily denied any association with Geller and accused him of jumping on a publicity band wagon. Hoddle, though, did anything but dissociate himself from Eileen Drewery. 'Once it was out he was asked about it a lot, but he seemed keen to develop the discussion and would spend forever talking about her,' recalls Henry Winter. 'He made her into a bigger issue than she needed to have been. I think if he had just said to the players, "Look, I think she can help you. If you want to go, go, but I'm not going to force you," that would have been fine.'

But reports began to emerge that far from being a last port of call, Drewery's healing room had become the first. Some players began to feel that unless they agreed to Hoddle's suggestion that they saw her, they would be undermining their chances of being in the squad or the team. Several players let it be known to reporters off the record that they had begun to feel uneasy about Drewery. (Arsenal's Ray Parlour at least saw the amusing side of it when he went for a session and asked for a short back and sides as Drewery laid her hands on his head. Robbie Fowler, though, said that if he wanted spiritual guidance he would go to his local priest.)

The shameless promotion of the merits of Drewery was another crucial mistake by the England coach that might easily have been avoided, according to Rob Shepherd. 'His belief in faith-healing was not a problem in itself, but it was the fact that he used the press to promote Eileen Drewery. No one forced him to talk about it. He would either bring it up himself or when asked about it he would talk about it *ad nauseam*. In my view, he did it to help promote her. If she had nothing to do with Glenn Hoddle, you might find her down the end of Brighton pier now. She was given football's equivalent of the royal seal of approval, which enhanced her reputation. There was a commercial spin-off for her from Hoddle's promotion. 'The Hoddle camp is now trying to make the point that it was just cynics out to rubbish faith-healing, but that's not what the dispute is about. It's using the position of England manager to promote a particular person. It was a kind of cronyism. Another problem with the faith-healing issue was the effect it had on the players. More than half his squad saw Eileen, and it was a bit of a problem for some players who might not have wanted to go and see her but felt that if they didn't it might impinge on their chances of being selected.'

One of the curious aspects of Hoddle's relationship with the press is that there did not appear to be anyone advising him on what to say and do, or rather on what not to say and what not to do. David Davies, the FA's Director of Public Affairs at the time, who found himself under fire after ghost-writing the coach's controversial World Cup diaries, believes Hoddle should have been more protected. 'People at the FA can give advice to an England manager, but it does not necessarily follow that the advice will be taken,' says Davies, who covered England for BBC Radio until joining the FA to help revamp their media operation after the Taylor years. 'People are individuals with minds and wills of their own. But contrary to what some people might say, Glenn Hoddle actually made much more effort with the media than he ever did in his Chelsea days. The question is whether Glenn ought to have been minded more and limited more in what he said. The truth of the matter is that there will always be tensions, but when the results start going awry there is little the England manager can do. If Glenn Hoddle had won a couple of key games after the World Cup, the question is whether he would still be doing his job. There are certain things you can do, but ultimately you are at the mercy of results.'

Davies believes that the intense scrutiny of the modern media has changed the coverage of the England set-up beyond all recognition from what it was like just fifteen years ago. 'The days of the press having bacon and egg sandwiches with the manager the day after the match are over,' he says. 'There is an understandable nostalgia in the press for those cosy days, but the sheer size of the modern media has put an end to that. You can't let just a few reporters have access like that. It would be very obviously unfair. The FA are constantly thinking of ways of trying to accommodate the different demands of such a vast group. When I first arrived at the FA at the same time Terry Venables took over, we considered all sorts of options for the media. We considered the "Barcelona option" where, rather than have five different media sessions with the various groups on the same subject, you have just one huge press conference. But the written press don't want that because it means that what is said just goes out live or is on the TV screens a few hours later. 'We've also tried to make all the England players available for interview in a room at once, but then what happens is that you get a hundred surrounding Beckham, seventy around Owen and Shearer, and then twenty guys leaning up against the wall twiddling their thumbs. Another suggestion is that the players have it in their contracts to talk to the press. We have looked at that, but it is unworkable. How do you force a player to speak? You can put him in front of the press, but he could just sit there saying, "Yes . . . no . . . yes . . . no . . . thanks, goodbye.' Even when we have suggested to the press that we will put a dozen or so players into a conference, they say they can't cope with having too many people. They can't be in five parts of the room at once.

'Some journalists have suggested to me that the players are bursting to come and talk to the press but that the so-called FA spin doctors are stopping them. That is not true. The players are not bursting to talk to the press by any stretch of the imagination. I think an important point to grasp in this debate is that England only have the players for about six weeks a year. For the other 46 weeks this relationship with the press is going on back at their clubs. The England players do not exist in a vacuum. They are involved in a relationship with the press all year around. I don't think there is any point in talking about the relationship between England players and the press without reference to the more general relationship. 'But you have to see the issue in a wider context. It's not just football. It's the rough and tumble of public life. I think there are responsibilities in public life, but some of the England players are young guys and are thinner-skinned than you might think, and if they get turned over it hurts them and their families as well.'

Brian Woolnough of the *Sun* says the current system is entirely unsatisfactory and that the situation has not been helped by the growing influence of agents in the game. Woolnough also feels that without the media high-profile figures in football would be considerably less rich, and that they conveniently tend to forget the countless occasions when they are praised, which he believes are far more numerous than the times when they are criticised. 'The relationship with managers and players has changed completely,' he says. 'You used to be able to sit down socially and talk to them. It's far more regimented now and there are far more agents involved deciding whether they should let their client speak to the press. If you go to the England camp now, you won't go to their hotel as in the past. You ask the FA if you can speak to Shearer and they say no, and they will wheel out David Seaman. It's organised for you, and there is a them-and-us situation which I don't like at all. As far as I am concerned football managers and players in this country get fantastic coverage and they don't appreciate it. They take it for granted. You always get a reaction on a negative story, but never after the hundreds and hundreds of times that you've written how good they are or what a great game they've had.'

Howard Wilkinson, the FA's technical director who took over as caretaker manager for the match against France at Wembley in February 1999 following Hoddle's abrupt dismissal, believes money and television have changed professional football for ever. 'Top football people are now in film star status,' says the former Leeds United and Sheffield Wednesday manager. 'We're dealing with millionaire players who have a completely different lifestyle to their predecessors just fifteen or twenty years ago. The England players and manager no longer arrive at Bisham Abbey on the train or in a Morris Oxford. At the same time, the communications industry has put these managers and players right under the microscope every minute of the day. When the World Cup squad went to Brazil in 1950, there were five or six journalists plus the guy from BBC Radio; when England went out to Rome for the last qualifier against Italy in 1997, the FA accredited 120 journalists for the flight out. The media demands in Sir Walter Winterbottom's time were ten per cent, at the absolute most, of what they would be today. The journalists in those days sent their stories by cable, and when they were abroad they would often arrive a day too late. You would get a brief news item about the match on the radio, but there was no analysis, no television and therefore England's performance did not make such a big impact. There wasn't the intense immediacy that there is today. Now the analysis is microscopic.'

Wilkinson, who was only in the England manager's job for a week but found it was still time enough to see himself caricatured as *Star Trek*'s Mr Spock on the front page of one paper, is convinced that knowing how to deal with the press is vital for the national coach. 'Dealing with the media is second only in importance to winning football matches,' he says. 'It's just arguable that people will put up with anything if you are winning all the time, but only just. If you look at France 98, 75 per cent of managers lost their jobs and some of them were successful managers whose teams had done better than expected, so maybe winning isn't enough any more. The media is important in that it can buy the manager time and lengthen the stay of execution. Clearly, the media presence is here to stay; there is nothing that the England manager or anyone else is going to do about it. It's like pretending it doesn't rain in England. The media criticism is just going to happen. The England manager should just face it, but he will need Wellingtons and an umbrella and he should make sure he's wearing them from the beginning.'

Both Hoddle and the press knew full well, however, that if he came back from France holding aloft the Jules Rimet trophy, then he could step off the plane wearing a long silk robe, *à la* David Icke, drink out of puddles and announce that he was Napoleon Bonaparte and no one would have cared. Hoddle's relationship with the press in France was uneasy from the outset after he took the decision not to let the accredited sports reporters travel with the squad on the plane, as they had done on every trip since the Second World War. 'That was a major blow because it was one of the few occasions where the press and players get together these days,' says Henry Winter. 'It was what I call the "carousel culture" where you would all hang around with each other waiting for your luggage. You would have a bit of a chat and a joke with the players and build up a bit of rapport. The plane trips was one of the few opportunities you had to mingle and bond with the players. It was always good to see them in that context because they were at ease and did not retreat into their shells like they did under the glare of the cameras at a press conference. By kicking us off the plane Glenn threw up an unnecessary barrier and created a bad atmosphere.'

Hoddle's relationship with the press was strained further by his treatment of David Beckham, whom he left out of the opening match against Tunisia in Marseilles on 15 June. Hoddle said of Beckham, arguably England's most technically accomplished player, that he was 'not focused' and 'vague' coming into the tournament. His comments prompted a very public row with Alex Ferguson, Beckham's manager at Manchester United, and Hoddle's standing among the players was not enhanced when he was said to have humiliated the young midfielder in front of the rest of the squad at a training session. The exclusion of Owen from the starting line-up against both Tunisia and Romania in the second group match also prompted severe criticism.

Much of the attention on Hoddle and his squad before England's opening match was diverted by the behaviour of 500 hooligans (out of an estimated total of 30,000) who ran riot in Marseilles for two days, creating scenes of mayhem not witnessed since the 1988 European Championships in Germany. England, though, came through the match against Tunisia without serious alarm with goals from Scholes and Shearer sealing a comfortable 2–0 win. They headed for Toulouse as firm favourites to beat Romania and book their place in the last sixteen. Once again, Owen and Beckham were left on the bench and this time their absence proved crucial. When Owen finally came on with twenty minutes to go and England trailing 1–0, he equalised almost immediately and then hit a post before a blunder by Graeme Le Saux allowed his Chelsea team-mate Dan Petrescu to seize victory at the death. Hoddle finally named Beckham and Owen in his starting line-up for the must-win final group match against Colombia in Lens on 26 June. England won the match 2–0 with goals from Darren Anderton and a stunning free-kick by Beckham in the team's best performance of the competition to date. Afterwards, Hoddle claimed that it had always been his intention to play the pair against the Colombians because of their pace against an ageing team.

Despite the pleasure at seeing England progress into the next round, where they would face a powerful but beatable Argentinian side, the press by now were heartily sick of Hoddle's almost comic campaign of misinformation. The idea was that he was fooling the opposition, but were they really quaking in their boots about whether Gareth Southgate was going to play? For all his virtues as a solid and composed defender, Southgate is no Ronaldo. And why, it was asked at the time, not play Owen and Beckham, two of the most talented players the country has ever produced, and let England's best team just get on with it? The contradictions and tortured explanations of Hoddle's selection policy had confused the players, the press and probably even himself – everyone, it seemed, apart from the opposition. Many felt it was another case of Hoddle simply trying to be clever to no apparent end. Ian Ridley, the chief football writer for the *Independent on Sunday*, had clearly had enough of the manager's ramblings when he began his preview of the Argentina game by saying: 'There are times when following England can be a maddening, frustrating occupation, the more so these days given Glenn Hoddle's cloak-and-dagger control-freak regime of attempted cuteness and cleverness in dissembling misinformation . . . It is time to shed the Camp Paranoia image that Hoddle has created around England – and which the majority of his bright and honest players find difficult to play along with. He should simply come out and say: "This is England. This is what we do well. Stop it if you can." '

Both Owen and Beckham started against Argentina, although only one would be on the pitch by the end of what many felt with hindsight was the best game of the entire tournament. Owen was outstanding. Seaman's bovine challenge on Diego Simeone had allowed Gabriel Batistuta to fire the South Americans into a sixth-minute lead, but within four minutes Owen had ensured England were back on terms when he used his pace and guile to win a dubious-looking penalty for Shearer to convert. It was a pulsating start to the match, and after sixteen minutes Owen scored the goal of France 98 when, released by Beckham, he set off like a rocket on a diagonal run that left Jose Chamot and Roberto Ayala trailing in his slipstream. He seemed to have taken the ball too wide as he sped into the right side of the area, but with a shot of exquisite precision he fired across the face of Carlos Roa's goal and into the top corner. Scholes had a gilt-edged opportunity to kill the match in the 37th minute, but missed from eight yards out with just Roa to beat. Argentina equalised on the stroke of half time when Javier Zanetti scored with a thundering drive after a delightfully crafted free-kick. England's hopes of victory suffered a major setback in the first minute of the second half when Beckham was sent off for an act of petulance that would make him Public Enemy Number One on his return to England. Brought down by a heavy challenge from Simeone, Beckham kicked out at the provocative Inter Milan hard man under the nose of Danish referee Kim Nielsen, who immediately reached for his red card. (Hoddle would say later that Beckham's fit of pique might have been avoided if the England coach had had the courage to take Eileen Drewery to France. Leaving her at home, he said, was his biggest mistake of France 98.) Hoddle quickly reorganised, ordering Owen and Shearer to alternate up front while the other dropped back into midfield. Adams and Campbell were outstanding at the heart of the defence as England's ten men produced an heroic performance which saw them keep out the Argentinians for the rest of the second half and then extra time. England were now back on equal playing terms as the match went to penalties, but for the third successive occasion in the finals of a major championship, England failed as Ince and Batty fluffed their efforts.

England flew home in Concorde to receive a hero's welcome from the public despite their worst performance in the World Cup finals since 1958. The dismissal of Beckham was blamed as the reason for England's premature exit, while the brilliance of Owen's goal and the courage and composure of the ten men left on the pitch allowed people to feel that England had been glorious, unlucky losers. It was football's Dunkirk. Hoddle brushed off criticism of England's perennial failure in penalty shoot-outs, claiming that practice was made irrelevant by the intense pressure felt by all the takers on the night. But many felt his comments made a nonsense of his claims that his England squad were the best prepared ever to enter a World Cup.

'The Argentina game was arguably one of Hoddle's best games,' says the *Daily Telegraph*'s Henry Winter. 'Tactically he got it spot on with the way he used Owen and Shearer making shuttle runs forward while the other dropped back to defend. That was very impressive and showed what a good coach he is. But I also thought that the fact they didn't practise penalties was arrogant and foolish and cost them the game. You would have thought that as a fine deadball player himself he would have had them practising. I found that extraordinary. I was sitting among the German press for the match, the last place you want to be as an Englishman when it comes to a shoot-out, and these guys from the Frankfurt Hamburger or wherever said, "Bad luck, you're going to penalties, you're going to lose." My immediate reaction was that there was nothing to worry about – until I saw the line-up and then I realised we didn't have a chance. I thought Glenn got the order wrong. I think you want to have all your best penalty takers to go first to try and build up some pressure on them. You don't have a weak one [Ince] going third.

'Afterwards Glenn was very dismissive about the need to practise penalties, but it is such an essential part of the World Cup. We bowed out of the 1990 World Cup and Euro 96 as a result of poor penalty taking. Argentina, coached by one of the great penalty takers, Daniel Passarella, practised them after every training session because they knew that a lot of games in the World Cup would be settled that way. They had a contest among themselves every time and they were very clever about it because they practised them at the end of a hard training session when they were tired, just as they would be in a match situation. It is just a little attention to details like that which make a difference. John Sadler of the *Sun* and I went for Glenn at the press conference afterwards, but he was very offhand about it. He kept saying England were the best prepared team ever to go to a World Cup. The penalty shoot-out showed that simply wasn't true.'

Having flopped at the World Cup and antagonised the press all the way, Hoddle was now a vulnerable figure, an easy target for the snipers who could point to the World Cup for proof of his failure. Hoddle needed all the friends and results he could get, but quickly managed to lose more of both. Shortly after France 98 Hoddle published his World Cup diaries for a reported sum of £200,000. They had been written in conjunction with David Davies, the FA's Director of Public Affairs, and were then serialised for another princely sum in the *Sun*, a paper which Hoddle had frequently criticised in the past. Their publication proved to be another public relations disaster for the England manager. He was accused of disloyalty and indiscretion towards his players as he revealed details of Gascoigne's tantrum when he told the temperamental midfielder that he was not in his final World Cup squad. His negative comments about Beckham and Chris Sutton were also seen as breaking the managers' convention of not criticising players in public.

If the players had reason to feel aggrieved, the journalists were furious, accusing him of withholding important information during the tournament so that his diaries would sell more copies. 'I thought the publication of his World Cup diaries was the beginning of the end for Hoddle,' says the *Express*'s Rob Shepherd. 'Firstly, if certain things were important at the time they should have been aired publicly. I think that made people feel as if they had been short-changed and lied to. I think it was an insult to England fans who would have felt a right to know about certain subjects at the time of the World Cup and were back in England hanging on every word, via the media, of what was happening in France. I think people had a right to feel unhappy that he saved things for the book to help it sell better. He should have waited like a prime minister or a president and published the book at the end of his tenure. I think that David Davies was in a position to advise him not to do the book and certainly he shouldn't have taken any part in its writing. Incredibly, Hoddle seemed amazed that when it was serialised the paper picked out the best bits about Gascoigne and so on. He later claimed he didn't want it in the *Sun*, but if he didn't then he should have taken it to another paper. But he went for the highest bidder, and quite rightly the *Sun* ran the most interesting parts of the book. A further contradiction thrown up by the diaries controversy was that although he moans about the press, he used the press to publicise his book and got paid handsomely for it.'

Any hope Hoddle had of remaining in charge was effectively ended when England's European Championship campaign got off to a disastrous start with defeat in Sweden and a goalless draw against Bulgaria at Wembley. Hoddle could not even claim that the public were on his side any more. When he left the pitch after the Bulgaria match boos and jeers rang in his ears, and pictures in the following day's papers showed a large group of fans giving him the masturbation hand gesture – the English football fan's equivalent of the Roman emperor's thumbs down in the gladiator's arena. A 3–0 victory in Luxembourg a month later suggested that the press campaign to oust him had gathered an unstoppable momentum. Reports circulated after the match that Shearer had clashed with Hoddle in the dressing-room and that the squad as a whole was on the verge of rebellion. Shearer's comments that 'what is said in the dressing-room, stays in the dressing-room' seemed only to confirm the rumblings of mutiny.

After a 2–0 victory in the friendly over the Czech Republic in November, there followed a three-month gap before England's next match against France. Hoddle kept a low profile at first, hoping that time would heal the festering sense of resentment and recrimination that had flared since the World Cup. When he finally emerged from his bunker, the snipers were waiting to ambush him. Hoddle gave an interview to Matt Dickinson in *The Times* in which, *inter alia*, he tried to explain his views on karma and reincarnation and offered his belief that disabled people were paying for their wrongdoings in a former life. Hoddle, who says he has a fair idea of who he was and what century he lived in in a former life, did not claim that he had been misquoted, only that he had been misinterpreted. His fumbling explanations of what he had in fact meant and his claim that the interview was meant to have been about football, attracted only more derision from all quarters. He said: 'The only reason people are saying I should resign is that they are saying I have come out and said that people disabled and handicapped have been paying for their sins and I have never ever said that. I don't believe that. At this moment in time, if that changes in years to come I don't know, but what happens here today and changes as we go along that is part of life's learning and part of your inner beliefs. But at this moment in time I did not say them things and at the end of the day I want to put that on record because it has hurt people.' It was difficult to know what Hoddle meant.

When Sports Minister Tony Banks and then the Prime Minister himself felt obliged to add their voices to the chorus of calls for his head there was no way back for Hoddle, and the announcement that his contract was being terminated 'by mutual consent' (legal language for 'sacked') was delayed only by negotiations over his pay-off, believed to be £500,000. Only Eileen Drewery seemed upset to seem him go as Hoddle found himself propelled through the revolving door at Lancaster Gate.

'I think the comments he made about disabled people became an excuse to get rid of him,' says Colin Malam of the *Sunday Telegraph*. 'I think he had become an embarrassment long before that. He had lost the dressing-room, he'd lost the press and he was in the process of losing the country. I think the players felt he had been a bit disloyal to them in the World Cup diaries. Then there was all this silly business about Owen not being a natural goalscorer. I don't think the way he treated Beckham pleased one or two of the players either. But even if he had managed to keep the press and the players sweet, it still boils down to results.' On his awkward relationship with the press, Malam says: 'Glenn was always a bit reserved as a player, although he also liked a drink and a bit more. He was quite a party animal. He was rather difficult to deal with, but strangely he was better in press meetings with the Sunday papers rather than the dailies, which were much larger gatherings. He seemed more comfortable with smaller groups of people. We saw the best side of him and he could even be quite chummy. I think it would be fair to say that he was not as articulate as he would have liked to have been. That was particularly true when he was talking about the very complicated, non-football issues towards the end of his time in charge.'

Henry Winter believes Hoddle's towering self-confidence, stubbornness and frostiness towards the press finally played a significant part in his fall from grace. 'Part of the problem was Glenn's arrogance. He found it difficult to understand that a journalist might have a legitimate point about football. I thought that was a major concern and I spoke to Glenn about his lack of media relations. We shouldn't really take any interest in an England manager's views on matters not relating to football, but if they make them, then those opinions are going to be reported. I'm amazed that an England manager should venture controversial opinions on other issues. I don't ask Tony Blair whether he thinks England's formation should be 5–3–2 or 4–4–2 and I think he would decline to give me an answer if I did, saying that it was the business of the England manager. It's not his job to know. In the same way it is not Hoddle's role to sort out the economy or use his position to advance his views on the country's spiritual well-being.

'In his defence, it should be said that in a press conference he can only answer questions asked of him, but he should have been more careful about what he said and he certainly should not have volunteered his thoughts as often as he did. Hoddle can believe what he likes, but I think the people close to him at the FA should have been warning him not to bang on about certain matters or he would end up in hot water. I think they probably did tell him not to rabbit on about his personal view of life, but he just carried on anyway. I think it was a sign of his arrogance and thick skin. He was so convinced that he was right, he couldn't possibly imagine how anyone was going to object to what he said.'

Brian Woolnough of the *Sun* believes Hoddle should have been protected from himself by the FA and his agent, Dennis Roach. 'His image was collapsing around him after the World Cup and the results were poor. I don't think he realised how important the media were, and I don't think he believed we reporters were important. You can't get away with that these days. That's not a threat, it's just a fact of commercial life. I think Hoddle needed help desperately and I think the FA and the people close to him, like his agent, have a lot to answer for in that respect.' Woolnough believes that an England manager, as a high-profile public figure, has a responsibility to the country to communicate with them openly through the media. 'I think its essential that the England manager has to be good at dealing with the press. The media side of football has become massive. Don't forget that on the back of coverage, these guys get massive sponsorship deals, television invitations, newspaper columns, books and so on, all of which make an enormous amount of money for them. You can't take on a massive job on a massive salary in a very public role and then say to yourself, "I enjoy doing this job, but I'm not going to do anything on the PR side." It goes with the job. The England manager is a very public figure and has important responsibilities. You don't give the England manager hundreds of thousands of pounds for him not to promote your product. I also think dealing with the press is the easiest thing in the world. It is essential that they give the media something and stupid if they don't. Put it like this: if they erect a brick wall in front of the media all that will happen is that the media will either climb over the wall or go around the back. If you're clever and just give the media something, then by and large they'll be happy.

'The relationship between Hoddle and the media was worse than I have known, no question about it. He couldn't handle it. He's a very private man and never came to terms with being a public figure. He couldn't grasp it at all. He thought he was articulate, but he wasn't. Hoddle lost it. He never had the same warmth as, say, Robson. I've known Glenn for twenty years and you never get close to him. Chelsea chairman Ken Bates is on record as saying he knew no more about Glenn Hoddle on the day he left than on the day he arrived. He couldn't grasp what was expected of him and he didn't like the media, and in the end, in trying to talk about something that wasn't important to football, it brought him down.'

Woolnough believes that his successor will show Hoddle that it is possible to be a good coach as well as a diplomatic communicator. 'Hoddle wasn't brought down just by his comments about invalid people, it was just the final mistake that he made. Hoddle also told the press lies about injured players and so on, and that never goes down well. In the end you didn't know if he was telling the truth or not. He was prickly all the time. It is such an easy thing to do to come and be bubbly with the press. Keegan will teach him how to handle the media. But it's not just about handling the media, it's about winning the games. But if you don't win the games and you start making mistakes in public life then you will get harangued for it.'

Jimmy Armfield, the former England international, FA technical director and now respected co-commentator for BBC Radio Five Live, disagrees with the view that an England manager needs to be good at dealing with the press. 'I don't see why a manager has to be good at dealing with the press. He's paid to be football coach. He's not paid to be Terry Wogan. You listen to these people on TV who never played football and they start to believe their experts. They're suddenly making statements about a profession they know nothing about. But because they're commentators or whatever they start to believe their experts. Well, if someone in football started talking about newspapers or TV or radio, all the journalists would start saying, "What the hell does he know about it?" One thing about being a footballer is that everyone knows your job better than you.'

Rob Shepherd believes that managers and players need to face up to the fact that their salaries nowadays are effectively being paid not just by the fans but also by the big media corporations, and that consequently they are under an obligation to make an effort with the media. 'Whether the players and managers like it or not, the World Cup is now the property of the TV companies and the sponsors who are bankrolling it. Billions of people around the world are interested in the World Cup and they want to be informed about what is going on, not just with their own team but others as well.' Shepherd also feels that it is wrong for players to complain that the English press are overly critical. 'Well over half the managers at the World Cup lost their job and came in for heavy criticism from their own national press. When Brazil went home their manager and coaches faced a civil action over the Ronaldo affair. Now that is serious. The press can upset people in this country, but they're getting off lightly compared to other countries like Brazil and Italy. Football people, especially those in the England set-up, get very well rewarded for what they do. The England manager gets a lot more than the Prime Minister, and he's never exactly going to be asked to press the nuclear bomb button. When you look it at like that, it's not *that* difficult a job.'

Index

Index